HEALING THE NATION

RELIGION IN NORTH AMERICA
Catherine L. Albanese and Stephen J. Stein, editors

HEALING

 the

NATION

LITERATURE, PROGRESS,

 *and*

CHRISTIAN SCIENCE

L. ASHLEY SQUIRES

INDIANA UNIVERSITY PRESS

This book is a publication of

Indiana University Press
Office of Scholarly Publishing
Herman B Wells Library 350
1320 East 10th Street
Bloomington, Indiana 47405 USA

iupress.indiana.edu

© 2017 by L. Ashley Squires

♾ The paper used in this publication meets
the minimum requirements of the American National Standard for Information
Sciences—Permanence of Paper for Printed
Library Materials, ANSI Z39.48-1992.

Manufactured in the United States of
America

Cataloging information is available from
the Library of Congress.

ISBN 978-0-253-02954-6 (cloth)
ISBN 978-0-253-03037-5 (paperback)
ISBN 978-0-253-03031-3 (ebook)

1 2 3 4 5 22 21 20 19 18 17

CONTENTS

ACKNOWLEDGMENTS

NEARLY A DECADE AGO, I embarked on an effort to comprehend every possible intersection between American literary and religious history. During that process, someone patiently pointed out to me that there was enough original material in the Christian Science chapter to fill an entire monograph, thus making possible the book you see before you. To Phillip Barrish and Brian Bremen, I owe a tremendous debt of gratitude for their patient collegial advice throughout the process of writing this book. Tom Tweed, likewise, opened the door to the field of religious studies for me and provided an indispensable model for how to write a book. I also thank Gretchen Murphy and Coleman Hutchison for their insightful feedback and Evan Carton and Christopher Ellison for reading early chapters. Michael Winship is to be thanked for helping my findings on Willa Cather and the authorship of Mary Baker Eddy's biography—which did not fit within the scope of this book—a proper home.

Also in my thoughts are my colleagues from the University of Texas at Austin, including the members of my writing group: Coye Heard, Sydney Bufkin, Rachel Wiese, Bradley King, and Ty Alyea—to name but a few—who have already read almost this entire book, though in pieces over the course of time.

Much of the primary research for this project was conducted at the Mary Baker Eddy Library in Boston, Massachusetts. This would not have been possible without the two fellowships they offered. I thank Sherry Darling for her guidance through that process and for making it possible for me to share my research with the community. Judy Huenneke, whose expertise in this area is unparalleled, was a tremendous resource to me during my residence, as were Research Room staff members Kurt Morris and Amanda Gustin.

The final stages of the writing and revision process were conducted during my first two years at the New Economic School in Moscow, Russia. I wish to thank my colleagues there as well as my research assistants Daniel Resnick and Kerry Matulis, who edited individual chapters and helped me track down primary sources. I am also blessed with a number of colleagues around the world who have contributed to this project in various ways, even just by chatting about it at MLA. I particularly want to recognize Anne Stiles for motivating me to press forward with this book with her interest in its topic as well as for her assistance with the Burnett chapter. Myles Chilton, who has been such a vital collaborator on other projects, also swapped book chapters with me and provided moral support. And finally, Melanie Haupt helped me get this manuscript into fighting shape, finding the mistakes and inconsistencies that I could not.

My family has borne witness to this entire process with the utmost forbearance. My husband, Edmond Squires, has given up many a vacation so that I could spend time writing, has tolerated many a foul mood, and has supported me unconditionally throughout this journey. My parents and siblings have also offered their views on the monograph from outside academia and have helped me continue to believe that it is interesting to real people.

Chunks of this monograph have appeared in other places, and I would like to thank the editors and reviewers at *American Literary Realism, Studies in the Novel,* and *Book History,* particularly Andrew Jewell for his work on the Cather issue in SITN. And finally, at Indiana University Press, Dee Mortenson provided patient guidance throughout the review process, and I am grateful to her and the peer reviewers for having very high standards and holding me to them.

HEALING THE NATION

Introduction

Restitution and Modernity

Since 2010, American actor Val Kilmer has toured the United States performing one-man shows in the character of Mark Twain. Bedecked in a white suit and disheveled wig, he portrays the familiar Sam Clemens of the turn of the century—curmudgeonly, lethally clever, skeptical of everything, and wrestling with his legacy as an author. Less familiar to audiences is the Clemens who was also deep in the throes of a vitriolic obsession with Mary Baker Eddy, the venerable leader of a growing religious movement called Christian Science. Kilmer's Twain is the man who had lost his daughter, a Christian Scientist, and his wife, a dabbler in various sectarian medical theories. He is also a writer whose preoccupation with Eddy exploded into print in a series of articles, a book-length screed published in 1907 as *Christian Science*, and lengthy correspondences with Eddy's friends and enemies, including one woman who claimed to have conceived her son, named Prince of Peace, through parthenogenesis. This is a Clemens who, at an earlier time, had written an article called "Mental Telegraphy," espousing the theory that minds could influence one another at a distance—a central principle in Christian Science—and was ignoring his memoirs while writing a never-to-be-finished story called "The Secret History of Eddypus, the World-Empire," conceived as a sequel of sorts to *A Connecticut Yankee in King Arthur's Court*.

Though entertaining in their own right, Kilmer's performances are part of an independent film project that has been gestating since 2002, an historical epic depicting the contrasting lives of two towering figures of fin de siècle American culture.[1] Whether the film ever actually graces theaters, it is difficult to deny that Kilmer, a Christian Scientist himself, has found in Twain and Eddy, both of whom died in 1910, a compelling set of foils. Here is Mark Twain: the avatar of late-nineteenth-century skepticism and hostility toward enchantment, irrationalism, and romanticism. And here is Eddy: self-proclaimed prophetess and instrument of the divine, leader of a religious movement that claimed to have found the secret of health not in germ theory or surgery, but in metaphysics. These are contrasts worthy of both romance and comedy.

But Mark Twain was hardly alone among literary figures of public note in his preoccupation with Christian Science. While Twain was penning polemics, respected novelist and *New York Times* correspondent Harold Frederic was dying slowly of complications following a stroke as doctors battled with the Christian Science practitioner who had been summoned by his mistress. Frederic eventually dismissed the doctors, and after he died, both women were tried for manslaughter but never convicted.

In 1907, the fully revised version of Twain's book on Eddy greeted the public, and Willa Cather, fresh off the success of *Alexander's Bridge*, joined the staff of *McClure's*. Her first assignment: editing a serial biography of Mary Baker Eddy by a young journalist named Georgine Milmine and previously edited by Ida Tarbell and Burton Hendrick.

During this same decade, Theodore Dreiser was visiting a Christian Science practitioner with his estranged wife, Sara, amid the ruins of their crumbled marriage and the intense personal crisis precipitated by the commercial failure of *Sister Carrie*. He wrote about this experience for eighty pages of the semiautobiographical novel *The "Genius,"* published in 1918. Frances Hodgson Burnett likewise became fascinated with Eddy's teachings, an interest made manifest in *A Little Princess*, *The Secret Garden*, and *The Dawn of a To-morrow*, novels that explore the ability of the mind to shape experience in the material world.

In 1918, Upton Sinclair came after Christian Science in the self-published work *The Profits of Religion*; in Europe, various members of Gertrude Stein's circle, including, to her consternation, her sister-in-law Sarah, were dabbling in Christian Science along with Vedanta. Ernest Hemingway and Hart Crane were both raised by mothers who were

Christian Scientists, and Christian Science was one of the many religio-medical theories adopted by J. D. Salinger. The list goes on.

The questions that animate this book are as follows: How did Christian Science—a movement that now numbers its members in the tens of thousands rather than the millions—become such a cultural phenomenon that it left virtually no corner of the early-twentieth-century American literary canon untouched? And why is almost no one in the field of literature talking about it? Of all of the interventions of major canonical writers into the debates surrounding Christian Science, Mark Twain's critique is still the best known and most frequently studied, but it is not particularly well understood. When not treated as straightforward misogyny, Twain's antagonism toward Eddy is almost invariably presented in stark Manichean terms: modern scientific rationalism versus religious mysticism.[2]

Perhaps because it emerged at a historical moment when the modern medical profession was just beginning to take shape, Christian Science has been easily characterized by twentieth- and twenty-first-century critics alike as an antimodernist throwback that resisted the tide of progress in favor of a more religiously centered model of healing and self-improvement. Its adherents still frequently, but not universally, eschew medical treatment in favor of spiritual healing, believing that human beings created by God are fundamentally perfect and that disease and disability are little more than the products of delusion. All that is necessary for healing, argues Eddy in her masterwork *Science and Health*, is the realization that one is actually well. For critics, Christian Science is therefore to be blamed for many preventable deaths. And for many of Eddy's contemporaries, it was considered a threat to the very fabric of modern civilization. Thus, to some scholars, the hostility of Twain toward Eddy and Christian Science, not to mention that of Upton Sinclair, Gertrude Stein, Edith Wharton, and Ernest Hemingway, has always seemed fairly straightforward and easy to explain. Likewise, the affinity for Christian Science manifested in the life and work of Theodore Dreiser, Harold Frederic, Frances Hodgson Burnett, and Mina Loy has always been a perplexing, even embarrassing, part of their legacies.

But to characterize the furor over Christian Science in those terms is to misunderstand something fundamental about the people who participated in it and the cultural landscape they occupied. During its heyday,

Christian Science was the epicenter of heated and wide-ranging public debates, which included manslaughter trials, sensationalistic newspaper headlines, internal battles in the American Medical Association, and legislative efforts to curtail the activities of religious healers. These debates were complex, with many intersecting interests in play. *Everyone*—doctors, lawyers, legislators, ministers, and the citizens they claimed to serve—had a stake in the large-order concerns they raised: freedom of religious expression, therapeutic choice, journalistic ethics, freedom of speech, the nature of professionalism itself, and the entrance of various minorities into white-male-dominated arenas. And what is surprising is the degree to which interests on *all* sides shared an investment in the idea of scientific progress and a kind of rationalized spirituality—distinguished by both Christian Scientists *and* their critics from "outmoded" forms of religion—as essential for the progress of humanity and the future of the United States in the world. Christian Scientists claimed the authority of both "Christian" and "Science" with equal fervor even as their enemies insisted they had the right to neither. The story of Christian Science and the furor that surrounded it is not the story of how the enlightened proponents of modern, secular, scientific ideals swept away a particularly pernicious form of supernaturalism. It is rather the story of how various competing forces contended over *who had ownership* over the fundamental narratives of modernity. All appropriated the rhetoric of "progress," of the turning back of a bygone era in favor of a new one, even as they raged vehemently against one another over what that progress ought to look like.

The purpose of this book is to examine the relationship between American literary history and Christian Science by examining the narratives that were produced around it, from the story that Eddy shaped over the years of how she "discovered" Christian Science by healing herself of a supposedly fatal injury to the representation of her theories by doctors and journalists and by literary figures such as Twain, Dreiser, and Burnett. These investigations will elucidate texts that have thus far been nearly inaccessible because of poor contextual understanding—in particular, Twain's *Christian Science* and Dreiser's *The "Genius"* (by far the least studied of all his novels), not to mention the involvement of people like Cather and Tarbell in Eddy's biography. This inquiry will also enable a reexamination of the disciplinary assumptions that drive the field of American literary studies, where secularization narratives have remained surprisingly durable, given the ongoing importance of religion and spirituality in American public life.[3]

As Tracy Fessenden argues in *Culture and Redemption*, this lingering investment in a sharp distinction between religion and secularity betrays itself by the refusal to acknowledge any relationship of the former to the formation of the post-Emersonian canon.[4] Indeed, to refuse to treat religion as worthy of study in the context of American literature is to ignore how specific religious ideas have shaped the very idea of a "secular" that is presumed to be wholly disenchanted. According to Fessenden, what passes for secularism in the United States is perhaps a deinstitutionalized and unmarked form of Reformed Protestantism presenting itself as value free. This Protestantism that masquerades as religious neutrality is allowed to determine what actually counts as a religion and to exclude groups or belief systems deemed hostile to the emancipatory, "secular" democratic project: "the salutary transparency of good religion and the attribution of antidemocratic leanings to any other kind made it inevitable that, beyond the discipline of religious studies (and frequently enough within it), *all* visible forms of religion might easily be regarded as irrational, regressive, and threatening to the democratic project."[5] In her book, Fessenden demonstrates how this version of the secular defined itself against Catholicism, the authoritarian other to liberated, enlightened Protestantism. But it should be noted that Islam, the Latter-day Saints, Native American shamans, Chinese Buddhists, and yes, Christian Scientists frequently shared the pillory with the bishops, and hatred for any single one was often expressed in terms of its supposed similarities to other hated religious minorities.

Despite its status as a religious outsider, Christian Science nevertheless managed to penetrate to the heart of American culture in ways that have similarly gone unmarked. Linked to a broader tradition of idealism that goes back to Anglican bishop George Berkeley, to Emersonian romanticism, to nineteenth-century intellectual confidence in the promise of empirically derived truths to better the human condition, and to an emergent popular and scientific faith in the power of the mind to shape material reality, Christian Science was deeply engaged in producing many constituent parts of what we know as twentieth-century American culture. As Anne

Harrington and Barbara Ehrenreich have shown, belief in the power of the mind infuses American business culture, motivational literature, and recovery and addiction therapy.[6] But as distant as these populist theories may seem from a woman who died in Boston in 1910, every contemporary healer and self-help author, from Napoleon Hill to Deepak Chopra to Andrew Weil, "came out from under Mary Baker Eddy's petticoats." Blending science with spirituality,

> The idea that healing lies within the self has become a vessel capable of containing all manner of modern anxieties and needs. The self-healers of the twentieth century have touted their connection to the great god Science, a connection which, as Eddy perceived, would be the ultimate twentieth-century imprimatur. Even as they borrow from the prestige of science, they have also rejected the powerful authoritarian figure of the Doctor/Scientist jealously protecting the inner sanctum of a fearsomely complex, secret knowledge. Anyone can have that knowledge, they say. Anyone.[7]

Mary Baker Eddy and other mental and metaphysical healing figures like P. P. Quimby and Warren Felt Evans are the direct intellectual ancestors of Norman Vincent Peale, author of *The Power of Positive Thinking* (1952), and Rhonda Byrne, author of *The Secret* (2006). Bill Wilson, one of the founders of Alcoholics Anonymous, was also influenced by the writings of Mary Baker Eddy, attesting to how the central assumptions of Christian Science have penetrated mainstream therapeutic vocabularies that are now simply taken for granted.

Though it has received attention from scholars in religious studies, particularly as a feminist recovery project, Christian Science remains poorly understood by the broader scholarly community and the public as a whole.[8] One need only look to the frustratingly enduring usage of the 1907 *McClure's* biography as an authoritative source (not to mention its problematic attribution to Cather) for evidence of scholarly ignorance.[9] The first question I get from many people who hear about this project usually involves Tom Cruise, which says almost everything you need to know about the rest. Indeed, just as Christian Science is often confused with Scientology (to which it bears some passing similarities, despite emerging on the scene almost a century prior), it is also often confused with the many contemporary movements that Mary Baker Eddy both influenced and defined herself in opposition to. These included Theosophy, spiritualism, New Thought, mind cure, and divine healing. Scholars who are sensitive to these distinctions have done much to illuminate them, and where it is prudent and necessary, I will underline the differences as well.[10]

On a broader level, I am interested in Christian Science not only as a discrete set of doctrines, beliefs, and practices codified by a single authority, but also as a social and cultural phenomenon. I am interested in how it codified and proliferated itself in the form of institutions, publications, and narratives, but I am also interested in how people put it to use. Christian Science as it was operationalized in the broader culture was frequently heterodox, not always staying within the boundaries defined by Mary Baker Eddy. What's more, it was frequently syncretic. As we shall see, individuals like Burnett and Dreiser were avid readers of Eddy and frequently invoked her name, but their interest in Christian Science was of a piece with their interest in other forms of religious experience. Affiliations in fin de siècle American religious culture could be loose and dynamic, full of experimentation and shifting affinities. Amy Voorhees portrays this tendency to conflate Christian Science with contemporaneous movements as mere "cultural confusion" stemming from their shared unorthodoxy and female leadership.[11] But I suggest that these conflations also occurred because individuals found similarities that helped them make meaning out of a frequently confusing religious (and scientific) landscape, highlighting similarities as they found them in order to fulfill a desire to find in all religions some kernel of fundamental truth. This study aims to portray that complexity while maintaining distinctions where they truly matter.

In many ways, the same applies to Mary Baker Eddy. As Voorhees also states, Mary Baker Eddy's biography has been an object of far greater interest to scholars outside the church than the movement she founded. Though this book establishes certain central facts and arguments about Eddy's life, it is certainly not a biographical treatment, nor does it pretend to offer new information on her life. As with Christian Science, I am interested in the cultural role that Eddy has played. The picture of her that I present in this book is based on her many biographies as well as my own reading of her works.[12] But to a very real extent, the Eddy that emerges in some of these chapters is as much the Eddy of folklore as the historical

Eddy. As I argue in chapter 4, even the most ardent realists of the era could not, at times, resist thinking of Mary Baker Eddy as a literary construct, as the central character in an unfolding romance.

This is part of the rationale for using literary studies as a lens for examining the cultural impact of Christian Science. But extending that rationale further, we can look not only at the fact that Mary Baker Eddy and Christian Science served as the subject of narrative but also consider the centrality of narrative to the movement's appeals to potential converts. At the center of Christian Science and all of the talk that surrounds it are stories of sickness and healing. For all the intellectual appeal it had for individuals like Dreiser and Burnett, one of the primary motives for conversion remained tied to the experience of radical delivery from chronic suffering and death. These stories of healing exist as literal accounts by individuals who wrote about their healing experiences in letters to Mary Baker Eddy and to local healers, in the pages of the *Christian Science Journal*, and in testimony delivered in court. In *The Wounded Storyteller*, Arthur Frank calls these kinds of accounts "restitution narratives," because they tell the story of ill bodies that are returned to their preferred, supposedly "natural" state of wellness: "Anyone who is sick wants to be healthy again." But the restitution narrative also serves a social and cultural function: "Contemporary culture treats health as the normal condition that people ought to have restored. Thus the ill person's own desire for restitution is compounded by the expectation that other people want to hear restitution stories."[13]

But behind all these individual testimonials was an even bigger restitution narrative about the ability of Christian Science to heal the nation and the world, to bring it out of a period plagued by war, crime, alcoholism, madness, corruption, and, of course, sickness and death to a shining era of perfection. As Christian Scientist Carol Norton declared in an 1899 lecture in Concord, New Hampshire:

> We live in an era of progress, scientific development, and mental expansion. In the universe of Mind new worlds are being constantly discovered. The psychological unfolding of mentality is world-wide. Universal consciousness is throwing aside its swaddling clothes. The ghostly shapes of religious superstition, medical vagaries, and absurd and materialistic scientific speculations are fast being relegated to the realm of oblivion.

Divine rationality, demonstrable religion, and scientific mental therapeutics are assuming their rightful place as the righteous rulers of this world.[14]

It is no accident that this narrative mapped perfectly onto other evolutionary narratives of advancement that drove so many Progressive Era
reforms. Reeling from the Civil War, the tumult of the Industrial Era,
and the abandonment of Reconstruction, the United States was in search
of a restitution narrative. Those narratives were provided in various ways
by the projects of national expansion, technological innovation, moral
reform, and the rationalization of almost every part of human life from the
home to the workplace to the prison. These were the narratives of modernity, what Zygmunt Bauman characterizes as a "drive to mastery; a mode
of being shot through with hope, ambition, and confidence—a behavioral-
attitudinal complex correlated with what Francois Lyotard described as
the Cartesian determination to graft finality upon a time-series ordered
by subordination and appropriation of 'nature.'"[15] Christian Scientists
and their contemporaries envisioned a better, even perfect, world, and
they believed in the power of both science and religion to drive humanity
forward. This is why, in their own unique ways, progressives like Dreiser and Burnett found Christian Science appealing, and it is why Mark
Twain's invective against Eddy—which was rooted in a more fundamental
distrust of the broader restitution narrative—is so deeply misunderstood.

For as Samuel Clemens knew all too well, healing narratives have their
limitations. Even though William James lumped her in with the "healthy-
minded," Eddy's own life, like James's, was marked by bitter struggle.
Though some of her followers believed that she would never die, she was
decidedly mortal, passing away in 1910, the same year as Clemens. And the
decade that followed their deaths seemed to vindicate the cynic's view of
the world rather than Eddy's, closing not with heaven on earth but in the
aftermath of a devastating world war. However, even that calamity, for
some, meant the culmination of the restitution narrative was deferred,
not problematic at its core. In the modern world, suggests Bauman, death
is a scandal, "an emphatic denial of everything that the brave new world
of modernity stood for, and above all of its arrogant promise of the indi-
visible sovereignty of reason."[16] Like the invention of antibiotics and the
development of cybernetics, Christian Science can be seen as another one

of humanity's bids for immortality, an attempt to conquer contingency by aligning the mind with a higher reality, a divinely ordained reality that they believed to also be scientifically knowable. Thus, its failures should prompt not only reflection on the limits of the mind-body theories that attained such a durable place in American culture but, perhaps, the limits of the restitution narrative itself.

NOTES

1. Val Kilmer, "Mark Twain and Mary Baker Eddy," accessed June 14, 2015, http://twaineddyfilm.com.

2. An example of this treatment can be seen in the introduction to the 1997 Oxford edition of *Christian Science*. Mark Twain, *Christian Science*, ed. Shelley Fisher Fishkin (New York: Oxford University Press, 1997).

3. See Winfried Fluck's history and critique of the field in *Romance with America: Essays on Culture, Literature, and American Studies* (Heidelburg: Winter, 2009).

4. Tracy Fessenden, *Culture and Redemption* (Princeton, NJ: Princeton University Press, 2007), 13–14. See a similar argument in Joanna Brooks, "From Edwards to Baldwin: Heterodoxy, Discontinuity, and New Narratives of American Religious-Literary History," *American Literary History* 22, no. 2 (2010): 439–53, and Jenny Franchot, "Religion and American Literary Studies," *American Literature* 67, no. 4 (1995): 833–42.

5. Fessenden, *Culture and Redemption*, 14.

6. Barbara Ehrenreich, *Bright-Sided: How Positive Thinking Is Undermining America* (New York: Picador, 2010); Anne Harrington, *The Cure Within: A History of Mind-Body Medicine* (New York: Norton, 2008).

7. Caroline Fraser, *God's Perfect Child: Living and Dying in Christian Science* (New York: Picador, 1999), 14.

8. For examples of this feminist recovery work, particularly as it manifested in the 1980s, see Mary Farrell Bednarowski, "Outside the Mainstream: Women's Religion and Women Religious Leaders in Nineteenth-Century America," *Journal of the American Academy of Religion* 48, no. 2 (1980): 207–31; Penny Hansen, "Women's Hour: The Feminist Implications of Mary Baker Eddy's Christian Science Movement, 1885–1910" (dissertation, University of California Irvine, 1981); Susan Hill Lindley, "The Ambiguous Feminism of Mary Baker Eddy," *Journal of Religion* 64, no. 3 (1984): 318–31; Jean A. McDonald, "Mary Baker Eddy and the Nineteenth-Century 'Public' Woman: A Feminist Reappraisal," *Journal of Feminist Studies in Religion* 2, no. 1 (1986): 89–111; Gail Parker, "Mary Baker Eddy and Sentimental Womanhood," *New England Quarterly* 43, no. 1 (1970): 3–18.

9. See Ashley Squires, "The Standard Oil Treatment: Willa Cather, the *Life of Mary Baker G. Eddy*, and Early Twentieth Century Collaborative Authorship," *Studies in the Novel* 45, no. 3 (2013): 1–22.

10. Strong work that places Christian Science in the context of this constellation of innovative, woman-led spiritual and medico-religious movements, clarifying what Christian Science actually is and what it is not, includes Catherine Albanese, *A Republic of Mind and Spirit: A Cultural History of American Metaphysical Religion* (New Haven, CT: Yale University Press, 2007); Stephen Gottschalk, *The Emergence of Christian Science in American Religious Life* (Berkeley: University of California Press, 1978); Pamela E. Klassen, *Spirits of Protestantism:*

Medicine, Healing, and Liberal Christianity (Berkeley: University of California Press, 2011); Amy Voorhees, "Writing Revelation: Mary Baker Eddy and her Early Editions of *Science and Health, 1875–1891*" (dissertation, University of California Santa Barbara, 2013).

11. Voorhees, "Writing Revelation," 170.

12. The biographies I have relied on most heavily for this project are Gillian Gill, *Mary Baker Eddy* (Reading, PA: Perseus, 1998); Stephen Gottschalk, *Rolling Away the Stone: Mary Baker Eddy's Challenge to Materialism* (Bloomington: Indiana University Press, 2006); and Robert Peel, *Mary Baker Eddy: Years of Authority* (New York: Holt, Rinehart and Winston, 1977).

13. Arthur Frank, *The Wounded Storyteller: Body, Illness, and Ethics* (Chicago: University of Chicago Press, 1995), 71.

14. Carol Norton, "Lecture in Concord," *Independent Statesman* (Concord, NH), January 5, 1899 (newspaper clipping, Alfred Farlow Scrapbooks, Mary Baker Eddy Library for the Betterment of Humanity, Boston).

15. Zygmunt Bauman, *Mortality, Immortality, and Other Life Strategies* (Stanford, CA: Stanford University Press, 1993), 132–33.

16. Ibid., 134.

1

The Falling Apple

The Rise of Christian Science

The origin story of Christian Science was refined over time, but the final and best-known version goes like this: On February 3, 1866, Mary Patterson—the future Mary Baker G. Eddy[1]—was rendered unconscious after falling on a patch of ice in Lynn, Massachusetts. She was taken to the home of her friends and treated by Alvin M. Cushing, who considered her injury to be serious.[2] Despite the protests of Dr. Cushing, she insisted on being taken home, where she was treated by two neighborhood women. These caregivers reportedly despaired for their charge's life, claiming that Patterson had broken her back. Three days after the accident, Patterson asked for her Bible and dismissed everyone from her room. Hours later, the woman thought to be suffering from a spinal injury left her bed unaided. This incident—retold in Mary Baker Eddy's autobiography and every account of her life since—eventually became the founding myth of Christian Science, the moment when, as its architect claimed in her autobiography, "my immediate recovery from the effects of an injury caused by an accident, an injury that neither medicine nor surgery could reach, was the falling apple that led me to the discovery how to be well myself, and how to make others so."[3]

As Amy Voorhees indicates, the dating of the discovery to this precise event had both a personal and rhetorical purpose. On a personal level, it signaled Mary Baker Patterson's growing independence from her mentor,

Phineas Parkhurst Quimby, whose influence framed accounts of her innovation prior to 1872.[4] Voorhees also highlights a shift from "a narrative about a phenomenological discovery to an explicitly religious one," but what is truly remarkable about the 1866 account is the way it blends the tropes of religion and science to create a restitution narrative that addressed the perceived inadequacies of those offered by institutional religion and orthodox medicine.[5] In its most essential elements, the story of "The Falling Apple" follows the pattern laid down by so many other religious origin stories, from Paul on the road to Damascus to Joseph Smith and the Golden Plates. Its rhetorical function is to assert the status of the protagonist as prophet, the epiphany as divine intervention. But through the apple metaphor, which calls back to another origin myth—Isaac Newton's "discovery" of gravity—Eddy attempted to distinguish her particular revelation from those of others by arguing that the event was a miracle "in perfect scientific accord with divine law," not a temporary suspension of the divinely ordained laws of nature, but in perfect keeping with them.[6] She called her system "Christian, because it is compassionate, helpful, and spiritual."[7] But she called it Science because its methods were supposedly true to natural laws that she believed to be empirically observable and verifiable. Christ's "demonstrations" were not supernatural events, she argued, but acts in keeping with laws of nature that humans were no longer able to access because of sin and ignorance.[8]

This chapter provides historical background for the literary analysis that follows, and it explores how Christian Science healing narratives responded to a historical moment that demanded restitution narratives that provided solutions to the problems of contingency, mortality, and human existence in ways that encompassed reason and affect, science and faith. Dating Eddy's discovery to 1866 places it at a sensitive moment in American history and culture, right at the end of the Civil War, which had introduced carnage and suffering into the lives of ordinary Americans in a way that shattered conventional faith and placed institutions in a state of disarray.[9] Amid this landscape, Christian Science satisfied the desire for, in the words of historian Drew Gilpin Faust, "an explanation that satisfied hearts as well as minds."[10]

PROFESSIONAL CRISIS AND
THE RELIGIO-MEDICAL MARKET

One of the ubiquitous tropes of Christian Science narrative is medical failure, signaled in Eddy's claim that her injury was one that "neither medicine nor surgery could reach." This likely surprised very few of her contemporaries. To be in the care of a doctor with conventional training in the middle of the nineteenth century was not necessarily to be set up for the best of all outcomes, and the many alternative therapeutic movements that populated the scene leveraged their stories of success against the inadequacy of doctors. To quote feminist historians Barbara Ehrenreich and Deirdre English, "Not until 1912, according to one medical estimate, did the average patient, seeking help from the average American doctor, have more than a fifty-fifty chance of benefiting from the encounter."[11] Physician and Emmanuel Movement leader Richard C. Cabot, critiquing Christian Science in the pages of *McClure's* in 1908, similarly confessed, "It is impossible to study the evidence for and against the so-called Christian Science cures without crossing the track of many an incapable doctor. Indeed, there can be no candid criticism of Christian Science that does not involve also an arraignment of existing medical methods."[12] At the time Cabot was writing, the field of medicine was coming to the end of several decades of deep soul searching, defined not only by changes to the field's methods and theories but a wholesale redefinition of what it meant to be a member of the profession. This period of professional crisis opened up a space in which alternative therapies that had emerged early in the century could continue growing and flourishing while new approaches were invented. The consolidation of medicine as a modern profession at the end of the nineteenth century served as the backdrop against which struggles over lay healing and therapeutic choice played out.

The concept of "professionalism" as it applies to medicine requires some explanation here, as its development over the course of the nineteenth century had profound implications for Christian Science and other forms of lay and alternative healing. The crisis of professionalism helped make those alternatives both possible and necessary, just as the resurgence of professional culture also beleaguered them by the century's end. Likewise, professionalism provided a rhetoric and a narrative that Christian

Scientists at least partially appropriated even as they challenged the exclusivity of mainstream medicine. Professionalism also shaped the careers of many people of letters and is a concept I will revisit in the context of journalism in chapter 4.

The word "professional" does not simply mean one who has completed specialized training and obtained a set of qualifications that make him (and at this historical juncture, it was almost always a "him") suitable for a job. As historians Burton Bledstein and Samuel Haber define it, the professional is a third category of working person who is neither businessman nor laborer. He owns his own labor, but his allegiance is to a code of honor rather than the market. In short, professionalism is as much a claim to prestige as it is an occupation or a predefined field of knowledge. In the eighteenth and early nineteenth centuries, the major professions were medicine, ministry, and law, though the category later expanded to include academics, journalists, editors, and other "brain workers" whose allegiances were supposed to be to a professional "code" rather than monetary gain.[13]

In eighteenth-century Europe, the professions were limited to and therefore derived their authority from the genteel classes, and in the United States leading up to and just after the Revolutionary War, professions largely followed this European model. In late-eighteenth-century London, medicine, law, and the ministry were the few learned occupations considered respectable enough for gentlemen. Even within those professions, there were strata that distinguished the learned practitioner from the technician. A physician, for example, would have been classically educated and acquired "some medical training" in various casual ways. He attended to internal diseases and prescribed drugs; yet, as a gentleman, he did not work with his hands as surgeons and apothecaries did. Surgeons, who attended to injuries and "external disorders," were trained through apprenticeships rather than a liberal arts education, whereas apothecaries were simple businessmen who required no formal education. Social status and education level also determined one's potential rank within the clergy. Bishops were noblemen whose "preeminence contrasted sharply with the wretchedness of the deacons, who . . . in the eighteenth century had become a fixed 'clerical proletariat.'"[14]

Few nobles or gentlemen migrated to the American colonies, however, which meant that the professions in this expanding society had to be filled by relatively ordinary men. That period of leveling, however, was more a matter of necessity than a full-scale assault on the systems of privilege that underwrote the eighteenth-century concept of professionalism. Rather than lowering the status of physician, lawyer, or minister as professional titles, acquiring those distinctions raised the status of the individual who acquired them by attending one of the newly established universities, linking professionalism to social mobility. The professions, with their institutionalized associations with status and privileged knowledge, helped create the elite classes of early American society. Yet this ruling class would not exactly mirror that of Europe. American doctors never duplicated the occupational ranks of physician, surgeon, and apothecary, just as "the attempt to set up a cohesive elite of Anglican priests and to bring a bishop to America failed."[15] The emerging professional class did, however, succeed in establishing collegial organizations in the style of the Royal College of Physicians and the Inns of Court. These organizations helped establish licensing laws and raise the prestige and, at times, the incomes, of their members.

This state of affairs was not to last. The precipitous decline of the professions beginning in the 1820s is attributable to the broader leveling impulses of the post-Revolutionary and Jacksonian periods. Yet, Haber notes, this was an "equivocal egalitarianism" that "mixed a vague animus for leveling with a distinct eagerness for rising in the world." Thus, institutional gateways into the professions and the social standing those professions could confer were collapsed, but only for white men. Rather than abolishing the notion of social hierarchies, "the expansion of political democracy in this era, through suffrage extension and the new political devices that accompanied it, to all appearances made most white males, irrespective of social standing, religious belief, merit, and even virtue, members of the ruling class." Any "well-behaved white male" could be a gentleman, and the traditional professions increasingly became a model for gentlemanly behavior for the emergent middle class. This had the dual effect of rendering professional status desirable and elite while simultaneously lowering the standards for entry into those professions.[16]

Evangelical Protestantism was both an impetus for and a beneficiary of these processes. American evangelicalism largely eliminated denominational (Anglican) hierarchies. While elite divinity schools such as

Harvard and Yale continued to produce learned clergymen in the tradition of the Puritans, the Second Great Awakening—an explosion of Protestant revivalism in the early nineteenth century—saw, in the words of evangelical historian Nathan O. Hatch, "a style of religious leadership that the public deemed 'untutored' and 'irregular'" become "successful, even normative in the first decades of the republic."[17] New Protestant sects like the Millerites, the Latter-day Saints and the Holiness and Restorationist movements emerged under the leadership of religious visionaries who defined themselves against those elite institutions. American Protestants tended to emphasize the personal, unmediated relationship of the individual Christian with both the biblical text and even God himself, and these individuals based their claims to authority not on classical learning but on direct knowledge of the divine.[18]

Just as populism and sectarian innovation had profound implications for the future of American Protestantism,[19] so similar forces shaped nineteenth-century medicine. Animating each tiny revolution was the promise of redeeming predecessors' mistakes and democratizing communities of science as well as faith. Increasing emphasis on technical know-how over elitist classical education led to a proliferation of training colleges—more accessible alternatives to elite universities such as Harvard and Yale—opening the medical field to nearly all white men and even some women who wished to pursue medicine as a career.[20] However, the ultimate outcomes of democratization in the medical profession were paradoxical, for accompanying that expansion of opportunity was a relaxation of standards that proved almost catastrophic for both doctors and their long-suffering patients. Attacks on medical licensure, for example, began as a way of *ensuring* competence, as popular opinion held that a medical license was "an expression of favor" rather than a certification of skill.[21] As medical historian Paul Starr argues, a medical license was only meaningful "if it was accepted as evidence of objective skill. But the belief that medical societies and boards of censors were merely closed corporations, like the banks and monopolies, utterly subverted their value as agencies of legitimation."[22] Abolishing licensure was a means of forcing traditional medical practitioners to compete on the market with other approaches, reaffirming the belief that rational knowledge ought to be accessible to the layman, free from "all the traditional forms of mystification that medicine and other professions had relied upon." This shift in attitudes was, in fact, a crucial turning point that enabled mid- and late-nineteenth-century doctors and researchers to challenge "outdated bases of legitimacy" and build a profession based on modern science, which "shares with the democratic temper an antagonism to all that is obscure, vague, occult, and inaccessible." However, that same populist shift also hampered those very scientific developments, which, in their constantly compounding specificity, give "rise to complexity and specialization, which then remove knowledge from the reach of lay understanding."[23] Through this complex interplay of sociocultural forces, the mid-nineteenth century—that tumultuous period between the decline of eighteenth-century professionalism and the rise of what we might recognize today as the modern medical profession—saw that profession first reach its nadir in terms of both authority *and* competence.

Like the clergy, doctors during this period found themselves competing with various medical sects, and the religious connotation of the term "sectarianism" is not an accident. Starr argues that medical pluralism bore a great resemblance in both inspiration and practice to the explosion of religious sects: "A sect, religious or professional, is a dissident group that sets itself apart from an established institution—a church or a profession; its members often see themselves as neglected and scorned apostles of truth." It was also hardly unusual for religious sects to adopt a particular form of medical practice that suited their theology: "The Mormons favored Thomsonian medicine and the Millerites hydropathy. The Swedenborgians were inclined toward homeopathic medicine." The reason for such an affinity between religion and medicine is that the care of the body and the care of the soul were seen as linked enterprises. While the "pastor-physicians" of the eighteenth century—professionals with both theological degrees and medical credentials who attended to the physical and spiritual needs of the community—are largely gone today, "in America, various religious sects still make active efforts to cure the sick."[24] As Pamela Klassen argues,

> within Christian communities, healing, as the art and science of mending, or at least alleviating physical suffering, has long been considered the responsibility of both religious and medical specialists. Loosely defined as

the restoring of physical or emotional wellbeing with recourse to medical, symbolic, or religious means, anthropologists have usually distinguished healing from curing as a therapeutic approach with broader goals than the cessation of particular physical ailments. In Christianity the distinction between medical technique and miraculous healing has been especially blurred, as the earliest Christians combined curing and exorcising by means of relics and charismatic authority with the techniques of hospitals and Galenic medicine.[25]

Emmanuel Movement historian Sanford Gifford takes a particularistic view of the situation in the United States. Arguing that the traditional antagonism between science and the state churches in Europe necessitated that scientists "establish a secular basis for their discoveries, free from moral and religious judgments," he suggests that the egalitarian spirit of the United States, "with its traditional belief that each man is free to create his own religion," made it the sort of place where "the same kind of person who was attracted by new religious enthusiasms was almost equally susceptible to innovations in science and political theory." Thus, "America generated unusual combinations of religious, scientific and political radicalism, creating some unlikely intellectual bedfellows."[26] Gifford's gloss of this history has a certain exceptionalist appeal to it (if you like that sort of thing), but it is an oversimplification. As we shall see later in this chapter, the consolidation of the medical profession as a true profession in the United States *was* often predicated on a secular ideal. What's more, these movements that linked health, religion, and reform traveled and found welcoming homes across the Atlantic and all over the world. Frances Hodgson Burnett is one such transatlantic figure. But the situation in the mid-nineteenth-century United States certainly saw both religious and therapeutic communities competing in the very marketplace that modern professional medicine had only lately and gradually come to dominate. These included not only more radical movements like spiritualism but also groups like the Emmanuel Movement, a form of lay group therapy that anticipated later developments like Alcoholics Anonymous, which sought cooperation with the medical profession and defined itself against radical Christian Scientists and Pentecostal faith healers.

These groups offered themselves as either an alternative or a supplement and often established their credibility in contrast to a medical profession that had been stripped of its long-held signifiers of authority and had become conspicuously incoherent and ineffective. Charles Rosenberg's *The Cholera Years* provides a vivid portrait of the state of the medical profession in the mid-nineteenth century through the lens of the three major cholera epidemics of 1832, 1849, and 1866. During that final epidemic, which occurred the same year as Mary Baker Eddy's "Falling Apple" incident, "the American medical profession was in transition. . . . the critical temper productive of the scientific advances that have so transformed the status of the American physician in the twentieth century served in 1866 merely to underline the profession's real, if transitory, inadequacies." Rosenberg's portrait of the 1849 cholera epidemic is chilling. "More damaging to the medical profession," he says, "than either lack of education or of ethical standards was the practice of the average physician. His ministrations provided neither cure nor the illusion of competence and consistency." The so-called heroic treatments for cholera were diverse and brutal. High doses of calomel (mercury chloride) were administered with the intent of inducing mercury poisoning: "a common rule of thumb warned that the drug had not begun to take effect until the patient's gums bled." Other common treatments included bloodletting, tobacco smoke enemas, and high doses of laudanum. Needless to say, these treatments were as ineffective as they were unpleasant: "The lack of dignity and of education, even its harsh remedies, could have been forgiven the medical profession had it produced results. But its failures were too conspicuous."[27]

Physicians themselves were aware of the serious inadequacies of most medical treatments. According to Haber, "a leading physician of the Massachusetts Medical Society announced that 'the amount of death and disaster in the world would be less, if all disease were left to itself.'"[28] Therefore, even if the resistance of some religious groups to medical treatment seems foolish to us today, resistance to the medical treatment provided by the average nineteenth-century doctor seems entirely sane: "Popular resistance to professional medicine has sometimes been portrayed as hostility to science and modernity. But given what we now know about the objective ineffectiveness of early nineteenth-century therapeutics, popular skepticism was hardly unreasonable."[29]

EARLY MIND-BODY MEDICINE AND
THE ROOTS OF CHRISTIAN SCIENCE

In this context, Mary Patterson, the future Mary Baker Eddy, having struggled with ill health the majority of her life, turned to Dr. Phineas Parkhurst Quimby for help, forming a relationship that became critical to her emergence as a major innovator in the field of metaphysical healing. Eddy suffered throughout her life from various neurasthenic complaints and experienced no small amount of personal tragedy. As a very young woman, she became both a mother and a widow within a span of months. Because of her poor health and an unsupportive family, her son was placed in the care of a former family servant. He was reunited with his mother only in adulthood.[30] Mary Baker eventually remarried only to see her husband, homeopathic physician Daniel Patterson, get captured by Confederate forces during the Civil War.[31] Patterson returned only to abandon his wife for another woman shortly after. The strain produced by such events no doubt exacerbated her depression, which manifested in various physical ways. Conventional medicine failed to alleviate her condition, so she became one of her generation's many experimenters with alternative forms of healing. In 1862, she sought treatment for the first time from P. P. Quimby.

Quimby's postmesmeric healing methodology was rooted in a nineteenth-century preoccupation with the powerful relationship between mind and body. Indeed, Eddy was an important member of a lineage of mind-body healers—not just Christian Scientists—who laid claim to the authority of science in efforts to redeem the physical and spiritual woes of the individuals who followed them. Christian Science emerged in a mid-nineteenth-century context in which, as Philip Cushman notes:

> The mind was becoming a thing in its own right, in contact with but separate from the body. This modern mind was not so much a battleground in which God and the devil contended; instead it was an entire realm that was governed by the natural laws of science and logic, and it was superior to the body and other aspects of the world of matter. Slowly, the mind began to show up as the most important quality of the human being. It was through the mind that logic and science were exercised, and thus through the mind that the world of matter was dominated and controlled. Because

domination and control were the order of the day in the emerging capitalist economy, the mind, as the instrument of domination, was becoming
the *essential* quality of the self. It was to become the most studied, focused
upon, worried over, experimented with, and revered subject of the modern
era. Those who were thought to understand it, and were responsible for
healing it, became increasingly powerful.[32]

In her history of mind-body medicine, Anne Harrington traces the roots
of nineteenth-century mesmerism, mind cure, Christian Science, psychotherapy, and ultimately the twentieth-century philosophy of "positive
thinking" all the way back to the confrontation between German exorcist
Father Johann Joseph Gassner and Viennese physician Franz Anton Mesmer. In the wake of Reformation-era challenges to Catholic authority and
practice, skeptics began to question the previously unassailable demonstrations of exorcism as practiced by European priests. This skepticism
regarding counterfeit claims of demon possession gave rise to a narrative
about the "power of suggestion," a paradigm in which the signs of the
body could no longer be taken at face value, and the symptoms of demonic
activity began to be attributed to the influence of human promptings.
Though remembered for their dubious claims and theatrical demonstrations, Mesmer and other early forerunners of modern psychology saw
themselves as replacing the mystical regime of religion with rational, scientific explanations for human distress.

Eighteenth-century exorcism was part religious ritual and part spectacle, a space in which the body exhibited the necessary signs that proved
both its disordered state (demonic possession) and its restitution. Gassner
could produce a variety of symptoms in his patients, including convulsions and the raising and lowering of heart rates on command, and Mesmer's contribution to the debunking effort was his ability to produce these
same symptoms through wholly unspiritual means. Mesmer, who exists in
the modern memory as "a charlatan, or a showman, or maybe as someone
who discovered the existence of psychological processes that he did not
himself properly understand," styled himself as the consummate scientist
in the tradition of Isaac Newton. Particularly intrigued by Newton's theories of gravitation, Mesmer experimented with moving magnets across the
bodies of his patients, who "reported experiencing strong sensations of
energy moving through their bodies" and exhibited similar symptoms to

those exhibited during an exorcism, including "violent convulsions." Yet these same patients always reported feeling much better after this treatment. Mesmer later discovered that he could produce the same effects merely by moving his hands over a patient's body, manipulating these invisible energies without the aid of the magnets. This force was later known as animal magnetism.[33]

Despite its scientific pretensions and its role in challenging the presence of demonic influence in explanations of physical disorders, mesmerism retained a mystical flavor. Mesmerism combined a theory of the mind as scientifically knowable and therefore subject to discipline with a popular conception of the mind as a repository of the same sort of mysterious forces that produced the effects of gravity and electricity. According to Robert Darnton, Mesmer postulated a "superfine fluid that penetrated and surrounded all bodies." This fluid was the source of gravity and magnetism and could be used, he believed, to treat sickness, which "resulted from an 'obstacle to the flow of the fluid through the body, which was analogous to a magnet. Individuals could control and reinforce the fluid's action by 'mesmerizing' or massaging the body's 'poles' and thereby overcoming the obstacle, inducing a 'crisis,' often in the form of convulsions, and restoring health or the 'harmony of man with nature.'"[34]

Such crises were part of the theater that Mesmer created around his methods. As Darnton indicates, "Everything in Mesmer's indoor clinics was designed to produce a crisis in the patient. Heavy carpets, weird astrological wall decorations, and drawn curtains shut him off from the outside world and muffled the occasional words, screams, and bursts of hysterical laughter that broke the habitual heavy silence." Groups of patients gathered, holding hands, around great tubs, "usually filled with iron filings and mesmerized water contained in bottles arranged like the spokes of a wheel. They stored the fluid and transmitted it through movable iron rods, which the patients applied to their sick areas." A patient who collapsed was carried off to the crisis room, "and if his spine still failed to tingle, his hands to tremble, his hypochondria to quiver, Mesmer himself approached, dressed in a lilac taffeta robe, and drilled fluid into the patient from his hands, his imperial eye, and his mesmerized wand."[35]

Critics and later reformers of mesmerism found much that was tawdry and suspect in this method. On the European continent, attempts to domesticate Mesmer's wild approach are epitomized in the work of the French neurologist Jean-Martin Charcot, infamous for his work with female hysterics.[36] Mesmer's methods were adapted and transported from Europe to the United States by Charles Poyen, who was briefly followed on his tours about the country by Phineas Parkhurst Quimby, Mary Baker Patterson's future mentor.

The American approach to mind-body healing, in keeping with the spirit of the Jacksonian period, framed itself in a more individualistic fashion, basing its authority on a democratic approach that empowered each individual and deemphasized the role of charismatic healers like Mesmer and Charcot, though charisma and rapport clearly played an enormous role in Quimby's successes. Despite his early interest in mesmerism, Quimby was deeply skeptical of his intellectual forbears, as was his student, the future Mary Baker Eddy, for whom malicious animal magnetism (MAM) represented the closest thing to demonic forces in Christian Science theology. This she described as a form of mind control, reflecting deep anxieties about the authoritarian implications of mesmerism. Quimby's contribution to the evolving field of mind cure was to "relocate the primary cause of emotional distress: mesmerism's theoretical emphasis on unbalanced magnetic fluids was replaced with an emphasis on outmoded or incorrect (negative) ideas about life."[37] Cushman claims that Quimby launched mesmerism from a system of mere symptom relief to a broader philosophy of life and wellness that emphasized the correction of erroneous thoughts over the production of altered mental states. Adherents of Quimbyism "learned to control the material conditions of their lives through the thoughts and wishes of their conscious mind."[38] Quimby's method, in fact, looks something like a reversal of the talking cure. A circular that reached Mary Patterson in New Hampshire and was probably written in 1860 describes his treatment thus: "He [Quimby] gives no medicine and makes no outward applications, but simply sits down by the patients, tells them their feelings and what they think is their disease. If the patients admit that he tells them their feelings, &c, he changes the fluids and the system and establishes the truth, or health. The Truth is the Cure."[39] The key to health, in this system, is for the suffering individual to realize the error of his or her belief in illness or injury, and that the healer is there to guide that realization.

These methods were profoundly successful in the case of the ailing Mary Patterson, allowing her to go about rituals of daily life that previously had been impossible. Patterson was in the midst of trying a variety of therapeutic solutions for her constant fatigue and pain, including homeopathy and water cure, when she learned of Dr. Quimby through one of his patients. Desperate for a solution, she wrote to Quimby and declared her determination to "use her last strength" to reach his office in Portland, Maine. The change was almost immediate. She notes in a letter to the Portland *Evening Courier* on November 7, 1862, her newfound ability to climb the 182 steps to Portland City Hall as evidence of her sudden transformation. She also often spoke of Quimby and his methods in spiritual terms: "At present I am too much in error to elucidate the truth, and can touch only the key note for the master hand to wake the harmony. May it be in essays, instead of notes, say I. After all, this is a very spiritual doctrine—But the eternal years of God are with it and it must stand first as the rock of ages. And to many a poor sufferer may it be found as by me, 'the shadow of a great Rock in a weary land.'"[40] Her initial cure was not permanent, however, and Patterson continued to correspond with Quimby from her home. Quimby, in turn, continued to heal her via "absent treatment," which was an accepted practice among mental healers: "Quimby firmly believed that he had clairvoyant powers and he could help others to recover their health, whether he was in the same room with them or separated by many miles."[41] Absent treatment became a hallmark of Christian Science methodology from its inception, a boon to those who—because of geography or disability—could not travel to see a practitioner.

The "Falling Apple" incident occurred almost immediately after the death of Phineas Quimby in January 1866. The traumatic loss of her mentor combined with her abandonment by Daniel Patterson brought Mary Patterson to a point of physical and spiritual crisis, culminating in her injury and cathartic healing. Prior to the incident, alone and destitute, depending on the hospitality of others in order to avoid homelessness, she contacted Julius Dresser, one of Quimby's other students (and one of her future rivals) to ask him to heal her. He announced that he had no intention of carrying on Quimby's methods. Thus, her "discovery" of Christian Science marks the point at which the future Mary Baker Eddy began adapting Quimby's legacy for her own specific purposes, an act that enabled her to survive without relying on her mentor and endowed her life with purpose. It not only gave her back her health, it gave her an occupation, and a remunerative one at that. From that point on, she dedicated herself to teaching her methods and writing furiously on the document that eventually became *Science and Health with Key to Scriptures*, first published in 1875.

Eddy's writings and healing methods attempted to harmonize her Congregationalist upbringing and the postmesmeric methods she learned from Quimby. Though Quimby occasionally spoke of his work in Christian terms, he never saw himself as the leader of his own religion. It was Mary Baker Eddy who turned metaphysical healing into a fully fledged theology. Whereas Quimby spoke of suffering as "error" that could be corrected by reorienting the thoughts of the patient, for Eddy all reality and all goodness emanated from God, and it was only through the internalization of the truth that one could be returned to one's natural state of divine perfection: "all real being is in God, the divine Mind," and "[it is true] that Life, Truth, and Love are all-powerful and ever-present; that the opposite of Truth,—called error, sin, sickness, disease, death,—is the false testimony of false material sense, of mind in matter; that this false sense evolves, in belief, a subjective state of mortal mind which this same so-called mind names *matter*, thereby shutting out the true sense of Spirit." The religion she developed was unorthodox, to be sure. Through it, she declared, "religion and medicine are inspired with a diviner nature and essence; fresh opinions are given to faith and understanding."[42] But it remained a thoroughly Christian (even Calvinist) invention, which distinguished it from many of the more religiously eclectic movements that followed in its wake.[43]

Though she was undoubtedly exposed both to theological liberalism and Transcendentalism, unlike many of her competitors, she never truly embraced either. Her Christ was not merely a human exemplar, nor did she read the Bible as essentially a work of literature. But she also wasn't exactly a biblical literalist. Eddy's entire system was rooted in a belief that God is an active and intervening presence in the world, the source of goodness and of reality itself. But her God was not interventionist in the manner presumed by faith healers. The healing that both she and Christ performed was assumed to be in keeping with a set of eternal laws. She believed that the miracle accounts in scripture were descriptions of actual events, but "she interpreted them as manifestations of eternal divine law and power, not as unrepeatable evidence of Jesus' supernatural authority."[44] In *Science and Health*, she describes Christ's atonement thus:

> The atonement of Christ reconciles man to God, not God to man; for the divine Principle of Christ is God, and how can God propitiate Himself? Christ is Truth, which reaches no higher than itself. The fountain can rise no higher than its source. Christ, Truth, could conciliate no nature above his own, derived from the eternal Love. It was therefore Christ's purpose to reconcile man to God, not God to man. Love and Truth are not at war with God's image and likeness. Man cannot exceed divine Love, and so atone for himself. Even Christ cannot reconcile Truth to error, for Truth and error are irreconcilable. Jesus aided in reconciling man to God by giving man a truer sense of Love, the divine Principle of Jesus' teachings, and this truer sense of Love redeems man from the law of matter, sin, and death by the law of Spirit,—the law of divine Love.[45]

What she means here is that Christ's role was not to propitiate the sins of man in order to raise humanity in the eyes of God. For God to become reconciled to man would be for divine Truth to reconcile with material error, an impossibility in Eddy's theology. The role of Christ was rather to demonstrate for mankind the way to realize and access the divine Love and divine reality of God, a reconciliation that is demonstrated in the act of healing, of physical/spiritual restitution. Christ, for her, was divine, but divine in the way that all humans might become. Likewise, Eddy viewed the Bible as the facilitator of her initial healing experience, but she "did not regard all of the Bible as inspired nor even the inspired portions of it as equally inspired. And though she spoke of the Bible as her authority, she by no means conceived of it as an absolute authority."[46] Though true in the most basic sense, Eddy interpreted the Bible in a way that got at the "spiritual" meanings she saw in its accounts, its demonstration of truths that human beings had simply lost. In this way, she saw herself as restoring a form of primitive Christianity.

Eddy also went much further than Quimby in rejecting mesmeric ideas and practices. Whereas Quimby had viewed them as essentially foolish, to Eddy they were a form of sin or evil. A few years into her healing practice, she stopped touching patients with her hands and instructed students to stop doing so as well. She later extended this prohibition even to the moving of hands over the body of the individual without direct contact. This change has been regarded by some of Eddy's less sympathetic biographers as at best a trivial difference between her practice and Quimby's. But as Amy Voorhees argues, it represented an important rejection of human agency in the healing process in favor of the divine: "it [touching patients] broke the first commandment by making electricity and the physical sense of touch a god that could heal, whereas her method worshipped God as Spirit completely and totally, making no concessions."[47] Though Quimby did not believe that touch was the mechanism of healing, he understood its suggestive role and used it to build rapport with patients. For Eddy, this was an exceedingly grave mistake. In her chapter on animal magnetism, she says that "if animal magnetism seems to alleviate or to cure disease, this appearance is deceptive, since error cannot remove the effects of error. Discomfort under error is preferable to comfort. In no instance is the effect of animal magnetism, recently called hypnotism, other than the effect of illusion. Any seeming benefit derived from it is proportional to one's faith in esoteric magic."[48]

Though she thought of mesmerism as essentially a superstition, Eddy believed very strongly that the human mind had extraordinary powers, including the ability to influence the embodied experience of other human beings at a great distance. But whereas mind cure and New Thought attempted to leverage this power in order to improve the health and well-being of its adherents (and humanity as a whole), Eddy insisted on subordinating the human mind to the source of Mind itself, which was God. Mesmerism and mental influence, at its worst, took the form of MAM, and Eddy's writings warn of the danger that it represented. As Stephen Gottschalk and Catherine Albanese indicate, she retained a Calvinist's sense of the world as a battleground between forces of good and evil. Her writings, says Albanese, "hid a Calvinist devil lurking beneath the metaphysical surface, an evil that played a very tangible presence."[49] In fact, Eddy attributed various setbacks in her work and in her life, including the premature death of her third husband, Asa Gilbert Eddy, to MAM.

Despite the strongly religious character of her work, Eddy firmly believed that what she was doing was also science. As Gottschalk explains, the term "science" is a slippery one, but in Eddy's usage "it meant the certain knowledge of universal law." Furthermore, Christian Science provided "a method or rule for demonstrating universal divine law. Closely associated with her use of the term *science* as method was her use of it to imply the certainty with which the method could be applied. Her references to her teaching as a science often imply her view that it is infallible, absolute, and exact."[50] She believed it was a divine truth that was verifiable just as a mathematical proof is verifiable: "My conclusions were reached by allowing the evidence of this revelation to multiply with mathematical certainty and the lesser demonstration to prove the greater, as the product of three multiplied by three, equaling nine, proves conclusively that three times three duodecillions must be nine duodecillions,—not a fraction more, not a unit less."[51]

Eddy explicitly presented her work as both scientific discovery and spiritual revelation, a rhetorical strategy that is, again, exemplified in the story of the "Falling Apple" moment. As a scientific discovery, it was unusual because it was derived intuitively through a process of developing acquaintance with the ultimate reality of God. And as a revelation, it was presented as "a gradual process of unfoldment in which she had played an active part." She saw herself as both prophet and researcher, her revelation both a gift from God and a thing that required constant processing, interpretation, and study. She viewed herself as uniquely equipped to perform that sort of work, not merely the instrument of God but an active participant in the ongoing task of understanding the Truth. In her analysis of the major revisions of *Science and Health*, Voorhees notes how the language Eddy used to describe her work shifted back and forth between the words "revelation" and "explanation," "which she seems to have viewed as cognates." This, Voorhees argues, "offers a helpful window into her sense of revelation: it was not a blinding gift from above that obviated or suppressed individual agency, as in trance, but an apparently mysterious gift from above with a divine rationale that required divinely sourced individual agency to clarify and explain."[52]

But ultimately, it was less in the realm of theory than in the realm of pragmatic results that Eddy felt the scientific credibility of her teachings lay. Writing to Julia Field-King after the controversial death of novelist Harold Frederic in the care of two Christian Scientists, Eddy lamented the fact that members of her movement seemed more inclined to teach than to heal, reducing the number of qualified healers in the field: "we need good safe practitioners more than teachers, a million times more.... No person ought to teach who is not the very best healer."[53] Throughout the last decade of her life, she continually warned her followers against the crisis that would inevitably ensue if Christian Science ceased producing "demonstrations" and became a theoretical rather than a practical religion. As she told Augusta Stetson, who had charge of New York's First Church of Christ, Scientist, in 1903, "healing the sick and reforming the sinner demonstrate Christian Science, and nothing else <u>can</u>."[54]

Healing, she told her students, was a calling far higher than preaching or leadership, because it was the best tool for growing the faith. As she told Archibald McClellan, head of the Christian Science Publishing Society, "Healing is the best sermon, healing is the best lecture, and the entire demonstration of <u>C.S.</u>"[55] Likewise, she wrote to Ezra Buswell, another high-ranking member of her movement, "Preaching and teaching are of no use without proof of what is taught and said."[56]

At the heart of Christian Science is the "demonstration," the act of healing. The process of healing oneself or another is a process of persuasion, of contesting the evidence of illness or injury with the "Truth" of Science. The efficacy of the method is proved through either the immediate or gradual abatement of erroneous physical symptoms:

> When the first symptoms of disease appear, dispute the testimony of
> the material senses with divine Science. Let your higher sense of justice
> destroy the false process of mortal opinions which you name law, and then
> you will not be confined to a sick-room.... Suffer no claim of sin or of
> sickness to grow upon the thought. Dismiss it with an abiding conviction
> that it is illegitimate, because you know that God is no more the author of
> sickness than He is of sin. You have no law of His to support the necessity
> either of sin or sickness, but you have divine authority for denying that
> necessity and healing the sick.

This argument takes place in the mind of both the patient and the healer, though it is the healer's responsibility to enable the patient to cease believing in his or her own affliction: "The sick unconsciously argue for [the reality of] suffering, instead of against it. They admit its reality, whereas they should deny it. They should plead in opposition to the testimony of the deceitful senses."[57]

In the final edition of *Science and Health*, Eddy provides an "illustration" of how this works in practice. The healer begins by reassuring the patient "as to their exemption from disease and danger." She then contemplates the supremacy of Truth over suffering, "plead[ing] the case" and then challenging the patient's belief in the material: "Argue at first mentally, not audibly, that the patient has no disease and confirm the argument so as to destroy the evidence of disease. Mentally insist that harmony is the fact, and that sickness is a temporal dream." In Christian Science, the mental state of the healer (or of a parent, in the case of an infant) has the power to affect the mental state of the patient. Only once the patient is ready should the healer begin to impart Christian Science: "To fix truth steadfastly in your patients' thoughts, explain Christian Science to them, but not too soon,—not until your patients are prepared for the explanation,—lest you array the sick against their own interests by troubling and perplexing their thought." Once the patient is prepared, the healer can begin to explain the divine reality of Mind and empower her to conquer her beliefs in sickness and suffering. "Instruct the sick that they are not helpless victims, for if they will only accept Truth, they can resist disease and ward it off, as positively as they can the temptation to sin." If this seems like a difficult task, it certainly was, and Eddy never pretended otherwise. To realize the Truth was not merely to deny the reality of sickness or injury but to see the entire cosmos in a different way, to realize the spiritual reality that lay behind the veil of the physical world, the spiritual meaning behind the words of Scripture. To see the world as a Christian Scientist was to see the world as God saw it: perfect, unified, whole.[58]

THE REBIRTH OF PROFESSIONALISM

During the 1880s, the professional interregnum gradually came to a close, and the formation of licensing laws, professional societies, and stricter medical school requirements began to correct the excesses of midcentury anti-intellectualism and establish the foundations of modern scientific medicine. This meant that medical sectarianism and lay healing faced significant challenges, losing mainstream credibility due to scientific discoveries and also, in some cases, having their right to exist

legislated away. Yet the period between 1880 and 1910 was the most productive period of Mary Baker Eddy's life. During that time, membership in her movement exploded and gained an international presence.
She founded three periodicals, including an international newspaper,
and continued to revise *Science and Health* for future editions. Christian
Science became one of the most discussed cultural phenomena in the
United States, especially in Massachusetts and New York, where churches
counted prominent residents among their members. As professional culture resurged, controversies involving Christian Science also became ral-
lying points for doctors seeking to codify orthodox forms of healthcare,
establish barriers to entry, and forbid the practice of methods deemed
erroneous and inimical to public health.

Samuel Haber identifies two sociocultural trends at work in the restoration of the professions—particularly medicine—to a place of authority
and honor. First, the rapid pace of scientific discovery and the specialization of knowledge allowed professionals to once again make claims about
special competence derived from formal education and the ethos scientific
inquiry:

> Professionals argued that the disciplines upon which their work was based
> were becoming increasingly scientific and that scientific understanding
> could be best inculcated through formal education. Academic training,
> it was generally believed, brought dignity and social standing. . . . The
> professionals undoubtedly looked to the increased educational require-
> ments to enhance their honor and generally increase their income as well.
> Nonetheless it seemed obvious that the better educated the practitioner
> the more likely that he would be competent, and therefore society also
> benefitted. This last point was requisite to the wholeheartedness with
> which the professionals pressed their argument.[59]

Thanks to advances in physiology, germ theory, surgery, anesthesiology,
hospital organization, and public health, doctors "could lead in the re-
assertion of professional claims to authority and honor on a new basis
and with the new social supports that the American society of that era
provided." Thus, the restoration of the American Medical Association
(AMA), the push for federal licensing laws, and the effort to eliminate
sectarian movements were motivated in part by an effort to restore quality,
competence, and scientific rigor to the practice of medicine.[60]

Yet that motivation was accompanied by a desire to restore to professionals the status of gentleman, with all of the social and economic privileges that standing entailed. Thus, the end of the professional interregnum was also embedded in a fierce backlash against the "dogma of equality." The social taboos that prevented professions from establishing gatekeeping standards collapsed. Haber links this to the abandonment of Reconstruction in 1877, the point at which the subordination of the black population helped facilitate reconciliation between the North and the former Confederacy. Toleration of overt white supremacy required an ideology that naturalized social inequality, sanctioned paternalism, and presented equality as fundamentally more threatening to the republic than elitism. Meanwhile, the white majority in the North demanded tighter restrictions on immigration, and the burgeoning wealth of the industrializing nation became concentrated in the hands of a select few. Therefore, the professional standards that emerged out of this period were as much about dictating who a medical practitioner could be as they were about what a doctor ought to know and how he ought to practice. Those same doctors frequently appealed to principles that bore the mark of science—such as the supposed biological inferiority of women and nonwhites—in determining who was acceptable and who was not. Standards were created with the partial intention of transforming professionals into a new elite class, distinct from businessmen and those who worked with their hands, and linking the formation of that elite class to the progress of the nation and even the human race as a whole. Naturally, this meant closing the gaps that had allowed nonwhite males and women to enter the profession during the interregnum.[61]

Also key to the re-creation of the doctor as a specially endowed member of an elite scientific class was the reimagining of the scientific disciplines as wholly secular enterprises. According to Peter Harrison,

> The transformation of natural history into scientific "biology" was a vital part of this process. Whereas natural history had traditionally been dominated by the clergy, the new scientific disciplines of biology and geology gradually achieved independence from clerical influence while at the same time legitimizing a new set of non-ecclesiastical authorities. This was in fact the explicit mission of such figures as Thomas Huxley and his colleagues in the "X-Club," who sought with an evangelical fervor

to establish a scientific status for natural history, to rid the discipline of women, amateurs, and parsons and to place a secular science into the center of cultural life.[62]

Members of the new scientific class rhetorically positioned themselves as the vanguard of reason, invoking a supposedly age-old conflict between science and religion in a battle for human civilization. The story doctors told about themselves was therefore one of restitution and redemption from centuries of religious obscurantism. In an article denouncing sectarian "humbug" medical practices in an 1889 issue of the *New York Medical Journal*, a doctor named A. S. Coe wrote:

> There are many reasons why medical science is behind all other sciences in its development and practical application to the wants of the people. Since Hippocrates, the founder of rational medicine, no real advancement was made until within the last century. The chief reason is that it has been subordinated to vague speculations of philosophers and metaphysicians and the mysticisms of the priesthood, although long before the last century a solid foundation was being laid by the study of anatomy, physiology, histology, chemistry, and therapeutics, but no application of the knowledge thus obtained to the cure of diseases could be made until the teachings of medical science had become emancipated from the traditions of the past, and freed from their dogmatic spirit by rejecting all hypotheses and returning to the unbiased study of natural processes as shown in health and disease.[63]

Yet there is nothing inevitable about this narrative. For every Galileo there is a Gregor Mendel, the Augustinian friar who contributed to the study of genetics by growing pea plants in his garden. But, as Harrison reminds us, this narrative of transhistorical struggle served a profession that was attempting to redefine itself as a secular body of nonclerical (and nonamateur) members: "It served the political purposes of this clique to deploy a rhetoric of conflict between theology and science."[64]

Physicians saw themselves as foot soldiers in a battle, not only against alleged frauds like Mary Baker Eddy, but also against the credulity of the masses. Previously, the anti-elitist spirit of the Jacksonian era had mandated therapeutic choice based on the (perhaps naïve) libertarian notion that theories and treatments had to compete with one another in an open market of ideas, but in the 1880s and 1890s, doctors called for the regulation of healthcare delivery on the grounds that the public was incapable of making informed choices. Calling upon his profession to champion the legal curtailment of the activities of sectarian practitioners, a writer going by the initials H. G. W. railed in the *Long Island Medical Journal* against the "fresh exemptions permitted [by the New York state legislature] for unqualified half-educated parasites who want the profits of healing without its responsibilities." Later, he proclaims, "The issue is a vital one, for upon it depends the question of future trespasses upon the rights of physicians of all manner of fakirs."[65] The invocation of the fakir, like Coe's reference to "the mysticisms of the priesthood"—almost certainly code for Catholicism—demonstrates the manner in which these forms of obscurantism were particularly associated with racial and religious outsiders. As Klassen argues, this strategy of equating Christian Science with non-Protestant and nonwhite groups was pervasive among critics: "The homegrown 'heresy' of Christian Science thus became a cipher for Protestants to assert their racialized supremacy over all the world's religions."[66]

Doctors frequently expressed concern that the democratic process and the American judicial system were inadequate to regulate the practice of medicine in the way it needed to be regulated. The softness of legislators was frequently blamed for the exceptions granted to Christian Scientists under their right to freely practice their religion. Likewise, juries and even judges were blamed for failures to successfully prosecute Christian Scientists whose patients died. As one editorial writer for the *Buffalo Medical Journal* writes, commenting on the trial of Harold Frederic's mistress:

> The sympathy of a jury and the weakness of the bench often combine to render adequate punishment a rare sequel. In Kentucky the practice of medicine has been well defined to be any ministration that pretends to offer to cure bodily ills for pay. But, too often, either the court itself or some of the jurors fancy they have been benefited by christian science [*sic*], hence convictions are not easy. Even lawyers of reputation for intelligence on ordinary subjects become believers in this weak combination of medicine and religion, and are willing advocates of the "oppressed" defendant.[67]

The intervention of external legal bodies in medical matters was apparently both desired and feared. Though physicians frequently appealed to the legislature and the judiciary to determine who could and could not practice, they also despaired over the qualification of those bodies to perform that same duty given their members' lack of scientific training. As Edwin Mack lamented in a 1903 issue of the *Wisconsin Medical Journal*, the doctor had much to fear from the "tribunal" that tried malpractice cases: "For the question of the propriety of a physician's conduct must in case of suit be determined by a jury. The members of the jury are necessarily not only not learned in medicine, but usually uneducated and untrained men, whose judgment on matters involving technical questions can seldom be based on any intelligent analysis of the circumstances." For that reason, he argued, verdicts must be based upon the testimony of "competent expert evidence. . . . A physician can be adjudged negligent or unskillful only on the testimony of physicians as experts, that the practice adopted was not such as physicians and surgeons, or ordinary knowledge and skill would have followed."[68]

The regulation of the modern medical profession had implications beyond the elimination of patent medicines and other humbug cures. As Ehrenreich and English demonstrate, in many cases, it produced results that were *inimical* to the cause of public health even by scientific standards. The eradication of midwifery, for example, was a particularly regrettable event. In the first decade of the twentieth century, half of all babies were still delivered by midwives. But as outsiders in a medical paradigm that began demanding university education and as the primary form of competition for obstetrics as an emerging specialty, these members of a long-standing tradition were pushed out in the name of science. They were "ridiculed as 'hopelessly dirty, ignorant and incompetent'" and blamed for infections. Ehrenreich and English argue that the techniques for preventing infection were "well within the grasp of the least literate midwife. . . . So the obvious solution for a truly public-spirited obstetrical profession would have been to make the appropriate preventive techniques known and available to the mass of midwives. This was in fact what happened in England, Germany, and most other European nations."[69] In the United States, childbirth was brought into the hospital, and poor women were used as test cases in teaching hospitals.[70] The result was a decline in the standard of care for pregnant women: "In fact, a study by a Johns Hopkins professor in 1912 indicated that most American doctors were *less* competent than midwives. Not only were the doctors themselves unreliable about preventing sepsis and ophthalmia but they also tended to be too ready to use surgical techniques which endangered mother or child."[71] Quality of care did not necessarily rise in tandem with scientific discovery, especially during this period of transition.

The professional narrative of redemption from the superstitions of the past is also complicated by the ways in which doctors made common cause with certain medical sectarians. Attaining authority and honor frequently required the profession to cooperate with irregular practitioners who possessed a considerable amount of cultural capital and controlled a significant share of the healthcare market, regardless of their nonadherence to the standards of the AMA. Starr demonstrates how regular physicians collaborated with Eclectics and homeopaths to set licensing standards for each form of practice. These irregular practitioners were given seats on licensing boards, sometimes with the support of legal statutes and even the court system. Such a practice obviously flies in the face of the myth that "homeopaths and herbal doctors were suppressed by the dominant allopathic profession." Rather, "Despite their historic efforts to avoid contact with sectarians, the regular physicians now found that a single integrated board worked better than multiple separate boards in controlling entry into the profession. Accordingly, they set aside their scruples about consorting with heretics and made common cause with them." Starr's narrative suggests that this collaboration bore more fruit for the regulars than it would for the homeopaths, and that the market for the latter would decline into oblivion during the first two decades of the twentieth century. Yet a visit to one's local health food store will immediately suggest otherwise. While in some cases, such as the Emmanuel Movement, medical professionals were successful in either co-opting or driving away lay alternative therapies, a market for such continued to flourish on the margins, bolstered, perhaps, by an aura of notoriety.[72]

CHRISTIAN SCIENCE ANSWERS THE MEDICAL PROFESSION

Amid the ongoing inefficacies of "regular" medicine, Christian Scientists continued to push back by highlighting its visible failures and by providing what was for many a more attractive alternative. Throughout the first two decades of the twentieth century, well after the processes of modernization and professionalization had begun, doctors remained important characters in Christian Science narratives. The pages of the *Christian Science Journal* are full of testimonials that begin thus:

> I was taken sick about August 1901, and was treated by a physician.... There was no immediate improvement in my condition, but gradually I grew worse. Becoming discouraged, I changed physicians. The second one announced a complication of diseases, and there was no improvement under his treatment. In October, 1901, I went to Gilroy Hot Springs. Grew worse there and returned in a critical condition, gave up my practice and continued treatment,—medicine and washing out of the stomach, with a very limited diet. The doctor finally pronounced neurasthenia of the stomach. I got no better, and December 24, 1901, a consultation was held. They were at a loss to know what to do.[73]

Occasionally in these stories, a doctor will be summoned by a relative or friend only to prove themselves utterly useless:

> Early in April, 1905, our little boy, aged two years, was seized with high fever followed by violent spasms, from no apparent cause. A very serious nervous condition followed for four days, when a state of coma set in. The nearest Christian Science practitioner was asked to take the case, but the father, not being a Christian Scientist, insisted that *materia medica* should be well represented. One physician was in steady attendance, and four who were called in consultation pronounced the disease meningitis. They agreed that there was absolutely no hope, and that the best they could do for us was to wish that the child would lie in that state until he passed on, that all might be spared any form of violent agony before death came. They said it was impossible for him to recover and that we should be anxious for the end to come quickly, for if such a rare thing as his living through the illness occurred, he would necessarily be both mentally and physically deformed.[74]

All testimonials, accounts of hopeless situations in which benighted physicians make mistaken (and often contradictory) diagnoses and administer futile, painful treatments, invariably end with the intervention of a Christian Science practitioner, as in the case of the dying child just described:

> Medical skill having failed so entirely, the father was then willing to have Christian Science. I telephoned my teacher for help. The physician

continued in attendance, being deeply interested in seeing the effects of Christian Science upon the little patient. He eagerly watched the change, which he pronounced most marvelous, and frankly said no power but God's could bring it about. He watched with us as the demonstration was made that death is only a shadow and not a reality. Once, death apparently claimed the little one, but Christ, Truth, was strong to deliver, and error could not prevail.[75]

For the Christian Scientists who produced and read these stories, medical failure went beyond an outdated commitment to heroic treatments or ignorance of psychotherapeutics. It was the very narrative provided by physicians that proved unsatisfying. When the attending physician announced a "complication of diseases" or said the word "meningitis," illness could effectively become destiny. In the accounts of these patients and so many others, the part of the story that includes mainstream medicine is characterized by abandonment or consignment to fate, of being given up for dead by doctors or asked to accept death or permanent disability as inevitable. Says a writer going by the initials E. S. in March 1892: "For eight long years I searched for health, and found it not. Each and every physician told me the same story, viz: that I was diseased in every organ, and when free from pain ought to be satisfied, for I could never be strong; but none of them could even free me from the pain. Useless and miserable, I often wondered why God afflicted me so." By introducing Christian Science into the picture, these stories attempt to refute a narrative of biological determinism in which diagnosis becomes fate. After being treated by a Christian Science practitioner, E. S. "returned home, cured of my worst troubles, and able to walk as well as anyone. My friends all made fun of me, and said it was excitement that was keeping me up; that in a short time I would be as bad as ever,—but thank God, their prophecy has not been fulfilled." And while this prediction of relapse did come true—"Every old disease and pain came back to me that summer and fall, and many times I was tempted to give it all up and go back to medicine"—the story is transformed from one in which the teller must accept suffering as a fact of life to one in which "I am always sure of one fact: that these claims cannot stay long, and must finally disappear forever."[76]

Christian Scientists did not challenge physicalist medicine by positing a softer spiritual narrative over the cold empiricism of scientific medicine but by satisfying a need for *both* physical and spiritual restitution that medicine left unfulfilled. What's more, they used the alleged disparity in results in order to accuse doctors of practicing bad science. According to Anne Harrington, Christian Scientists maintain that their practice is "not just rooted in blind faith, but grounded in repeated personal experience. It is in this sense above all, they say, that Christian Science should be seen as a science, a form of Christianity that aims to demonstrate its truths through empirical demonstration."[77] Reflecting on the healing accounts produced by Christian Scientists and other mind cure movements, William James similarly stated, "these are exceedingly trivial instances, but in them, if we have anything at all, we have the method of experiment and verification."[78] As such, Christian Science was part of what Harrington calls "a third way of thinking about physical illness—and of telling stories about physical illness—that is neither the traditional way that has lost credibility, nor the standard physicalist way that lacks existential relevance. This third way also claims to be rooted in science. Indeed, it often claims to have a scientific understanding of illness that is more complete than that provided by the physicalist stories of mainstream medicine."[79]

For Eddy, medical language, the naming of concepts, was at the heart of medicine's failure: the labeling of the disease reified a set of mental abstractions and doomed the patient to a particular end. Concerned that the use of diagnostic terms had the power to induce illness, she asserted in *Science and Health* that the very "act of describing disease—its symptoms, locality, and fatality" is "unscientific."[80] She had a point. It is on this very basis that physician F. G. Crookshank insisted, "Medicine is not, and never will be one of the exact sciences." Medical knowledge is organized through the application of specific names to clusters of symptoms and/ or pathological agents and calling those "diseases." A problem occurs, however, when names or titles of convenience become confused with the things to which they refer and thereby take on realities and lives of their own: "But when, as so often happens, a *name* is illegitimately transferred from the *reference* it symbolizes to particular *referents*, confusion in thought and perhaps in practice is unavoidable." "Diagnosis," he says, "too often means in practice the formal and unctuous pronunciation of a Name that is deemed appropriate and absolved from the necessity of further investigation."[81] For Eddy, to pronounce that name was to induce the disease it described, to make what was only a thought concrete for both practitioner and patient and thereby give credence to the "error" that all physical symptoms were anything more than products of Mortal Mind. She blames the naming of new diseases for propagating certain trends in ill health: "It does this by giving names to diseases and by printing long descriptions which mirror images of disease distinctly in thought. A new name for an ailment affects people like a Parisian name for a novel garment. Every one hastens to get it."[82]

In early issues of the *Journal*, healing accounts appeared with the names of the diseases healed above each testimonial in bold print—"A Case of Scrofula," etc. By 1893–94, this practice was dropped, and in 1906, Eddy instructed the editors of her periodicals to "keep out of them all descriptions of shocking suffering and the symptoms of disease" because "rehearsing error is not scientific."[83] In place of the specific diagnostic language of medicine, Christian Science developed a vocabulary of its own that acolytes and patients were required to master. "Claim" or "belief" was used to describe physical ailments, which, according to Eddy, were illusions caused by the human inability to realize the Truth. Thus, one had a "belief in blindness," a "claim of tuberculosis," and so on. While specific diagnostic language does appear, it is never without a qualifier that reminds both writer and reader that the name of the disease is fundamentally symbolic.

Although the process of healing was a process of coming into alignment with Divine Mind and not simply exerting the will of the human mind over matter, in *Science and Health*, Eddy did often slip into language that granted an individual mind agency over the physical condition of the body. The empowerment this bestowed upon the patient during treatment was, in fact, an important distinction between Christian Science and modern medicine: "At the right time explain to the sick the power which their beliefs exercise over their bodies. Give them divine and wholesome understanding, with which to combat their erroneous sense, and so efface the images of sickness from mortal mind." Fear of coercion and the ability of that fear to produce adverse physical responses were, indeed, part of Eddy's opposition to medicine. She cites the case of a woman who was "compelled by her physicians" to take ether for an operation and died: "Her hands were held, and she was forced into submission. The case was brought to trial. The evidence was found to be conclusive, and verdict was returned that death was occasioned, not by the ether, but by fear of inhaling it." Christian Science demanded that its practitioners treat every patient as a mind, that is, as a subject rather than as "so much mindless matter, and as if matter were the only factor to be consulted." Even the hypnotist, she says, "dispossesses the patient of his individuality in order to control him. No person is benefited by yielding his mentality to any mental despotism or malpractice." Insofar as Christian Science subordinates the body to the mind, so it protects both from the violent intrusions, humiliations, and dismissals of modern medicine.[84]

Despite the counternarrative it provided, Christian Science participated along with the medical profession in the production of what Arthur Frank calls the modern experience of illness,

> when popular experience is overtaken by technical expertise, including complex organizations of treatment. Folk no longer go to bed and die, cared for by family members and neighbors who have a talent for healing. Folk now go to paid professionals who reinterpret their pains as symptoms, using a specialized language that is unfamiliar and overwhelming. As patients, these folk accumulate entries on medical charts which in most cases they are neither able nor allowed to read; the chart becomes the official story of the illness.[85]

Indeed, it would be easy to interpret Christian Science as a return to the premodern model of domestic and family-centered treatment, in which, according to Michel Foucault, "the natural locus of disease is the natural locus of life—the family: gentle, spontaneous care, expressive of love and a common desire for a cure, assists nature in its struggle against the illness itself to attain its own truth."[86] Christian Science, while perhaps more domestic and family-centered in some respects, constructed its own norms of scientific, clinical practice, born out of the modernist desire for expertise, for professionals who reinterpret the illness experience according to a specialized language. In the case of Christian Science, this is the language of *Science and Health*, in which Mind, Love, and Truth, used with Eddy's precise spiritual definitions in mind, become the terms of power. Christian Science's claim to being a better science was based on the performance of expertise on the part of practitioners, not simply a rejection of medicine's primary investment in physiology.

For practitioners, adopting the role of the expert was a way of ensuring economic survival and claiming cultural authority. Through the

Massachusetts Metaphysical College, Eddy conferred the authority of licensure. And, as it turns out, these signs of competency proved critical in getting some patients to submit to treatment and tell their stories in the practitioner's terms. Though Christian Science restores the agency of the patient, there is a still a need for what Arthur Frank calls "narrative surrender" to a professional with some kind of institutional imprimatur, "the central moment in the modernist illness experience." That surrender is both an agreement to submit to particular forms of treatment and to tell a story in the terms defined by the healer. For the patient of a medical doctor, "'How are you?' now requires that personal feeling be contextualized within a secondhand medical report. The physician becomes the spokesperson for the disease, and the ill person's stories come to depend heavily on repetition of what the physician has said."[87] In some instances, the practitioner literally does become the spokesperson. Many of the *Journal*'s narratives were written or passed along by practitioners who recontextualize the patient's experience according to the narrative template required by Christian Science. It is the practitioner, not necessarily the patient, who emerges as the hero, rescuing the patient from the physician who has condemned him or her to death. As Frank argues, this is a hallmark of modern restitution or recovery narratives, which "bear witness not to the struggles of the self but to the expertise of others: their competence and their caring that effect the cure."[88]

Indicative of the centrality of expertise is the tension between "true" and "false" Scientists that emerges in patient narratives and in discussions among Christian Scientists. Some patients depict "true" practitioners (trained in Eddy's school) as essential to their individual progress in realizing the Truth and demonstrating over material circumstances. For example, in August 1893, Mary A. Shearer of Geneseo, Illinois, writes:

> She [the healer] treated me for several weeks and I was healed, but as my home was far from there and no Scientist near the old troubles came back; then I took medicine, but finally had to go to a Scientist again. I never responded to treatment as quickly as many do, so I often became discouraged, and indeed, sometimes wished I had never heard of Christian Science. I had much to discourage me, for I attended lectures with two different teachers (both having been highly recommended to me), who were Christian Scientists in name only. One had been Mrs. Eddy's student, but

had drifted away from her teaching to a line of thought of his own. I was
unable to demonstrate over the false claims that were constantly coming
up. However, I had learned that after once starting there was no real going
back. I must press on, and in the past few months I have had such marvelous demonstrations that I am overwhelmed with the thought of what
Truth will do when we understand and are faithful.[89]

The existence of illegitimate practitioners, of "Christian Scientists in
name only," is indicative of the importance of institutional sanction to the
success of the healing endeavor. Not only did certification confer honor
on the practitioners, operating in an environment in which such signifiers
mattered; it was essential for the patients themselves. They required these
outward signs of legitimacy in order to be able to buy into the enterprise.

THE SCANDAL OF MODERNITY

Both doctors and Christian Scientists positioned themselves as the
fulfillment of a teleological progress narrative, and both used one another
as foils to demonstrate the past mistakes that were in the process of being redeemed. But in similar ways, that narrative broke down once death
entered the scene. Failure to heal was a difficult thing for Christian Scientists *and* modern physicians to account for and became an occasion for
blame, recrimination, and heated rhetoric. But as insurgents who, in the
perception of the public, promised total liberation from physical suffering
through the application of their theories, Christian Scientists suffered the
most in the public eye. Sensational reports about the deaths of individuals
from treatable diseases in Christian Science homes have garnered media
attention from Eddy's time to our own, resulting in memoirs like Lucia
Greenhouse's *fathermothergod: My Journey Out of Christian Science.*[90] But
in order to demonstrate just how messy the cases of wrongdoing on the
part of Christian Science healers could be, let us take as a case study the
widely publicized death in 1898 of novelist and *New York Times* correspondent Harold Frederic and the trial of Kate Lyon and Athalie Mills, the
Christian Scientists who treated him.

At the time of his death, Frederic was financially supporting two families: his legitimate family in London and his household with Lyon, his

mistress, in Surrey. According to Bridget Bennett, Frederic's biographer, the author's health began declining in 1898, largely as a result of the stress of his double life: "In March he began to lose weight rapidly, and a dose of what he believed to be food poisoning in early summer resulted in what was probably a minor stroke." This was followed by a much more severe stroke on August 12, which left him paralyzed on one side of his body. Kate Lyon treated Frederic through the methods of Christian Science, but Dr. Nathan Ellington Boyd was also involved in the case. Boyd recommended a "restricted diet," but Frederic refused to comply. On August 16, Lyon enlisted the help of Athalie Goodman Mills, a local Christian Science practitioner, who enjoined Frederic to give up medical treatment but eventually granted him special dispensation to continue receiving the services of Dr. Boyd in addition to Christian Science treatments.

On the 17th, Frederic requested a solicitor in order to dictate his will, and Dr. Boyd summoned Dr. Hubert Montague Murray to diagnose Frederic with "paralysis and an 'affectation of the heart.'" Frederic consistently refused to follow the orders of his doctors. On the 19th, he dismissed Boyd entirely in a fit of rage, saying that "doctors were killing him but Christian Science could cure him within two days. Boyd wrote to Lyon warning her that if Frederic died, she would probably be tried for manslaughter. She wrote back requesting that he stop attending Frederic." He was treated thereafter by Drs. Brown and Freyburger, who also prescribed dietary restrictions and bed rest and also found the patient noncompliant. According to Bennett, "Freyberger was convinced that Frederic was not in his right mind and that he was being unduly influenced by Kate Lyon—he claimed at one point that she formulates his thought for him." By September 20, Frederic had renounced medical treatment entirely in favor of Christian Science, and by late October, he was dead.[91]

Bennett argues that Frederic's turn to Christian Science was the act of a desperate man: "[Frederic] was not a Christian Scientist although he was interested in the successful cures that it claimed for itself. His mother had been a great believer in the power of the mind (positive thinking), and Frederic had inherited a belief that mental attitude could influence the physical state of the body." Dr. Freyburger, who attended him in his final moments, reported that Frederic denounced the treatment of Mrs. Mills as not a "bit of good."[92] His death was reported in the New York Times, the beginning of a two-month campaign covering the deaths of patients under the care of Christian Scientists. A long investigative piece on the branch churches in New York was published on November 13, 1898, following the appearance of the indelicately titled "Faith Cure Murders" two days prior. Lyon and Mills were eventually tried for manslaughter but ultimately acquitted for lack of evidence, even though a coroner's inquest had originally found them guilty. As with many prosecutions of Christian Scientists, the case involved complex questions of informed consent, the mental competence of the patient, therapeutic choice, the likelihood that the patient would have improved under the exclusive care of his regular physicians (far from certain), and the potentially coercive influence of Christian Scientist caregivers. One editorial in *The Outlook* formulated the problem thus,

> If a sane man chooses to eschew all physicians, to refuse all means of cure, to deny himself all remedies, and to depend wholly upon means unrecognized by modern science to effect a cure, may the law interfere? If he should determine to live without eating, or in a winter climate without fuel—and it is difficult to see why hunger and cold are not "mortal thoughts" as truly as disease—must the law leave him to starve or freeze to death? If not, is there any more reason why it should allow him to die of disease which science could remedy if he would take the remedies? In short, what are the rights and the duties of the community in protecting an individual from inflicting what the community believes to be needless and perhaps fatal injuries upon himself?[93]

The author offers no answers.

Many critics of Christian Science saw the Frederic case as a clear indicator that legal action must be taken to curtail the activities of irregular practitioners. A writer for one medical journal called the restraint of the law a "scandalous inadequacy." Rather than a matter of informed consent and therapeutic choice, the writer depicts Frederic's death as a case of brainwashing: "But for the fatal interference of the Christian Scientists, both Major Lester and Mr. Harold Frederic would, in all probability, still be with us, doing their good work."[94] The *Medical Herald* (reprinting an item from the *Philadelphia Medical Journal*) similarly called Frederic a "victim" of Christian Science and insisted that the case proved "that an erartic [*sic*] mind may coexist with considerable literary talent and that a sick man is not fitted to be trusted with his own disabled body."[95] The *New York Times* declared that "the largest liberty of opinion in matters of faith and religion must be accorded to the people of all free countries" and that there "should be absolute freedom of choice among the several schools of medicine." However, legal tolerance of Christian Science was quite simply beyond the pale: "the most liberal theory of law and public policy would never sanction the issue of licenses to 'healers' whose system bears no closer relation to recognized therapeutics than the incantations of an Indian medicine man. If the thing cannot be licensed it cannot be tolerated. Its evil and fatal effects have been demonstrated."[96] Not all commentators saw the problem in such stark terms, however. The Chicago-based legal journal *The Public* argued that therapeutic freedom—even the freedom to refuse treatment or pursue unconventional treatments—was, in fact, essential to scientific progress:

> The real difficulty in determining the relation of the healing phase of Christian Science to the law, does not rise out of cases like that of Harold Frederic, in which a sane man, in the exercise of his undeniable right to belief, deliberately refuses the assistance of doctors and puts his trust in Christian Science. It is no function of the public to force doctors upon such a man. Not only is it his right to decide for himself, but if he were denied that right the healing profession might be stagnated. Had police regulations successfully interfered with freedom of choice in this respect in the past, the new schools of medicine that have from time to time challenged and ultimately modified the old, would have been suppressed; and like the law-protected Chinese, we might still measure the usefulness of a physician by the amount of blood he draws and the virtues of drugs by their nastiness.[97]

For Christian Scientists, the response to such high-profile cases was always to disavow the practitioner rather than to question the efficacy of the method. At the time of the Frederic scandal, Eddy enjoined Julia Field-King to "teach your dear students, whom I deeply pity, <u>wisdom</u>, to be as wise as serpents. Never to take a case of so doubtful a kind and conspicuous and with so many minds turned on it without counting the cost and knowing that they can hold it and heal it."[98] Christian Scientist parents also frequently blamed themselves in cases where they or their own children failed to get well. The cases involving children are especially wrenching,

and many *Journal* accounts concerning sick children are saturated with
the anxiety of adults simply trying to do what is best for their offspring,
trying to determine the best course of treatment based on mixed experiences with both traditional and nontraditional forms of care. John Ellis of
Lynn, Massachusetts, whose adult daughter died under the exclusive care
of doctors, wrote this harrowing tale in 1893:

> About nine years ago our daughter passed on; just before her earth life
> closed, she asked to have a Christian Science healer; it was the first time
> our attention had been called to the subject (supposing it was some 'ism').
> We were told that before the healer would take the case we must discharge
> the M.D.s, which, with our understanding, we could not do; consequently,
> we are left to mourn the loss of our daughter."[99]

Ellis was explicit about his sense of regret in obviating his daughter's therapeutic choice, convinced that his unwillingness to allow a Christian Scientist free rein in the case resulted in her death. This harrowing experience
naturally shaped his decision-making process later on when his infant
granddaughter became ill:

> I have a granddaughter who was nine months old in August, 1891, having
> been sickly from her birth. Her father at this time put her under the care
> of the best medical treatment; the doctor called the disease indigestion;
> he consulted the best writings known to medical science and prescribed
> food that was decided by the best medical authorities to be the nearest to
> mother's milk. The child grew worse all the time. She slept but little and
> what little food she took caused severe suffering. It was decided she could
> live but a few hours. As a last resort it was determined to turn to Christian
> Science; a healer from Boston was called, who ordered clear milk and any
> other food that the child could take, which never distressed her in the
> least; she began to recover immediately. The change was so rapid that it
> could hardly be credited. In less than six weeks she was entirely healed. In
> June, 1892, the child was again, taken very ill. For the sake of speed a doc-
> tor was called, who said that there was no hope of saving her, and desired
> a consultation; the most skilled physician was called; she grew worse.
> Seeing her growing worse, her father desired to have the same Christian
> Science healer as before and asked me to go for him. I told him that in my
> opinion it was his duty to go; he did not hesitate but went at once to the
> healer's house. By comparison it was found that very soon after the father
> reached the healer's house the child began to improve, and in three weeks

she was in perfect health and remains mentally and physically a monu-
ment of the power of Truth through Christian Science.[100]

Christian Science attributed the illness of minors not to a lack of understanding or belief on their own part *but on their parents' part*. Therefore,
a parent whose faith was insufficient was guilty of injuring or killing his
child. This probably accounts for the grandfather's insistence that the
father go see the healer out of "duty," to serve as a sign of his own commitment to Science and to the ultimate recovery of his child.

On the other side of the debate, parents were blamed—and frequently
prosecuted—if their child died under the care of a Christian Scientist.
Even the writer of the aforementioned editorial in *The Public*, who de-
fended therapeutic choice as an essential feature of democracy, insisted
that the treatment of children must, to some degree, be regulated by the
state: "Because mature persons have the right, in the treatment of their
own ills, to ignore public sentiment as it at any time exists, it by no means
follows that they have the right to do so in the treatment of the ills of their
children.... society owes to the child the duty of protecting its right to life
not only against what may appear to the community to be the malice of
parents, but also ... their foolishness."[101] As Rennie B. Schoepflin indicates,
the rise in activism on the behalf of children during the late nineteenth
century led to increased concerns about how the unorthodox therapeutic
choices of parents affected their offspring, a heated and emotional debate
that continues to play out today. Children became central to the public
debates over informed consent, parental responsibility, and the regulation
or criminalization of Christian Science activities. According to Schoepflin,
"Of the thirty-six pre-1921 Christian Science cases involving healing practices that I have identified, twenty-one (58.3 percent) involved a sick child,
and in at least sixteen (44.4 percent) the death of a child precipitated the
trial."[102] Eight of the ten manslaughter charges involved the death of children. These cases sparked widespread public outrage, aided by the efforts
of muckrakers and yellow journalists. As William Randolph Hearst's *New
York Evening Journal* editorialized following the death of a seven-year-old
to diphtheria under the care of her Christian Scientist parents, the child

was allowed to die, and it did die, while a so-called faith-curer, or alleged
"healer," prayed and went through various incantations as senseless, as

hopeless, and as vicious in a case of diphtheria as would be the contortions of some negress of the voodoo faith twisting serpents around her neck to achieve a medical result. . . . An example is needed now. If any alleged healer, pretending to cure that child, deprived her of medical aid, and without legal license pretended to practice the healing art, he should be convicted of manslaughter and put in jail for a term sufficiently long to act as a preventive to him and A WARNING TO OTHERS.[103]

These heated accusations were not enough to persuade certain medical and legal experts that Christian Scientist parents ought to be jailed for imposing their therapeutic and religious beliefs on their children. Christian Scientists fought back by insisting that people died in the care of doctors as well. An item appearing in the *Christian Science Journal* after the death of Harold Frederic states that all Christian Scientists knew "that the general practice of medicine is experimental; that good results are obtained every day by regular practitioners from the use of harmless and non-medical tinctures. We also know that oftentimes prescriptions which cure or modify the symptoms of one patient signally fail in another case of the same character."[104]

Questions of public policy in matters concerning Christian Science have always been complicated by the simple fact that it is difficult to determine in any given case whether a patient's recovery could be guaranteed under a different form of treatment. It is a problem that continues to arise in medical malpractice cases to this day. Nevertheless, on March 23, 2010, the *Times* reported that "faced with dwindling membership and blows to their church's reputation caused by its intransigence concerning medical treatment, even for children with grave illnesses, Christian Science leaders have recently found a new tolerance for medical care."[105] Reportedly, church leaders encourage parents to follow the dictates of their conscience, and anecdotal evidence suggests that many Christian Science parents use some combination of regular medical treatment and spiritual healing, though many refuse to carry health insurance or vaccinate their children.[106]

As Catherine Albanese states at the beginning of her history of American metaphysical religion, "American metaphysics," of which Christian Science is a significant part, "formed in the midst of a yearning for salvation understood as solace, comfort, therapy, and healing." For many nineteenth-century Americans, the healing of the body, the salvation of the soul, and the redemption of human society were linked enterprises. Healing was a space in which science, theology, and reformism merged: "In the context of metaphysical naturalism in the materialistically oriented United States, sin and loss were graphically re-understood in social, cultural, and somatic terms."[107] This new understanding emerged from a deep desire to see the evidence of redemption borne out pragmatically. This is why the confrontation between Christian Science and its various opponents occurred in a rhetorical space in which it was possible for each to accuse the other of both bad science and bad faith and of holding back human progress. Though doctors frequently accused Christian Scientists of backwardness (and did so by equating them with racial and religious others), at its heart, this was a struggle over who was allowed to structure and deliver modernity's master narrative, which promised both the rational mastery of the body and of human relations.

We have seen this play out in the story that the medical profession told about itself and the narratives that Christian Scientists produced to make sense of their experiences of suffering and salvation. Both had the concept of restitution at their core. The remaining chapters will investigate this through the work of those who made storytelling their vocation, though not all of them took the inevitability of restitution for granted.

NOTES

1. Mary Baker G. Eddy was married three times. She married George Washington Glover in 1844. He died, probably of yellow fever, in the same year. A decade later, in 1853, she married the dentist and homeopath Daniel Patterson, but the two separated and eventually divorced in 1866 because of Mr. Patterson's affair with another married woman. She married her final husband, Asa Gilbert Eddy, one of her own students, in 1877. In the tradition of Eddy's biographers, I will refer to her by the chronologically correct name when discussing specific events in her life and in the history of Christian Science. The name Mary Baker Eddy, however, will be used when talking about her general ideas.

2. Gillian Gill, *Mary Baker Eddy*, 162.

3. Mary Baker Eddy, *Retrospection and Introspection* (Boston: Stewart, 1912), 24.

4. Amy Voorhees, "Writing Revelation," 40.

5. Ibid., 12.

6. Eddy, *Retrospection and Introspection*, 24.

7. Ibid., 25.

8. As Stephen Gottschalk claims, "The healing that she associated with this revelatory breakthrough was not, however, on the order of a dramatic 'road to Damascus' experience or

a turning point as clear-cut as Luther's decision, upon being struck by lightning, to become a monk." Gottschalk, *Rolling Away the Stone*, 78.

9. As Voorhees argues, this war "demanded new identities and new theologies and shook open a space where Eddy could ask the questions about certainty and uncertainty, freedom and enslavement, mortality and immortality, truth and error, God and creation, body, thought, identity, health, and salvation that came into increasing focus for her during and just after this time." Voorhees, "Writing Revelation," 227.

10. Drew Gilpin Faust, *This Republic of Suffering: Death and the American Civil War* (New York: Knopf, 2008), 174. Faust points to spiritualism as one other unorthodox answer to this problem that "offered belief that seemed to rely on empirical evidence rather than revelation and faith."

11. Barbara Ehrenreich and Deirdre English, *For Her Own Good: Two Centuries of the Experts' Advice to Women* (New York: Anchor, 1978), 32.

12. Richard C. Cabot, "100 Christian Science Cures." *McClure's* 31, no. 3 (July 1908): 475.

13. Burton Bledstein, *The Culture of Professionalism: The Middle Class and the Development of Higher Education in America* (New York: Norton, 1976).

14. Samuel Haber, *The Quest for Authority and Honor in the American Professions: 1750–1900* (Chicago: University of Chicago Press, 1991), 4–5.

15. Ibid., 9.

16. Ibid., 96.

17. Nathan O. Hatch, *The Democratization of American Christianity* (New Haven, CT: Yale University Press, 1989), 5.

18. This commitment to populism among American Protestants was hardly universal or uniform. The established clergy predictably responded to these movements with suspicion and hostility, yet those divisions followed class lines as much as they did theological ones. As Nathan Hatch states in *The Democratization of American Christianity*, the established clergy feared that "the wrong sort of people had joined Methodism—people who rejected social authority's claim to religious power." Ibid., 14.

19. See also William R. Hutchison, *Religious Pluralism in America: The Contentious History of a Founding Ideal* (New Haven, CT: Yale University Press, 2004).

20. Because most medical care in the eighteenth century was rendered at home, women occupied important—though nonprofessional and underappreciated—roles as lay practitioners and midwives. The rise of obstetrics eventually made midwives and nonprofessional female practitioners obsolete in certain areas, particularly among the middle classes. However, the 1840s saw the first women obtaining formal medical training in the United States and the founding of the first medical college for women, the New England Medical College.

21. Paul Starr, *The Social Transformation of American Medicine* (New York: Basic Books, 1982).

22. Ibid. S. Weir Mitchell mocks the standards of this period in "Autobiography of a Quack" by having his protagonist present this portrait of medical school: "Dissecting struck me as a rather nasty business for a gentleman, and on this account I did just as little as was absolutely essential. In fact, if a man took his tickets and paid the dissection fees, nobody troubled himself as to whether or not he did any more than this. A like evil existed at the graduation: whether you squeezed through or passed with credit was a thing which was not made public, so I had absolutely nothing to stimulate my ambition. I am told that it is all very different today." S. Weir Mitchell, *Autobiography of a Quack and Other Stories* (New York: Century, 1905), 14.

23. Starr, *Social Transformation of American Medicine*, 59.

24. Ibid., 95.

25. Klassen, *Spirits of Protestantism*, 45.

26. Sanford Gifford, *The Emmanuel Movement: The Origins of Group Treatment and the Assault on Lay Psychotherapy* (Boston: Harvard University Press, 1996), 6.

27. Charles Rosenberg, *The Cholera Years: The United States in 1829, 1842, and 1866* (Chicago: University of Chicago Press, 1987), 156–57, 244.

28. Haber, *Quest for Authority and Honor*, 106.

29. Starr, *Social Transformation of American Medicine*, 56.

30. Mary Baker Eddy and her son were reunited after the establishment of her church, when the latter was an adult, but the two never had a close relationship. Critics of Eddy would use the supposed "abandonment" of her son and her chilly adult relationship with him in order to paint her as an indifferent mother, but Gillian Gill's biography of Eddy has revealed that the circumstances were far more complicated, that the young Mary Glover (her first married name) struggled to care for her son as an invalid and relinquished him unwillingly and under intense pressure from the family members with whom she was living. See Albanese, *Republic of Mind and Spirit*, 284.

31. For the impact of the war on Mary Baker Eddy's life, see Voorhees, "Writing Revelation," chap. 1.

32. Philip Cushman, *Constructing the Self, Constructing America: A Cultural History of Psychotherapy* (Boston: Addison-Wesley, 1995), 93.

33. Harrington, *The Cure Within*, 41–42.

34. Robert Darnton, *Mesmerism and the End of the Enlightenment in France* (Boston: Harvard University Press, 1986), 3–4.

35. Ibid., 6.

36. Charcot attempted to locate the mechanism for hypnotic and mesmeric states in the physiology of the brain itself, and in doing so became convinced that such states "could *only* be produced in patients suffering from hysteria. It consisted of discrete phases—catalepsy, lethargy, and somnambulism—each of which could be identified by special physiological signs and provoked by stimulating the nervous system in specific differentiable ways." Rather than a healing method, susceptibility to these states became a sign of (usually distinctly female) pathology. As Harrington argues, "Charcot had succeeded in doing two things: giving an aura of respectability to the subject [of hypnosis]; and staking a clear claim to the medical profession's exclusive competency to deal with it." Charcot became famous for his photographs of hysterical patients, taken in the midst of his efforts to develop an anatomy of hysteria and analyzed to great effect by feminist literary critic Evelyn Ender. He also became famous for his own (unsettlingly familiar) brand of showmanship: public displays of symptomatic female patients performed for groups of physicians, medical students, and even members of the general public. However, he consistently denied the influence of doctor-patient rapport in this work: "As he saw it, his exhibitions were not interpersonal dramas, but demonstrations of a tool capable of revealing certain laws of physiology under pathological conditions." Harrington, *The Cure Within*, 55–57. See also Evelyn Ender, *Sexing the Mind: Nineteenth-Century Fictions of Hysteria* (Ithaca, NY: Cornell University Press, 1995).

37. Cushman, *Constructing the Self*, 124.

38. Ibid., 125.

39. Qtd. in Gill, *Mary Baker Eddy*, 129.

40. Ibid., 131.

41. Ibid., 134. Quimby's writings revealed that he thought of his contribution in metaphysical, even quasi-religious terms. He dabbled in spiritualism and claimed to have the abilities of

a medium. In her analysis of his private papers, Albanese argues that he "betrayed a kind of messianism in which he identified himself with the biblical Christ, at the same time typically separating Christ, as identical to Science, from sole attachment to the historical Jesus." Albanese, *Republic of Mind and Spirit*, 288.

42. Mary Baker Eddy, *Science and Health with Key to Scriptures*, (Boston: Church of Christ, Scientist, 1910), 107.

43. This is particularly true of New Thought, which was never explicitly Christian in its conception. Adherents freely experimented with Buddhism, Vedanta, Theosophy, and other forms of Eastern-inspired mysticism. That said, one of the critiques of Christian Science made by Protestant clerics was that one didn't have to be a Christian in order to follow it. The differences between New Thought and Christian Science will be discussed at greater length in the next chapter.

44. Gottschalk, *Emergence of Christian Science*, 23.

45. Eddy, *Science and Health*, 18–19.

46. Gottschalk, *Emergence of Christian Science*, 19.

47. Voorhees, "Writing Revelation," 54.

48. Eddy, *Science and Health*, 101.

49. Albanese, *Republic of Mind and Spirit*, 290.

50. Gottschalk, *Emergence of Christian Science*, 26.

51. Eddy, *Science and Health*, 108.

52. Voorhees, "Writing Revelation," 32, 43.

53. Mary Baker Eddy, *Advice to Healers: Selected Letters by Mary Baker Eddy*, Vol. 2: 1870–1910 (Mary Baker Eddy Library for the Betterment of Humanity, Boston), 71.

54. Ibid., Vol. 3, 51.

55. Ibid., 54.

56. Ibid., 56.

57. Eddy, *Science and Health*, 390, 394–95.

58. Eddy, *Science and Health*, 411, 412, 414, 420.

59. Haber, *Quest for Authority and Honor*, 201–2.

60. Ibid.

61. Ibid., 197.

62. Peter Harrison, "'Science' and 'Religion': Constructing the Boundaries," in *Science and Religion: New Historical Perspectives*, edited by Thomas Dixon, Geoffrey Cantor, and Stephen Pumfrey (New York: Cambridge University Press, 2010), 27.

63. A. S. Coe, "Modern Medical Science," *New York Medical Journal* (October 1889): 406.

64. Harrison, "'Science' and 'Religion,'" 27.

65. H. G. W., "Church Healing," *Long Island Medical Journal* 10, no. 1 (January 1916): 491.

66. Klassen, *Spirits of Protestantism*, 112.

67. "Harold Frederic and Christian Science," *Buffalo Medical Journal* 38, no. 5 (December 1898): 378.

68. Edwin S. Mack, "The Law in Its Relation to Medicine," *Wisconsin Medical Journal* 1 (January 1903): 199.

69. Ehrenreich and English, *For Her Own Good*, 34.

70. The use of indigent patients as test or teaching cases in the advancement of medicine is a history fraught with sorrow and irony, as some of the treatments responsible for improving the quality of life of so many people, rich and poor, were purchased with the lives of the most

vulnerable. As one physician has said to me quite eloquently, "The rich pay for medical care with their money. The poor pay with their bodies." That continues to be true in the United States today.

71. Ibid.

72. Starr, *Social Transformation of American Medicine*, 107.

73. "Testimonies from the Field," *Christian Science Journal* 24, no. 1 (April 1906): 35.

74. Ibid.

75. Ibid.

76. "Notes from the Field," *Christian Science Journal* 9, no. 12 (March 1892): 512.

77. Harrington, *The Cure Within*, 115.

78. William James, *The Varieties of Religious Experience* (New York: Penguin, 1982), 121.

79. Harrington, *The Cure Within*, 18.

80. Eddy, *Science and Health*, 79.

81. C. K. Ogden and I. A. Richards, *The Meaning of Meaning* (New York: Harcourt, 1923), 341–43.

82. Eddy, *Science and Health*, 197.

83. Eddy, *Advice to Healers*, Vol. 3, 101.

84. Eddy, *Science and Health*, 396, 159, 375.

85. Frank, *The Wounded Storyteller*, 5.

86. Michel Foucault, *The Birth of the Clinic: An Archaeology of Medical Perception* (New York: Vintage, 1994), 17.

87. Frank, *The Wounded Storyteller*, 6.

88. Ibid., 92.

89. "Notes from the Field," *Christian Science Journal* 11, no. 5 (August 1893): 229.

90. Lucia Greenhouse, *fathermothergod: My Journey out of Christian Science* (New York: Crown, 2001).

91. Bridget Bennett, *The Damnation of Harold Frederic: His Lives and Works* (New York: Syracuse University Press, 1997), 51, 53–55.

92. Ibid., 55.

93. "Harold Frederic and the Christian Scientists," *The Outlook* 60, no. 12 (November 1898): 710.

94. "The Christian Scientist Fraud," *Medical and Surgical "Review of Reviews"* 1, no. 2 (November 1898): 86.

95. "A Victim of Christian Science," *Medical Herald* 17 (December 1898): 508.

96. "Faith Cure Murders," *New York Times*, 11 November 1898.

97. The racist references to Indians and Chinese in these last two quotes are so blatant that they barely require analysis. "Christian Science and the Law," *Public: A Journal of Democracy* 1, no. 35 (3 December 1898): 7–8.

98. Eddy, *Advice to Healers*, Vol. 2, 71.

99. "Notes from the Field," *Christian Science Journal* 11, no. 7 (October 1893), 326–27.

100. Ibid.

101. "Christian Science and the Law," 7–8.

102. Rennie B. Schoepflin, *Christian Science on Trial: Religious Healing in America* (New York: Johns Hopkins University Press, 2003), 184.

103. Ibid., 187. And yet again, we have an example of opposition to Christian Science packaged with explicit racism.

104. "The Harold Frederic Case," *Christian Science Journal* 26, no. 9 (December 1898): 622.

105. Paul Vitello, "Christian Science Church Seeks Truce with Modern Medicine," *New York Times*, 23 March 2010.

106. Val Kilmer, currently among the highest-profile Christian Scientists in the United States, told Chuck Klosterman, "There is a big misnomer with Christian Science. People used to say, 'Christian Science. Oh, you're the ones that don't believe in doctors,' which is not a true thing. It's just a different way of treating a malady. It could be mental, social, or physical. When Wesley [Kilmer's brother] was diagnosed [with epilepsy], he was given medical treatment. When he was in school, they would stop the treatment. Then periodically, he would go back and forth between Christian Science and medical treatment." When asked if Val Kilmer would treat his daughter with antibiotics if she had a sore throat, "he tells me that because he's divorced, he doesn't have complete control over that type of decision. But he says his first move in such a scenario would be to pray, because most illness comes from fear." Chuck Klosterman, "Crazy Things Seem Normal . . . Normal Things Seem Crazy," *Esquire*, 1 July 2005.

107. Albanese, *Republic of Mind and Spirit*, 15.

2

Build Therefore Your Own World

The Restitution Narratives of Frances Hodgson Burnett

I n the climactic scene of Frances Hodgson Burnett's *The Secret Garden* (1911), the young invalid Colin rises from his wheelchair to walk before his father, a grief-stricken widower whose impenetrable sorrow has contributed to the neglect of his son and brought about the decay of his manor house and its abandoned gardens. Colin's ailment is psychosomatic, however, the result of absorbing a belief in his imminent death from the adults around him. Having endured the ineffectual treatment of doctors for years, Colin recovers under the tutelage of his cousin Mary and her friend Dickon by making himself "believe that he was going to get well, which was really more than half the battle."[1] Colin's restitution narrative explicitly links both sickness and health to the workings of the mind. And for this reason, *The Secret Garden* is considered, if not an exact novelistic rendering of Mary Baker Eddy's theology, the most "Christian Science-y" of Burnett's novels.

Though she was well acquainted with the work of Mary Baker Eddy, Burnett never converted to Christian Science. Her son Vivian, who served as the inspiration for the novel *Little Lord Fauntleroy* (1886), actually did. Burnett herself maintained a lifelong interest in various forms of metaphysical healing and was consistently associated with it in the public mind. At the height of her fame, someone suggested she apply her literary gifts to the subject of Christian Science. She refused, declaring that "such an article could only come convincingly from a person who had long known Mrs. Eddy as a friend and had personally watched the development and effect of her work."[2]

It is tempting to wonder if at the moment she made this refusal, Burnett was aware of how much she and Eddy had in common. Though they were born a generation apart, their periods of greatest productivity and fame roughly coincided. Both were women who made a prodigious living off their writings. Both experienced prolonged bouts of ill health and sought relief in theories of mind and body that circulated during their day. Both had divorced and remarried. And both had experienced the crushing loss of children. And, because of their wealth and fame, both of them were targets of scandal-mongering in the press.

Born in Manchester, England, in 1849, Frances Hodgson immigrated to Knoxville, Tennessee, with her family at the end of the Civil War. Her father had died just a few years after her birth, and the family struggled with poverty for most of her childhood. At nineteen, she began writing and selling stories in order to help support the household, publishing regularly in *Godey's Lady's Book*, *Harper's Bazaar*, *Scribner's Weekly*, and *Peterson's*. She continued writing even after she married Swan Burnett, a doctor and close family friend, in 1873. As a writer, she was extraordinarily prolific, turning out multiple novels in a single year. But this productivity also proved to be exhausting, and Burnett suffered chronically from neurasthenic episodes that descended on her after intense periods of work. Writing to a friend in June 1880, she complained in her characteristically wry and self-deprecating manner:

> My backbone disappeared and my brain and when I found they were really gone I missed them. Their defection seemed so curious that I began to try to account for it & finally rambled weakly round to the conclusion that it might be because I have written ten books in six years & done two or three other little things. . . . I have about three hundred pages of a book done and generally I don't seem to care about it. There's a good deal of it in one place and another if I could find any brains and my wrists didn't seem to dangle so. I generally lie on my back and despise myself.[3]

In 1883, after publishing *Through One Administration* to mixed reviews, she suffered a collapse and was unable to write for several years. Several months into this episode, she began patronizing Anna B. Newman, a mind cure practitioner who treated Louisa May Alcott, also suffering from "literary overwork."[4]

Burnett swore that these treatments were helpful for her (Alcott was far more skeptical). She eventually began studying the writings of Mary Baker Eddy, mingling a blooming interest in metaphysical healing with Hindu philosophy, Theosophy, spiritualism, and other alternative faiths. But she always maintained that she was not a healer herself and never formally joined Christian Science or any of the New Thought organizations: "While I would not call myself a Christian Scientist, I believe in its principle because it is the exposition of the pure Christ-spirit applied to the needs of today." For Burnett, these needs extended to every part of life. In addition to her chronic health problems, she divorced Swan, remarried, and divorced again. In 1890, her eldest son, Lionel, died of tuberculosis, an event that shattered her emotionally while deepening her need for spiritual relief.[5]

According to her biographer, "her long struggle with the God who had allowed her son to die" was worked out both in her spiritual seeking and, importantly, in her writing.[6] For Burnett also saw a deep affinity between the spiritual comforts offered by her beliefs about the human mind and in the regenerative capacity of imagination and literary creation. Though not hostile to science, she felt that literature opened up humanity to insights "that have a far greater significance to the happiness of men and women than any scientific discovery can give them."[7] This preference for the affective sources of meaning derived from spirituality, literature, and (as we shall see) nature speak to a romantic sensibility that we might also recognize as Emersonian, appealing to the ability of art to throw "a light upon the mystery of humanity."[8] But in suggesting that art, nature, and the imagination produce real-world effects, Burnett's novels also reflect the pragmatic spirit of late-nineteenth- and early-twentieth-century US culture.

One of the other things that Burnett shares with Mary Baker Eddy is a history of being read within the confines of Victorian sentimental rhetoric and aesthetics.[9] As women who made a living from their writing and their ideas, they both crossed the boundaries of conventional womanhood and yet tended to adopt conservative personas that conformed to sentimental ideals. *Little Lord Fauntleroy*, the book that made Burnett's reputation, is full of sentimental tropes about childhood. The iconic image of the title character dressed in ruffles with soft, long curls framing his face became a Victorian cliché (and it haunted Vivian Burnett, who was Fauntleroy's model, for most of his life). Likewise, Burnett's biographer, Gretchen Gerzina, attributes her lack of acceptance among modernist intellectuals to the fustiness of her religious beliefs: "Belief and faith, it seemed, were difficult concepts in these disillusioned postwar years, but her audience was a wide and general one. There is no doubt that [Burnett's] kind of book was not in favor with the postwar intelligentsia, who rejected what they saw as the wordy sentimentalism of the Victorians and Edwardians."[10]

John Seelye, on the other hand, makes a strong argument for viewing Burnett's faith and aesthetics as part of a different sort of avant-garde: "Only seven years older than Sigmund Freud, Burnett was drawn to movements that were acting to open up late Victorian culture to alternative faiths, aspects of romanticism that stressed the therapeutic benefits of association with the natural world, emphasized the power of the imagination especially when expressed through creativity, and acknowledged that reason does not account for all that happens in this complex world."[11] Indeed, it is possible to see Burnett and Eddy as part of a developing conversation between romantic/idealistic and materialistic/pragmatic philosophies. As the previous chapter argued, Eddy saw her work as a practical demonstration of spiritual principles. And as Burnett's life became more complicated, her work became darker, her fictional children decidedly less angelic, and her books began to explore not only the powerful relationship between mind and body but the pragmatic implications of belief itself.

CHRISTIAN SCIENCE OR NEW THOUGHT?

Scholars of Burnett's work have differed on the question of whether Burnett's personal religion is more closely aligned with Christian Science or New Thought. Burnett disavowed any formal affiliation with either, though it was always apparent that she had been inspired by them. I first became aware of Burnett's connection to Christian Science at the Mary Baker Eddy Library, where clipped advertisements for the theatrical version of *The Dawn of a To-morrow* are visible in the scrapbooks kept by Eddy and her secretary, Calvin Frye. Christian Scientists felt a resonance between the religious messages that shaped her work and their own faith. Some scholars, however, have placed her in the New Thought camp. Anne Stiles, for example, reads both *The Dawn of a To-morrow* and *The Secret Garden* as "New Thought novels" in the tradition of the New Thought leaders who had literary aspirations, such as Ursula Gestefeld, Helen Van-Anderson, and Alice Bunker Stockham.[12]

The difference between New Thought and Christian Science and the history of their antagonism toward one another is worth detailing here because of their implications for how we understand not only Burnett's beliefs and how they shaped her work but those of other authors in this study. But both need to be understood as almost genetically related responses to religious and intellectual crises, responses that did much to bridge nineteenth-century Emersonian romanticism and early twentieth-century philosophical pragmatism. Both are the results of Mary Baker Eddy and other thinkers taking the Transcendentalists' tendency to speak of experience in terms of mind and suggesting that this might actually have real implications for experience.[13] This contribution to ways of thinking about thinking and thinking about living had the most profound impact on Burnett's life and work.

As is the case with virtually all new religious movements, Mary Baker Eddy faced, from the very beginning, challenges to her authority and to the doctrine she was attempting to codify. Even as she was laboring to define the boundaries of orthodoxy in Christian Science, various challengers arose with their own interpretations of her teachings. In some cases, these were former students. Two famous examples were Emma Curtis Hopkins and Ursula Gestefeld, each of whom studied under Mary Baker Eddy before making successful careers for themselves as healers, teachers, and writers. For these women, as well as other ex-students, the reasons for their separation from Eddy had to do with both personal independence and religion. Many of them chafed under Eddy's leadership: "These people wanted to write their own pamphlets, develop their own healing methods and ideas, teach their own students, and set up practice where they wished."[14] Furthermore, they felt limited by Eddy's commitment to biblical Christianity, finding inspiration in Buddhism, Vedanta, and Theosophy. Judging by the contents of the scrapbooks kept by Eddy throughout her life, she had a limited interest in Eastern religions as well, though perhaps more as an appealing supplement to, rather than on equal footing with, the Bible.

Similar challenges came from individuals who might accurately be considered Eddy's classmates, though they ultimately made common cause with (and in some cases exercised leadership over) her former students. Julius and Annetta Dresser were acolytes of Phineas Parkhurst Quimby, and in the mid-1880s, nearly twenty years after their mentor's death, they began promoting their own mind cure methods, which they defined in distinction to Eddy's. There is some controversy over whether the Dressers were capitalizing on a fad for metaphysical healing that Eddy had done so much work to bring to life. Indeed, Julius Dresser, who was approached by a suffering Mary Patterson in 1866, expressed no interest in continuing Quimby's work immediately after his death.[15] Yet two decades later, the Dressers brought charges of plagiarism to Eddy's door, arguing that she lifted significant parts of *Science and Health* from Quimby's private papers.[16] The Dressers and many New Thought leaders who followed them consistently looked back to Quimby as a more suitable forerunner for their movement, which came to be called New Thought.

But the difference proved difficult to sustain. Eddy's former students continued to use the name Christian Science even though their work was not sanctioned by the church or its founder. Emma Curtis Hopkins established a Christian Science Theological Seminary in Chicago, and various "unofficial" Christian Science periodicals began circulating in the 1880s. In the 1890s, when Eddy copyrighted the term "Christian Science" in order to prevent unsanctioned teachers and healers from using it, "the groups' leaders united their separate faiths in a loose national alliance and agreed upon 'New Thought' as the umbrella term for their movement."[17] Yet while the members of this group shared certain metaphysical preoccupations, the term "New Thought" describes neither a coherent set of doctrines nor a consistent healing methodology. What it drew from Eddy vs. Quimby is grounds for a substantial debate. Stephen Gottschalk, for example, notes that Julius Dresser himself had difficulty separating Quimby and Eddy in his mind and in his own writing:

For not only did Dresser read Mrs. Eddy in terms of Quimby, he also read Quimby in terms of Mrs. Eddy. That is, his teaching of supposedly pure Quimbyism was interlaced with terms and ideas of Mrs. Eddy which were quite foreign to Quimby. For example, Quimby never used the triad of terms "sin, sickness, and death" which was so conspicuous in Mrs. Eddy's vocabulary and also became a part of Dresser's teaching. Dresser's son Horatio (who was born shortly before the date the Mrs. Eddy gives as the discovery of Christian Science) continued, like his father, to read into Quimby theological and metaphysical ideas drawn from other courses, including Christian Science.[18]

Catherine Albanese, on the other hand, sees New Thought's ecumenical openness and capacity for holding the ideal and the material in tension— as opposed to Eddy's idealist absolutism—as the movement's inheritance from Quimby, who "straddled both worlds—affirming a wisdom beyond sense and matter and yet introducing sensate concepts as palpable, lived metaphors for the experience of wisdom."[19] Yet she also notes the ways in which individuals like Hopkins and Gestefeld acknowledged (and even paid homage to) Eddy's example.

The responses of orthodox Christian Science and New Thought to Emersonian Transcendentalism (and Emerson did in fact become the patron saint of New Thought) emerges as, perhaps, the signal difference between them. Emerson's *Nature* is, of course, famous for the ambivalence toward idealism and materialism that characterizes what Albanese calls "the classic crack."[20] It is a problem that runs throughout his opus. For instance, Emerson begins "The Transcendentalist" by neatly dividing all of the intellectual world into Materialists and Idealists: "the first class founding on experience, the second on consciousness; the first class beginning to think from the data of the senses, the second class perceive that the senses are not final and say, The senses give us representations of things, but what are the things themselves, they cannot tell."[21] Characterizing the Transcendentalist mind-set, Emerson says that "mind is the only reality, of which men and all other natures are better or worse reflectors."[22] Emerson, of course, never wholly embraced a truly Berkeleyan notion of the material world's unreality. As Lawrence Buell reminds us, Emerson's essay "Idealism" "entertains the Berkeleyan thesis that the mind creates the world, only to reject it for leaving 'God out of me' and alienating me from nature."[23] Yet Emerson's work reflects a lifelong effort to come to terms with the unreliability of perception and the illusory quality of embodied experience. The essay "Illusions," Buell argues, is where the author learns "better how to live with unreality. He can contemplate entrapment within the labyrinth of one's perceptions, the 'necessary film' that 'envelope[s] the soul' as Whitman called it, without the same compulsion to dispatch it or to bewail its horror."[24]

For Emerson, the advantage offered by idealism is that it

> presents the world in precisely that view which is most desirable to the mind. It is, in fact, the view which Reason, both speculative and practical, that is, philosophy and virtue, take. For seen in the light of thought, the world always is phenomenal; and virtue subordinates it to the mind. Idealism sees the world in God. It beholds the whole circle of persons, and things, of actions and events, of country and religion, not as painfully accumulated, atom after atom, act after act, in an aged creeping Past, but as one vast picture which God paints on the instant eternity for the contemplation of the soul.[25]

Never wholly in the idealist camp, Emerson nevertheless explores the tension between the actual and the perceived, "how nature remains an unfathomed mystery, how nature might not even exist except as a mental construct, how our moods do not believe in each other, how the world I live in is not the world I think, how even those I love seem more phenomenal than real."[26]

It is important to understand the degree of moderation with which Emerson takes idealist claims in order to appreciate precisely how radical Mary Baker Eddy's innovations were. She took Emerson's paraphrase of the idealist viewpoint, "Mind is the only reality, of which men and all other natures are better or worse reflectors," and advanced it several steps forward: "Theology and physics teach that both Spirit and matter are real and good, whereas the fact is that Spirit is good and real, and matter is Spirit's opposite."[27] One important distinction between Christian Science and New Thought is that the Emersonians in the New Thought camp still believed that there was some reality in matter, even if that reality was always mediated by perception. They also believed that through thought, human beings could shape both matter and material experience. As Gottschalk explains, Eddy "declared that matter was completely unreal, the erroneous sense of true substance":

> The physical senses, she taught, could not discern the reality of man; for the spiritual fact of man's being could be known only through revelation and discerned only through spiritual sense. Hence, in Christian Science treatment, denial of material sense evidence plays an important part as a preparation for the discernment of what man really is. What is denied, however, is not the body but its corporeality. In Christian Science, bone or any part of the body may hint some spiritual actuality, some real aspect of man's true functioning and formation. But considered as a *material* substance, even one expressive of thought, bone is definitely unreal.[28]

Putting the implications of this difference for healing practice more succinctly, he says, "What the Christian Scientist saw as a manifestation of a *false belief* that must be dissolved, the mind-curer saw as an *actual* condition that could be overcome by the power of thought."[29]

Another major distinction between New Thought and orthodox Christian Science had to do with the nature and existence of evil. Again, Emerson stated in a divinity school address that "all evil is so much death or nonentity. Benevolence is absolute and real."[30] Likewise, Eddy wrote, "We must learn that evil is the awful deception and unreality of existence. Evil is not supreme; good is not helpless."[31] But there is an important difference to be noted here. Whereas Emerson dismisses evil as "nonentity," Eddy, in referring to it as "the awful deception," indicates that evil—for all its unreality—still has important consequences for lived experience. As Gottschalk says, "she puts this important qualification on her statement of the unreality of evil: though it is nothing to God and has no intrinsic reality, it *is* a terrible reality to mortals; it confronts them with nothingness—'no-thing-ness.' If its claims are ignored, if men do not challenge them specifically, they will be overcome by them and will not be able to demonstrate the 'somethingness' of Spirit."[32]

Eddy's conception of evil is made most apparent in her doctrine of malicious animal magnetism (MAM). Critics of Christian Science have picked up on MAM as evidence of Eddy's paranoia. But even if it was sometimes a convenient tool for dealing with criticism, it was also the tool Eddy used to make an account of the inevitable *experience* of suffering in the context of a theology that claimed that suffering was fundamentally illusory. It was, in other words, her form of theodicy. Furthermore, the need to strenuously work against the influence of MAM distinguished her form of Christian Science from the seemingly blithe optimism of New Thought. As Gillian Gill writes,

> It is perhaps in her consistent and frequent refusal of the idea that God is immanent in man that Mrs. Eddy separates herself most sharply from the New Thought people who see God in everyone and indeed in everything and believe that by following one's natural bent, listening to one's inner deity, one can and will easily achieve health, happiness, goodness, and so forth. Mrs. Eddy returns constantly to the fact that the path to Christian Science is arduous and painful.[33]

Finally, New Thought tended to evolve in a more secular direction, whereas Christian Science remained a fundamentally religious movement. New Thought had no codified religious doctrine: "The only item of faith which could be called dogma for them was antidogmatism itself, a liberal eclecticism that stood firmly opposed to all religious authority. The very term New Thought, wrote Dresser, was adopted in 1895 as the name for the 'liberal wing of the therapeutic movement.'"[34] New Thought was therefore compatible with many other religious faiths and mystical practices. Individuals who pursued New Thought tended to blend it with Buddhism, Vedanta, Theosophy, and even spiritualism. Eddy's church, on the other hand, remained committed to biblical Christianity.[35]

The reason why the New Thought/Christian Science distinction mattered to Mary Baker Eddy is fairly obvious: as an emergent religious leader, she was attempting to get both arms around a movement that kept threatening to slip out of her control even though she and many of her followers saw her as the bearer of its founding revelations. What's more, she was confronted by plenty of well- and ill-intentioned misinterpretations of her teachings and wrongful associations with theories and healing practices she never actually sanctioned. Members of rival movements who were (or claimed to be) inspired by Eddy's teachings "sometimes advertised Mrs. Eddy's works right alongside those of her ex-students."[36]

Members of the New Thought movement, on the other hand, increasingly wished to advance the ideas associated with Christian Science while firmly distinguishing themselves from Mary Baker Eddy. But to a great many other people—including Burnett and many of the authors discussed in this volume—these distinctions really *didn't* seem to matter, and the distinctions between these movements as practiced by many people were less firm than they appear in a theological history text. Indeed, individuals who did not have a stake in the (sometimes actual) intellectual property disputes associated with this division quite freely mixed their readings of *Science and Health* with the readings of other teachers, attending séances while availing themselves of the healing services of Eddy's students. Mary Baker Eddy was a brand name and Christian Science was, in some cases, a metonym for a cluster of mind-body theories that could be traced back to her in some way or another. When *McClure's* and *Human Life* attempted to make some account of them, it was through the biography of Mary Baker Eddy. When William James runs through his list of "healthy-minded" religions, Eddy is the one religious leader he names. When Frances Hodgson Burnett first encountered spiritual healing, it was through a student of Mary Baker Eddy, and it was Mary Baker Eddy whom journalists asked her about when trying to come to some definite conclusions about Frances Hodgson Burnett's beliefs. Burnett, as we shall see, hews closer to Emerson and the New Thought leaders on the idealist/materialist spectrum, but *The Dawn of a To-morrow*, the most explicitly religious of her works, presents an unorthodox faith that nevertheless remains grounded in the Bible, as is Eddy's work. What's more, in keeping with Eddy, Burnett's narratives of healing and personal transformation are grounded in a notion of life as struggle and take place in a world in which there are evils and enemies that need to be overcome.

THE BEAUTIFUL THOUGHT

Burnett was inspired by Mary Baker Eddy, along with these other strains of romanticism, in the development of her own personal philosophy, which she eventually took to calling "the beautiful thought." What Burnett and so many of her contemporaries adapted from Eddy—whether in authorized or unauthorized ways—was the Berkeleyan/Transcendental tendency to speak of experience in terms of mind and suggest that that might have actual implications for experience itself. In other words, Eddy took the notion that the material world is not immediately accessible to us but only mediated through consciousness and argued that the material world as people experience it is fundamentally the *product* of consciousness, something that Berkeley and Emerson never advocated.[37] As Gottschalk states, "For all practical purposes, then, the idealism of Berkeley, Alcott, and Emerson did no violence to common sense perception. So too, the philosophic idealists who flourished in America during the last decades of the nineteenth century never really argued that physical percepts are not what they seem."[38]

On this basis, Gottschalk argues at the end of *The Emergence of Christian Science in American Religious Life* that Christian Science is "best understood as a *pragmatic interpretation of Christian revelation.*" He demonstrates that Christian Science and American pragmatism, rising from the same New England soil, emerged alongside one another (though not necessarily influenced by each other) in history. They share a prioritization of experience and a "disposition to think in terms of one order of experience, rather than in terms of two opposing orders of experience. In this sense it constitutes a rejection of the dualism of the secular and the sacred, earthly and heavenly, natural and supernatural and approaches the understanding of that which is ultimate in terms of that which is immediate—experienceable in man's present life-situation."[39]

Speaking in the voice of his prophetic poet, Emerson enjoins the reader of *Nature* to "build therefore your own world. As fast as you conform your life to the pure idea in your mind, that will unfold its great proportions." But even speaking in this register, he implies that this will result in the amelioration of present material circumstances:

> So fast will disagreeable appearances, swine, spiders, snakes, pests, madhouses, prisons, enemies, vanish; they are temporary and shall be no more seen. The sordor and filths of nature, the sun shall dry up and the wind exhale. As when the summer comes from the south the snowbanks melt and the face of the earth becomes green before it, so shall the advancing spirit create its ornaments along its path, and carry with it the beauty it visits and the song which enchants it; it shall draw beautiful faces, warm hearts, wise discourse, and heroic acts, around its way, until evil is no more seen. The kingdom of man over nature, which cometh not with observation—a dominion such as now is beyond his dream of God—he shall enter without more wonder than the blind man feels who is gradually restored to sight.[40]

The metaphysical healer might turn this into a mandate for mastery over embodied experience and even the transformation of human experience through the rejection of outmoded institutions. But it is also a call for art—particularly literature—for the creation of new worlds out of the raw material of the imagination. Thus in this section, I examine the worlds that Burnett creates in three novels written at the peak of her interest in metaphysical healing: *A Little Princess, The Dawn of a To-morrow,* and *The Secret Garden.* In these novels, Burnett links the amelioration of both physical and emotional suffering to the power of the mind. And that power enables her protagonists not only to imagine themselves well but to create new narratives that transform their lived experiences.

A Little Princess

A Little Princess (1905) is a very different novel from Burnett's first foray into children's fiction, though like *Little Lord Fauntleroy* it tracks the changing fortunes of a child who is almost impossibly clever and good. In *Fauntleroy,* Cedric, an impoverished child living with his widowed mother in New York, discovers that he is the son of a disinherited English nobleman. Following the deaths of his father's brothers, Cedric becomes the heir to the earlship of Dorincourt and goes to live with his crotchety grandfather, whom he teaches the values of compassion and charity. In *A Little Princess,* Sara Crewe is a wealthy heiress left at a posh boarding school run by the strict Miss Minchin and her sycophantic sister. Sara's father dies suddenly and penniless, leaving her in Miss Minchin's control. Sara is exploited as free labor until a friend of her father rescues her. As Cedric's fortunes change from bad to good to bad and then good again, he remains consistently angelic, and the narrative serves to reward him and those around him for their goodness, whereas with Sara, Burnett is more interested in exploring the psychological impact of the alterations in Sara's environment, for better *and* for worse.

Burnett's writing on children in between these two novels demonstrates her developing efforts to depict their inner lives. In 1893, a few years after *Fauntleroy* made her famous but more than a decade before she published *A Little Princess,* Burnett wrote a memoir called *The One I Knew Best of All: A Memory of the Mind of a Child,* which attempts to document not only what happened during her childhood but the psychological experience of being a child.[41] It was motivated by her strong conviction that childhood is a strange, overwhelming, confusing time. Speaking of her child-self in the third person, Burnett says that in going back and excavating her emotional life, "I found interest in her and instruction, and the most serious cause for tender deep reflection on her as a thing touching on that strange, awful problem of a little soul standing in its newness in the great busy, tragic world of life, touched for the first time by everything that passes it, and never touched without some sign of the contact being left upon it."[42] This memoir is an ambitious work of psychological realism, and its impact is evident in Burnett's later novels, especially (but not only) those about children, whose interior worlds are rendered in careful detail. Whereas *Fauntleroy* was a sentimental story about a model child, *A Little Princess* and later *The Secret Garden* flesh out that interiority, exploring the particular nature of childish perception and, most significantly, the power of a child's imagination. What's more, they do so in ways that reflect Burnett's evolving spiritual beliefs. Childhood intuitions and imaginings are presented much like structures of belief, not mere fantasies but things of actual pragmatic value.[43] Not only do they help the child navigate embodied experience and understand the world around her, these fantasies also help produce and transform that experience. Though the impact of Christian Science and metaphysical healing was most apparent in *The Dawn of a To-morrow* and *The Secret Garden*, the psychological groundwork for this pragmatic view of imagination and, ultimately, belief itself was being laid in *A Little Princess*.

The protagonist of the novel, Sara Crewe, begins the story as the worshipped daughter of a wealthy British imperialist who brings her from their home in India to London to attend a girls' boarding school. Sara is described as plain and rather "queer," unusually serious for her age and a great lover of books and of storytelling, "always inventing stories of beautiful things, and telling them to herself."[44] Sara is uncommonly generous and openhearted toward children who are less extraordinary than she is, readily befriending the social castoffs among her classmates as well as the young, mistreated scullery maid, Becky. Both the author and the character, however, are eager to call attention to how Sara's character is shaped by the circumstances of her upbringing, circumstances that are both unusual and entirely accidental. "A lot of nice accidents have happened to me," Sara tells her best friend, Ermengarde.

> It just *happened* that I always liked lessons and books, and could remember things when I learned them. It just happened that I was born with a father who was beautiful and nice and clever and could give me everything I liked. Perhaps I have not really a good temper at all, but if you have everything you want and everyone is kind to you, how can you help but be good tempered? . . . Perhaps I am a *hideous* child, and no one will ever know, just because I never had any trials.[45]

The second half of the novel attempts to resolve that uncertainty about nature/nurture as Sara experiences her profound reversal of fortune. Her father dies tragically after losing all of his wealth. The headmistress of the school, Miss Minchin, to whom Sara is now heavily in debt, keeps the girl on as a tutor and maid of all work. Sara sleeps in the rat-infested attic next to Becky and takes orders from the shockingly callous adults in the establishment. These trials consistently test the limits of Sara's tolerance and dignity. Each day in her life becomes a struggle not only to survive but to preserve a particular image of herself. Prior to her misfortunes, Sara imagines that she is a princess, which for her means not only carrying herself in a regal manner but exercising benevolence toward everyone around her, and this is a self-perception that she clings to as she becomes the object of charity rather than its agent.

This princess fantasy is the most important example of the one great gift that Sara possesses: her capacity for storytelling and imaginative play. Sara weaves tales for herself and her friends throughout the novel, and Burnett demonstrates that this activity serves a pragmatic function other than deception or mere entertainment. Sara distinguishes her storytelling from delusion and simple dishonesty and has a clear sense of what storytelling can and cannot accomplish when it comes to representing and ultimately shaping experience. When Miss Minchin and Sara meet for the first time, the headmistress tells her father that Sara is a beautiful child, an assessment that the girl believes to be a lie: "I should be telling a story if I said [Miss Minchin] was beautiful . . . and I should know I was telling a story. I believe I am as ugly as she is—in my way."[46] Stories, for Sara, are not a way of avoiding unpleasant truths but of coping with them.

Sara must continually confront grief, catastrophic loss, and physical pain in the novel, and her stories are a way of mitigating her circumstances even if she cannot completely change them. As she tells her friend Ermengarde early in the book, after her father's initial departure, "If I go on talking and talking . . . and telling you things about pretending, I shall bear it better. You don't forget, but you bear it better."[47]

In this way, the novel's use of storytelling comes to resemble William James's pragmatic assessment of religion: it is not a thing to be judged based on its correspondence to some external reality but on its ability to help human beings navigate experience. Indeed, something very like a Jamesian understanding of faith comes into play when Sara tries to comfort Lottie, whose mother is also dead, by telling stories about what their mothers are doing in heaven. Sara's vision of heaven is singular, not bound to any particular orthodoxy: "she had been told that her mamma was in heaven, she had thought a great deal about the matter, and her thoughts had not been quite like those of other people." Her story is as much a product of her imagination as her tales about mermaids. Sara's heaven is "a lovely country where real people were," where the spirits of the dead gather flowers and look down on those they have left behind, sometimes sending them messages. Sara's heaven, populated by departed souls who communicate directly with their loved ones, may reflect Burnett's experimentation with spiritualism, but it isn't explicitly tied to any particular religious tradition. It is rather the children's lack of dogmatism that is noteworthy. Lottie accepts the story not because she believes it to be true but because it "was prettier than most others."[48]

When Sara loses her father and her privileges, her imaginative resources help her cope. The fantasy that she is a "princess" runs throughout the entire novel, but the ability to sustain that fantasy enables her to survive her most difficult ordeal:

> It would be easy to be a princess if I were dressed in cloth of gold, but it is a great deal more of a triumph to be one all the time when no one knows it. There was Marie Antoinette when she was in prison and her throne was gone . . . She was a great deal more like a queen then than when she was so gay and everything was so grand. I like her best then. Those howling mobs of people did not frighten her. She was stronger than they were, even when they cut her head off.

In the dead of winter, Sara comforts herself and the abused scullery maid Becky, who lives in the adjacent attic room, by pretending that the two of them are prisoners in the Bastille or that they are deep in the jungles of India. Becky remarks that even the idea of the Bastille makes her feel warmer somehow. "That is because it makes you think of something else," Sara replies. "I've noticed this. What you have to do with your mind, when your body is miserable, is to make it think of something else." Imagining that she is a princess helps Sara retain her dignity and self-esteem, but it also inspires her to be decent to those around her: "While the thought held possession of her, she could not be made rude and malicious by the rudeness and malice of those about her."[49]

There are limits, however, to what Sara's storytelling can accomplish. Burnett does not invest creative play with the same power that she eventually gives it in *The Secret Garden*. Imagination cannot fully substitute for *actual* restitution. All it can do is make suffering bearable. Imagination cannot bring Emily, Sara's doll, to life in the way that Sara sometimes wishes it would: "She would have liked to believe or pretend to believe that Emily understood and sympathized with her. She did not like to own to herself that her only companion could feel and hear nothing." But even Emily's silence is productive so long as Sara is capable of using narrative to explain it. "I don't answer very often," Sara says to Emily, trying to comfort herself. "I never answer when I can help it. When people are insulting you, there is nothing so good for them as not to say a word—just to look at them and think. . . . There's nothing so strong as rage, except what makes you hold it in—that's stronger. It's a good thing not to answer your enemies. I scarcely ever do. Perhaps Emily is more like me than I am like myself. Perhaps she would rather not answer her friends even. She keeps it all in her heart."[50] Ultimately what imagination inspires individuals to do makes the most difference.

It is in this way that storytelling exerts the most dramatic impact on Sara's reality. Just as a story can help Sara maintain a quiet dignity in the face of mistreatment, so stories can model acts of heroism and uncommon generosity that other people might follow. This is demonstrated most poignantly through the side characters in Sara's narrative. At Christmas, a bleak point in Sara's career as a housemaid, one of the children of a family that lives near the school is inspired to give her assistance after

hearing so many stories about children who were poor and had no mam-
mas and papas to fill their stockings and take them to the pantomime—
children who were, in fact, cold and thinly clad and hungry. In the stories,
kind people—sometimes little boys and girls with tender hearts—invariably saw the poor children and gave them money or rich gifts, or took
them home to beautiful dinners. Guy Clarence had been affected to tears
that very afternoon by the reading of such a story, and he had burned with
a desire to find such a poor child and give her a certain sixpence he possessed, and thus provide for her for life. An entire sixpence, he was sure,
would mean affluence for evermore.

After accepting the sixpence from Guy Clarence, Sara later extends this
generosity to someone even worse off than herself. Indeed, though Sara
is naturally inclined toward such acts, the book reinforces the idea that
willpower and imagination enable her to sustain her generosity during
times of greatest difficulty. When she is running errands on a cold night,
having been deprived of dinner, Sara happens upon a four-penny piece
and wants to use it to buy food for herself at a nearby bakery. Her spirit
is tested, however, when a child even hungrier than herself appears. Sara
struggles to do what she knows is right, and the fantasy that she is a princess enables her to make a self-sacrificial choice: "If I'm a princess—when
they were poor and driven from their thrones—they always shared—with
the populace—if they met one poorer and hungrier than themselves. They
always shared."[51]

As this happens, Sara's new neighbors, Mr. Carrisford, another English-
man from India, and his Lascar servant, are also inspired to generous acts
by Sara's storytelling. Communicating via her attic window, Sara forms a
relationship with the Indian native Ram Dass, who listens to her "relate
her visions to her secret friends. Being sad one night, I lay close to the open
skylight and listened. The vision she related told what this miserable room
might be if it had comforts in it."[52] Deeply lonely and homesick himself,
Ram Dass then goes out of his way to try to make those visions a reality,
conspiring with Mr. Carrisford to provide bedding, clothes, and food for
Sara and Becky in secret.

Through human agency, Sara's stories become real and finally lead to
the culmination of Sara's restitution narrative. In the book's pivotal coin-
cidence, it turns out that Mr. Carrisford is her father's friend and has been

searching for her in vain for two years. What's more, it is revealed that Sara's fortune is not lost, and she is once again an heiress. Her restoration to her place as a kind of princess brings about healing in more than one quarter. Mr. Carrisford, who believes that he was the cause of Captain Crewe's death, is chronically ill, having nearly died of "brain fever." The discovery of Sara brings about his healing.

While not as explicitly "Christian Science-y" or "New Thought-y" as the novels written later that decade, *A Little Princess* shows Burnett working with this amalgam of romantic and pragmatic ideas about the mind and about the power of imagination and creativity. In addition to taking a rather Jamesian approach to storytelling and religion, we see Burnett, like Mary Baker Eddy, exploring the relationship between consciousness and experience. And while the idea that mind could shape matter pervaded the New Thought scene, despite the sunny ending, this is not "positive thinking."[53] Burnett shares with Eddy a felt sense of the world as a struggle between good and its absence. As John Seelye argues, this theme runs throughout her opus: "The selfish materialism of the earl of Dorincourt, the mean-spirited repressiveness of Miss Minchin, the self-defeating pessimism of Archibald Craven, the hysteric hypochondria of his son, these are the enemy and need to be exorcised. Love—*caritas*—whether figured by human affection, by benevolence, or by a more transcendent spiritual force, are the expressions of the universal Allness of Good and need to be promoted."[54]

The novel ends not only with Sara restored but with a bittersweet sense of what it cost her to get there and of the evildoers who must be punished for making her suffer. Sara must wrestle with Carrisford's culpability in her father's death, and she remarks again and again how close she was to him, understanding that her suffering might have been avoided but for a series of contingencies. Sara is never forced to reconcile with her tormentors, nor does Burnett have her bestow some token of mercy on Miss Minchin. Rather, Sara's good fortune brings about a reckoning between the headmistress and her meek sister, who tells her bluntly that she is at fault for destroying their business and their futures, now that Sara is in a position to bring their perfidy to light: "And it serves us right; but it serves you right more than it does me, for you are a hard woman, Maria Minchin—you are a hard, selfish, worldly woman."[55]

The Dawn of a To-morrow

Burnett, as we have already seen, suffered from bouts of neurasthenia, and her experience with mental illness is reflected in *The Dawn of a To-morrow*, a novella about a depressed man who has a chance encounter with a street urchin on his way back to the lodging house where he plans to commit suicide. The book is substantially concerned with the role that mind plays in shaping our mental, physical, and spiritual health. Indeed, it begins by addressing the relationship between health and perception of circumstances: "There are always two ways of looking at a thing, frequently there are six or seven." Burnett's narrator describes, as an example, the ways that emotional states can influence one's perception of the London fog: "If one awakens in a healthy body, and with a clear brain rested by normal sleep and retaining memories of a normally agreeable yesterday... Under such conditions the soft, thick, yellow gloom has its picturesque and even humorous aspect."[56]

The story's protagonist, Anthony Dart (later revealed to be Sir Oliver Holt), does not have a healthy body or a healthy mind. Dart is suicidally depressed and racked with insomnia, persecuted by a brain that is like an "infernal machine" whose "workings can only be conquered if the mortal thing which lives with it—day and night, night and day—has learned to separate its controllable from its seemingly uncontrollable atoms, and can silence its clamor on its way to madness."[57] Dart is unable to perform this service for himself, leaving him in a state of complete existential despair. He takes his suffering to be a sign of God's nonexistence: "If one believed in Deity, the living creature It breathed into being must be a perfect thing—not one to be wearied, sickened, tortured by the life Its breathing had created. A mere man would disdain to build a thing so poor and incomplete." Yet he is overpowered by a strong, intuitive sense—bordering on "religious monomania"—of some power external to himself: "Something which filled the universe had seemed to wait, and to have waited through all the eternal ages, to see what he—one man—would do."[58]

Looking to put the remaining cash in his pocket to good use, he winds up meeting a beggar girl named Glad and following her around as she spends his money on food and supplies for herself, the prostitute Polly, and Polly's baby, who occupy the same abandoned house in a slum called

Apple Blossom Court. Dart also meets a man driven by circumstances to petty thievery, and his despair and his determination to do some sort of good before he dies leads Dart to spend a considerable part of his day in the company of these unfortunates. While at Apple Blossom Court, Glad tells him about the unusual religion practiced and taught by Mrs. Jinny Montaubyn, a former dance hall prostitute and infamous alcoholic. Jinny Montaubyn's faith is what prompted many of Burnett's contemporaries to associate the author with Christian Science, and Burnett scholars consider it the clearest articulation of what she came to call "the beautiful thought."

Though the name of Mary Baker Eddy is never mentioned (neither is any other Christian Science or New Thought leader), the story Glad tells about how Mrs. Montaubyn came by these new beliefs would be familiar to many a Christian Science convert. After injuring herself falling down the stairs, she was taken to a hospital where a woman came to her bedside, instructed her in this faith, and gave her a Bible to read. What distinguishes this faith from orthodox Protestantism, according to Glad, is the fact that "There's no 'ell fire in it. An' there ain't no blime laid on Godamighty." As in Christian Science, this belief system refutes the notion that God is responsible for any of the bad things that happen to human beings. Glad applies it to an incident in which a little boy was crushed by a dray, and "the curick 'e ses, 'It's Gawd's will,' 'e ses—an' 'e ain't no bad sort neither, an' 'is fice was white an' wet with sweat—'Gawd done it,' 'e ses. An' me, I'd nussed the child an' I clawed me 'air sime as if I was 'is mother an' I screamed out, 'Then damn 'im!' An' the curick 'e dropped sittin' down on the curb-stone an' 'id 'is fice in 'is 'ands." For Mrs. Montaubyn and her "lady," the idea that God would have caused such a thing is unconscionable. They insist upon both the absolute goodness of God and his transcendent and immanent presence in the world: "Miss Montaubyn's lidy she says Godamighty never done it nor never intended it, an' if we kep' sayin' an' believin' 'e's close to us an' not millyuns o' miles away, we'd be took care of whilst we was alive an' not 'ave to wait till we was dead."[59]

The reason that bad things happen, then, is entirely attributable to the flawed human perception of God's absence and inefficacy. Mrs. Montaubyn expresses her faith using the language of struggle that Albanese identifies as critical to Mary Baker Eddy's writing, a Calvinist sense of human fallenness and need to be reconciled to the divine.

As Mrs. Montaubyn says of the problems of the world, "'E [God] never done the accidents and the trouble. It was us as went out of the light into the dark. If we'd kep' in the light all the time, an' thought about it, an' talked about it, we'd never 'ad nothin' else."[60] When questioned by Dart about the trouble and suffering of the world, she says, "There wouldn't be none if we was right—if we never thought nothin' but 'Good's comin'—good's 'ere."[61] Healing and redemption are brought about by staying "in the light," which reshapes human perceptions of the world around them and helps them see it as God sees it: "never think of nothin' else, an' then you'll begin an' see things. Everybody's been afraid. There ain't no need. You believe that."[62]

Mrs. Montaubyn speaks of her transformation in concrete terms—the healing of her broken legs, the curing of her alcoholism, and the changing of her luck. But the story is less interested in the kinds of dramatic healings that appear in typical Christian Science narratives than in demonstrating the capacity of Mrs. Montaubyn's faith to provide spiritual relief in critical moments. Near the end of the story, when a woman named Drunken Bet is fatally injured, Mrs. Montaubyn goes to her side to tell her "there is no death . . . 'In a minit yer'll know—in a minit. Lord.'" And in the end, it brings relief to the protagonist, who reveals himself to be Sir Oliver Holt, a wealthy financier: "Perhaps it was—perhaps to-day has strangely given a healthful jolt to my nerves—perhaps I have been dragged away from the agony of morbidity and plunged into new intense emotions which have saved me from the last thing and the worst—saved me!"[63]

As with Sara Crewe's heaven, the benefits of this new faith are laid out in pragmatic terms. For the characters, the utility of belief trumps absolute certainty about its basis in truth. As Glad says, "it was queer talk! But I liked it. P'raps it was lies, but it was cheerfle lies that 'elps yer." Comparing Mrs. Montaubyn's religion to that of the local Anglican priest, she says, "We ain't no more reason ter be sure of wot the curick says than ter be sure o' this. Dunno as I've got ter choose either way, but if I 'ad, I'd choose the cheerflest." Likewise, it is the impact that this belief has upon those who believe it that captivates the protagonist: "She believes—she thinks she knows her Deity is by her side. She is not afraid. To her simpleness the awful Unknown is the Known—and with her."[64]

The God Mrs. Mountaubyn worships is an explicitly biblical one. Mrs. Montaubyn's "lady" gives her a Bible and instructs her to read it, "an' I'd set 'ere an' read it, an' read it an' learned verses to say to meself when I was in bed—an' I'd got ter feel like it was someone talkin' to me an' makin' me understand."[65] And she later renders her confession of faith in God explicitly (and significantly) in the language of the Book of Job: "Im as stretched forth the 'eavens an' laid the foundations of the earth, 'Im as is the Life an' Love of the world, 'E's 'ere! Stretch out yer 'and,' she ses, 'an' call out, "Speak, Lord, thy servant 'eareth," an' ye'll 'ear an' see. An' never you stop sayin' it—let yer 'eart beat it an' yer breath breathe it—an' yer'll find yer goin' about laughin' soft to yerself an' lovin' every-thin' as if it was yer own child at breast. An' no 'arm can come to yer. Try it when yer go 'ome.'"[66] What's more, her beliefs take on the same millennial rhetoric that Amy Voorhees identifies in Eddy's writing. When she speaks of an ideal world in which "everyone of us thought it [Good]—every minit of every day," the narrator takes a moment to note that without being aware, "she was speaking of a millennium . . . and believing she was speaking of To-day."[67]

The Dawn of a To-morrow is the most explicitly Christian of all of Burnett's books. *The Secret Garden* presented similar spiritual concepts in a more pantheistic framework, though without demonstrating any overt animosity toward Christianity. Sara's imaginative world, Mrs. Montaubyn's unorthodox biblical faith, and Mary and Colin's healing "Magic" are all manifestations of Burnett's "beautiful thought," a set of Christian Science/New Thought–inspired beliefs, which could take many different forms. What determines how they are presented in these novels is the needs of the characters, how best the beautiful thought can serve them. Sara requires the narrative and imaginative resources to survive her harrowing circumstances. Mrs. Montaubyn requires hope in the goodness of God as well as Christian moral discipline to overcome alcoholism and loose living. And Mary and Colin, as we shall see, require contact with living, growing things.

The Secret Garden

Mary Lennox is Burnett's least appealing child heroine, having a "little thin face and a little thin body, thin light hair, and a sour expression." She is described as "sickly, fretful, ugly" as a baby and a "tyrannical and selfish pig" as a child.[68] Far from the cherubic Victorian orphan, Mary reaches age nine simultaneously cosseted and neglected, the failures of her parents registering in her poor health and poor character. She is then orphaned by cholera and packed off to live at Misselthwaite Manor, the shambling mansion of her mother's brother. Her new environment is one of stark contrasts from her childhood spent in India. The manor house itself is like something out of a Radcliffe novel, nearly empty and full of mystery, the deep absences in the space itself registering the emotional vacuum left by the former mistress of the property. But Mary also encounters here the natural wonders of the Yorkshire countryside and the progressive child-rearing philosophy of the rural Sowerby family.

Susan Sowerby, the matriarch of the clan and mother of seven children, is the mouthpiece of the novel's ideas about child-rearing. Described by Misselthwaite housekeeper Mrs. Medlock as "healthy-minded," she insists that what is best for children is good food, plenty of exercise, contact with nature, and not too much adult supervision. Two of her children become Mary's closest companions: Martha, the housemaid who encourages Mary to become more active and self-sufficient, and Dickon, the boy who tames animals and teaches Mary about the natural environment of the moor. Their influence brings about a dramatic physical and mental shift. The passages where Mary plays in the outdoors are reminiscent of the final chapters of *The One I Knew Best of All*, in which Burnett describes her days exploring the idyllic Tennessee wilderness after spending her early childhood years in an English factory town. The healing power of nature is demonstrated through the awakening of Mary's entire physical being: "She did not know that this was the best thing she could have done, and she did not know that, when she began to walk quickly or even run along the paths and down the avenue, she was stirring her slow blood and making herself stronger by fighting with the wind which swept down from the moor." Her appetite improves, and she remarks constantly that she is growing fatter.[69]

Mary eventually discovers the novel's titular garden, a walled-up space that has gone to ruin thanks to the death of its former mistress and the grief that prevents her widowed husband from caring for it. With Dickon, Mary begins to tend to it and bring it back to life, the resurrection of the garden mirroring Mary's own physical transformation. Soon after this, she discovers Misselthwaite's other big secret: the existence of Colin Craven, a lonely invalid who is kept out of sight because he reminds his father of the wife he lost. Burnett's portrayal of Colin is as bare of sentimental ideas about children as is her portrayal of Mary. Colin is an insufferable creature, the sickness of his body having corrupted his very personality, exacerbating his isolation. Martha calls him "th' worst young nowt as ever was," spoiled rotten and accustomed to ruling tyrannically over the servants because they are forced to do exactly as he likes.[70] Colin's illness, of course, is psychosomatic. He suffers because he believes that he is doomed: "If I live I may be a hunchback, but I shan't live."[71] This is a belief that he has acquired from the adults around him, most notably from the doctor who attends him, a close relation who "is quite poor and if I die he will have all Misselthwaite when my father is dead."[72] The doctor maintains Colin's belief in his condition by instructing the boy and those responsible for his care that "he must not forget that he was ill; he must not forget that he was very easily tired. Mary thought that there seemed to be a number of uncomfortable things he was not to forget."[73] His medical opinion, however, is challenged by another doctor who says that Colin has had "too much medicine and too much lettin' him have his own way."[74]

Colin's thoughts make his condition worse, just as Mary's negative attitude makes her frail and ugly. Indeed, the novel suggests that Colin's thoughts may even have the ability to kill him. He "says he's always thinking that if he should feel a lump coming he should go crazy and scream himself to death." According to Dickon, "No lad could get well as thought them sort 'o things."[75] Healing Colin and Mary thus means remediating their thoughts. Dickon himself supplies the example for how this might be done. Dickon claims that he never "ketched cold since I was born. I wasn't brought up nesh enough. I've chased about th' moor in all weathers same as th' rabbit does. Mother says I've sniffed up too much fresh air for twelve year' to ever get to sniffin with col. I'm tough as a white-thorn knobstick."[76] Dickon also "never talks about dead things or things that are ill. He is always looking up in the sky to watch birds flying—or looking down at the earth to see something growing."[77]

Mary succeeds in distracting Colin early on by telling stories about India or about the secret garden, and he begins to recognize the good that this does him: "When I lie and remember I begin to have pains everywhere and I think of things that make me begin to scream because I hate them so. If there was a doctor anywhere who could make you forget you were ill instead of remembering it I would have him brought here.... It is because my cousin makes me forget that she makes me better." But it is on his first visit to the garden that Colin begins to substitute a belief in life for his belief in death: "I shall get well! I shall get well!" he says to Mary and Dickon, "And I shall live forever and ever." This refrain is repeated at the end of the novel, when Colin, having regained the power to walk, bursts forth with "a sort of rapturous belief and realization" that he is well and that he shall live "to find out thousands and thousands of things."[78]

Mary and Colin describe the agency that brings all of this about as "Magic." When a robin leads Mary to the door to the secret garden, she is sure "that what happened almost at that moment was Magic."[79] Magic makes an appearance in *A Little Princess* as well. But for Sara, it is the force that gives imagination its power. When she, Becky, and Ermengarde pretend to make a grand feast for themselves on a night when Sara and Becky are starving, Sara pretends that the shabby furnishings in her room are actually luxurious: "Only the Magic could have made it more than an old table covered with a red shawl and set with rubbish from a long-unopened trunk."[80] In *The Secret Garden*, magic is something more. It is a natural force, something that can be observed and studied scientifically, but it also has mystical properties. Mary first hears about magic "in her Ayah's stories," connecting it to India and to Indian spirituality.[81] But it also becomes connected to Dickon.

Indeed, Magic, imagination, and "the beautiful thought" in Burnett's novels put individuals in contact with difference. Since her protagonists are well-to-do English people, this means contact with some enchanted Other—the Lascar for Sara, the destitute for Dart, and for Mary these agrarian Yorkshire folk, whose dialect is featured prominently throughout the novel.[82] Mary comes to believe that Dickon works the Magic: "She felt that his Magic was working all the afternoon and making Colin look like an entirely different boy." Dickon, however, corrects Colin when he asserts that his healing is Dickon's doing. Colin, according to Dickon, has only to stop being afraid before he can walk again. And the Magic that makes that happen is the "same Magic as made these 'ere [flowers] work out o' th' earth."[83]

Colin begins speaking of Magic as if it were a thing to be studied scientifically. After demonstrating that he can stand on his own feet for a few moments, he becomes determined to investigate this new development: "Of course there must be lots of Magic in the world . . . but people don't know what it is like or how to make it. Perhaps the beginning is to say nice things are going to happen until you make them happen. I am going to try and experiment." He declares that he shall become a scientist and that

> the great scientific discoveries I am going to make . . . will be about Magic. Magic is a great thing and scarcely any one knows anything about it except a few people in old books—and Mary a little, because she was born in India where there are fakirs. I believe Dickon knows some Magic, but perhaps he doesn't know he knows it. He charms animals and people. . . . I am sure there is Magic in everything, only we have not sense enough to get hold of it and make it do things for us—like electricity and horses and steam.

He offers a few possible definitions of this Magic, first as the horizon of his intelligence, that which lies beyond his powers of comprehension—"I don't know its name so I call it Magic." And that thing which he does not comprehend is the force that animates all life: "Sometimes I've been in the garden and looked up through the trees at the sky and I have had a strange feeling of being happy as if something were pushing and drawing in my chest and making me breathe fast." Magic is an immanent presence: "Everything is made out of Magic . . . So it must be all around us." But he becomes convinced that if he can get it into himself somehow by remembering every day, "as soldiers go through drill" that the Magic is in him, then he will be completely healed: "If you keep calling it to come to you and help you it will get to be part of you and it will stay and do things."[84]

Magic, then, works because people put it to work. Some human agency is required in order to use its healing power. Growing strong enough to pull weeds in the garden, Colin remarks, "The Magic works best when you work, yourself. . . . You can feel it in your bones and muscles." At this point, after his healing journey has been completed, Colin stops speaking of Magic as something that works upon him but as something that he himself performs: "I shall never stop making Magic." Yet this optimism about the positive results that can be achieved through positive beliefs and actions (a New Thought idea) is still suffused with Jinny Montaubyn's belief in human frailty and failure to fully recognize and put this power to use. In the final chapter of *The Secret Garden*, the narrator intervenes to explain the wonderful discovery that Colin's Magic represents and to show how the human mind is responsible for its own suffering:

> So long as Mistress Mary's mind was full of disagreeable thoughts about her dislikes and sour opinions of people and her determination not to be pleased by or interested in anything, she was a yellow-faced, sickly, bored and wretched child. Circumstances, however, were very kind to her, though she was not at all aware of it. They began to push her about for her own good. When her mind gradually filled itself with robins, and moorland cottages crowded with children, with queer crabbed old gardeners and common little Yorkshire housemaids, with springtime and with secret gardens coming alive day by day, and also with a moor boy and his "creatures," there was no room left for the disagreeable thoughts which affected her liver and her digestion and made her yellow and tired.
>
> So long as Colin shut himself up in his room and thought only of his fears and weaknesses and his detestation of people who looked at him and reflected hourly on humps and early death, he was a hysterical half-crazy little hypochondriac who knew nothing of the sunshine and the spring and also did not know that he could get well and could stand upon his feet if he tried to do it.

What Colin achieves is not a miracle but a "practical and simple" thing that could "happen to any one who, when a disagreeable or discouraged thought comes into his mind, just has the sense to remember in time and push it out by putting in an agreeable determinedly courageous one."[85]

Colin and Mary's autochthonous belief in a kind of pantheistic, Emersonian Magic that one encounters through nature lacks the explicitly Christian character of Jinny Montaubyn's faith in *The Dawn of a Tomorrow*. Rather, in this novel, Burnett is interested in showing children whose religion is primitive, derived from their own independent encounters with the world.[86] Like Sara's imagination, their Magic is produced through consciousness, but also has power over embodied experience. *The Secret Garden* offers this up as a theory of all religious belief. In the novel's only explicit reference to Christianity, Ben Weatherstaff suggests that the children sing the Doxology in celebration of Colin's healing. Dickon associates the song with church, but he says that his mother "believes th' skylarks sings it when they gets up i' th' morning." Colin speculates that it might mean "just what I mean when I want to shout that I am thankful to the Magic.... Perhaps they [God and Magic] are both the same thing." This transcendental pantheism is affirmed by Susan Sowerby, who calls it "Th' Big Good Thing," though she says it is called by many names: "It isn't like us poor fools as think it matters if us is called out of our names.... Never thee stop believin' in th' Big Good Thing an' knowin' th' world's full of it—an call it what tha' likes. Th' wert singin' to it when I come into th' garden."[87]

The resolution of novel—the spiritual and physical healing of Colin and Mary and the restoration of the garden—takes the Emersonian relationship between consciousness and a higher metaphysical reality as encountered through the natural world and links it to pragmatic, even Jamesian ideas about how spirituality functions in the life of the individual. Burnett takes from Christian Science and New Thought the ideas that best help make sense of human experience and alleviate human suffering. In contrast to Mary Baker Eddy's writing, Burnett's novels evince a still-strong belief in the material world even as she emphasizes the greater power of mind and spirit. Uncommitted to any particular denomination or movement, in *The Dawn of a To-morrow*, Burnett nevertheless demonstrates the ability to speak in the same Christological, even millennial language that Mary Baker Eddy used and to register the tropes of sin and struggle that permeate Eddy's work. At various points after her death, Vivian Burnett described his mother's life as an unhappy one, adding that she was in "real need of healing."[88] Frances Hodgson Burnett and Mary Baker Eddy shared not only a loose set of ideas but a deeply felt sense of what made their belief in metaphysical healing—both for the individual and for entire communities—a physical and spiritual necessity.

NOTES

1. Frances Hodgson Burnett, *The Secret Garden* (New York: Norton, 2006), 143.
2. Gretchen Gerzina, *Frances Hodgson Burnett: The Unexpected Life of the Author of* The Secret Garden (New Brunswick, NJ: Rutgers University Press, 2004), 241.
3. Ibid., 93.
4. Ibid., 103.
5. Ibid., 241.

6. Ibid., 242.

7. Ibid., 260.

8. Ralph Waldo Emerson, "Beauty," in *Nature, Addresses, and Lectures*, Vol. 1 of *The Collected Works of Ralph Waldo Emerson* (Boston: Harvard University Press, 1971), 16.

9. Beverly Lyon Clark's masterful history of Burnett's literary reputation is essential reading. See Beverly Lyon Clark, *Kiddie Lit: The Cultural Construction of Children's Literary in America* (Baltimore: Johns Hopkins University Press, 2003). For sentimental readings of Eddy, see Leslie Fiedler, *Love and Death in the American Novel* (Champaign, IL: Dalkey Archive Press, 1998); Parker, "Mary Baker Eddy and Sentimental Womanhood," 3–18; Claudia Stokes, *The Altar at Home: Sentimental Literature and Nineteenth-Century American Religion* (Philadelphia: University of Pennsylvania Press, 2014).

10. Gerzina, *Frances Hodgson Burnett*, 299.

11. John Seelye, *Jane Eyre's American Daughters: From the Wide, Wide World to Anne of Green Gables* (Newark: University of Delaware Press, 2005), 272.

12. Anne Stiles, "Christian Science versus the Rest Cure in Frances Hodgson Burnett's *The Secret Garden*," *Modern Fiction Studies* 61, no. 2 (Summer 2015): 295–319.

13. Gottschalk has broken a lot of the ground on the pragmatic implications of Eddy's work. See the conclusion of *Emergence of Christian Science*.

14. Gill, *Mary Baker Eddy*, 340.

15. Ibid., 159–60.

16. Though Eddy's radical claims to originality helped to create these problems, the theft allegations are not given much credit by serious scholars of Eddy's work. For a thorough examination of the documentary evidence, see Gill, *Mary Baker Eddy*, chaps. 7, 8, and 12.

17. Beryl Satter, *Each Mind a Kingdom: American Women, Sexual Purity, and the New Thought Movement, 1875–1920* (Berkeley: University of California Press, 1999), 3.

18. Gottschalk, *Emergence of Christian Science*, 136.

19. Albanese, *Republic of Mind and Spirit*, 301.

20. Ibid., 318.

21. Emerson, "The Transcendentalist," in *Nature, Addresses, and Lectures*, 201.

22. Ibid., 203.

23. Lawrence Buell, *Emerson* (Boston: Harvard University Press, 2004), Kindle edition, loc. 1511.

24. Ibid.

25. Emerson, "Idealism," in *Nature, Addresses, and Lectures*, 36.

26. Buell, *Emerson*, loc. 1805.

27. Eddy, *Science and Health*, viii.

28. Gottschalk, *Emergence of Christian Science*, 121.

29. Ibid., 122.

30. Emerson, "Address to Harvard Divinity College," in *Nature, Addresses, and Lectures*, 78.

31. Eddy, *Science and Health*, 207.

32. Gottschalk, *Emergence of Christian Science*, 128.

33. Gill, *Mary Baker Eddy*, 224.

34. Gottschalk, *Emergence of Christian Science*, 99.

35. Though Protestant critics of Christian Science frequently challenged it on the basis that one did not need to be a Christian in order to be a Christian Scientist. See Klassen, *Spirits of Protestantism*, 111–12.

36. Gill, *Mary Baker Eddy*, 112.

37. Indeed, when Bronson Alcott visited Mary Baker Eddy following the 1875 publication of *Science and Health*, he came away wary of "the radicalism of her teaching, and after his final meeting with her in 1878 wrote that there 'is perhaps a touch of fanaticism, though of genial quality, interposed into her faith, which a deeper insight into the mysteries of life may ultimately remove.'" Emerson likewise considered and rejected Eddy's innovations. See Gottschalk, *Emergence of Christian Science*, 78.

38. Ibid.

39. Ibid., 275, 227. Emphasis in original.

40. Emerson, *Nature, Addresses, and Lectures*, 45.

41. Sally Shuttleworth argues that this biography demonstrates Burnett's awareness of the scientific study of children at the time, though she "archly distances herself from its excesses." She "resists the categorization and medical labeling which can follow in the wake of professional child study, focusing rather, from the child's perspective, on the utter naturalness of the Small Person's behaviour." Sally Shuttleworth, *The Mind of the Child: Child Development in Literature, Science, and Medicine, 1840–1900* (New York: Oxford University Press, 2010), Kindle edition, loc. 3841.

42. Frances Hodgson Burnett, *The One I Knew the Best of All: A Memory of the Mind of a Child* (New York: Scribner's, 1893), 3.

43. The imaginative capacity of children was not always a thing to be celebrated in the nineteenth century. Fantasy and imaginative play, seen as a form of lying, came in for moral condemnation and were frequently treated as symptoms of mental illness or "moral insanity" in the middle of the century. See Shuttleworth, *The Mind of the Child*, chap. 3.

44. Frances Hodgson Burnett, *A Little Princess* (New York: Penguin, 2014), 4.

45. Ibid., 38.

46. Ibid., 8. This incident echoes and may have been directly inspired by a childhood experience Burnett describes in *The One I Knew Best of All*, in which she was told that one of her mother's friends had named her child Eleanor. When asked if she liked the baby and thought this was a pretty name, she struggled to come up with an answer that was both kind and sincere when the truth was that she did not like the name at all: "It was the first social difficulty of the Small Person—the first confronting of the overwhelming problem of how to adjust perfect truth to perfect politeness." Burnett, *One I Knew Best*, 11.

47. Burnett, *A Little Princess*, 36.

48. Ibid., 47–48.

49. Ibid., 164, 183, 165.

50. Ibid., 146–47.

51. Ibid., 142, 187.

52. Ibid., 200.

53. Indeed, the ending is bittersweet enough that the 1995 film adaptation merely gives Captain Crewe amnesia, swaps his identity with that of another man, and then restores his memory just in time to reunite him with his daughter.

54. Seelye, *Jane Eyre's American Daughters*, 272.

55. Burnett, *A Little Princess*, 281.

56. Frances Hodgson Burnett, *The Dawn of a To-morrow* (New York: Scribner's, 1906), Project Gutenberg, 8.

57. Ibid., 10. Interestingly, Burnett refuses to name his illness even though she says that physicians would have. The name itself is presented as a source of fear for Dart: "He had heard these names often—applied to men the strain of whose lives had been like the strain of his own, and had left them as it had left him—jaded, joyless, breaking things. Some of them

had been broken and had died or were dragging out bruised and tormented days in their own homes or in mad-houses. He always shuddered when he heard their names, and rebelled with sick fear against the mere mention of them."

58. Ibid., 11–12.

59. Ibid., 51–53.

60. Ibid., 56.

61. Ibid., 64.

62. Ibid., 57.

63. Ibid., 72, 85.

64. Ibid., 50–53, 63.

65. Ibid., 61.

66. Ibid., 57.

67. Ibid., 64; Voorhees, "Writing Revelation," 84–94.

68. Burnett, *The Secret Garden*, 3.

69. Ibid., 71, 27.

70. Ibid., 82.

71. Ibid., 77.

72. Ibid.

73. Ibid., 88. Anne Stiles sees Dr. Craven's treatment as a form of Silas Weir Mitchell's rest cure and reads the novel as a refutation of Mitchell's theories. Cure, in this novel, emphasizes vigorous activity and creative production rather than physical and mental rest. It also reverses the conventional gender dynamics of the rest cure, which has been seen by former patients like Charlotte Perkins Gilman as a tool of patriarchal oppression, designed to keep women docile and inactive. See Stiles, "Christian Science versus the Rest Cure."

74. Burnett, *The Secret Garden*, 82.

75. Ibid., 95.

76. Ibid., 63.

77. Ibid., 86.

78. Ibid., 113, 124, 158.

79. Burnett, *A Little Princess*, 62.

80. Ibid., 224.

81. Burnett, *The Secret Garden*, 45.

82. And which Mary learns to imitate. This is yet another reference to Burnett's childhood, when she herself learned the Lancashire dialect from working class children.

83. Ibid., 127, 131.

84. Ibid., 138–39.

85. Ibid., 163.

86. Keith Lois emphasizes the secular, self-authorizing nature of the children's belief as well as the utility that it has for them in circumstances where "they do not receive any worthwhile moral or spiritual guidance from the adults around them." This claim is not completely true. Susan Sowerby has a great deal of influence over the children, though at a considerable distance. She is not seen in the novel until the penultimate chapter, but characters are constantly talking about her and repeating her beliefs about children and the natural world. What is important about these beliefs isn't that they completely lack external influence but that they are allowed to grow and flower without immediate coercion. Keith Lois, *Take Up Thy Bed and Walk: Disability and Cure in Classic Fiction for Girls* (New York: Routledge, 2001), 120.

87. Burnett, *The Secret Garden*, 158, 161.

88. Gerzina, *Frances Hodgson Burnett*, xvi, 377.

Error Uncovered

Mark Twain and the Limits of Demystification

In 1899, Josephine Woodbury, one of the great heretics of Mary Baker Eddy's movement, sued her former mentor for libel. She was represented by a Boston attorney named Frederick Peabody, and together, they stood at the center of a public relations fiasco for the Mother Church that metastasized throughout the first decade of the twentieth century. Woodbury became something of a religious visionary herself, gathering a large following of individuals who practiced asceticism and sought mystical experiences. Ten years before the suit, Woodbury began having an affair with one of her students, a relationship that she invested with apocalyptic significance. When Eddy confronted Woodbury about it, the latter said that she and her lover were "acting out roles scripted in the Book of Revelation." Woodbury's paramour was widely considered to be the father of her child, though she claimed that the baby was conceived immaculately, an event thought by some to be theoretically possible in Christian Science though likely beyond the capacity of any living human. Followers were instructed to venerate her son, named Prince of Peace, "as Jesus had been."[1]

The Mother Church in Boston sought to discipline Woodbury by placing her church membership on probation twice, but Eddy remained reluctant to excommunicate her former student. Attempts to bring Woodbury back into line went on for a few years, and in 1899 things came to a head. In June of that year, Eddy gave her annual communion message a particularly millennial bent, referring to the new age that Christian Science had inaugurated and the struggle faced by the faithful to fulfill the mission laid out for them. Speaking of enemies and obstacles to the movement's progress, Eddy referred to the "Babylonish woman" of the book of Revelation. Even though her name was never mentioned, Woodbury assumed that she was the target of the reference.[2] Her libel suit was directed at Mary Baker Eddy's remarks, but for many opponents of Christian Science, including Woodbury's lawyer, Frederick Peabody, it seemed to offer a much sought-for opportunity to subject the tenets of Christian Science to the rational judgment of the courtroom.[3] According to Robert Peel, "the action was clearly a propaganda move. . . . Mrs. Eddy was, as her distinguished Boston attorney Samuel J. Elder put it, 'the only mark they are aiming at.' And Mrs. Eddy not as an individual but as the Discoverer and Founder of Christian Science."[4] In other words, this trial was presented as an opportunity for skeptics to debunk Mary Baker Eddy's religious claims, to prove her to be either a fraud or a madwoman.

The suit, however, was dismissed for lack of evidence after a single week, before any of the defense's witnesses were even called. Nevertheless, Peabody went on to make a career as one of the most prolific anti–Christian Science pundits in the church's history, giving lectures, writing pamphlets, and providing information to journalists.[5] Peabody contributed heavily to the research performed by Georgine Milmine and the rest of the team at *McClure's* magazine, the subject of the next chapter. But his most famous correspondent was none other than Samuel Clemens, who was, at the time, working on a series of articles on Mary Baker Eddy for *North American Review* and *Cosmopolitan*. These were released in book form in 1907 under the title *Christian Science*. At the time, Twain was also writing a short story called "The Secret History of Eddypus, the World Empire," conceived as a sequel of sorts to *A Connecticut Yankee in King Arthur's Court*.

The Woodbury trial is a critical piece of context for the creation of what many Twain critics feel is some of his most vexing and incomprehensible work. While some readers have taken Twain's hostility toward Mary Baker Eddy as sort of the default rational response to something like Christian Science, confusion frequently arises from what appear to be contradictions in Twain's stated positions. On the one hand, Twain accepted many of Christian Science's healing claims and frequently expressed admiration for Eddy, but on the other hand, he was prone to making pronouncements about the threat that the movement and its leader posed to American democracy.[6] This tension between Christian Science as a potentially effective healing system (though not for all ailments) and Christian Science as apocalyptic threat is challenging to reconcile. Echoing a rather common sentiment among Twain scholars, Laura E. Skandera-Trombley calls *Christian Science* "almost unreadable."[7] Some of the author's contemporaries agreed. William McCracken, a member of the Christian Science Publishing Society and one of Twain's other major informants, thought that he was writing under conditions of extreme mental disturbance: "In one of their conversations, Clemens told him how time and again he would be roused out of a sound sleep at night by an 'impelling force' which would send him downstairs to his library to dash off abusive letters to 'the woman in Concord' in a torment of rage."[8]

Looking for clarity and context, many scholars turn to the author's biography. Mind cure and Christian Science were among the many unorthodox medical treatments the Clemens family used throughout their lives, and two of the Clemens daughters were personally connected with Christian Science. After her father's death, Clara Clemens wrote a book called *Awake to a Perfect Day* about her devotion to the religion. Susy Clemens sought the treatment of a Christian Science practitioner in Connecticut on the recommendation of her father during a prolonged bout of depression and then again during the final disease (probably meningitis) that killed her. This has prompted many scholars to point to Susy's death as at least a proximate cause of the author's crusade against Eddy during the final decade of both of their lives.[9]

But it would be a mistake to write off this segment of Twain's work as merely incoherent rage or grief. Despite Susy's death, a belief that Christian Science and similar methods could be effective stayed with Twain until the end of his life. Indeed, during his wife's final illness, when he was working on his Christian Science essays, Clemens wrote to his friend, the Congregationalist minister Joe Twichell,

> The physicians are doing good work with her, but my notion is, that no art of healing is the best for all ills. I should distribute the ailments around: surgery-cases to the surgeon ... nervous prostration to the Christian Scientist; most ills to the allopath & the homeopath; & (my own in particular case) rheumatism, gout & bronchial attacks to the osteopathist.[10]

At the very least, this tremendous loss—and Susy was but one tragedy during this period—is only part of the context that produced these essays and stories. For a fuller picture, we must look to the libel suit and the influence of Frederick Peabody and Josephine Woodbury. Both delivered volumes of information to the writer's doorstep and helped shape his image of Eddy as a demagogue who exercised tyrannical control over her organization.[11] Clemens hearkened to their charges that Eddy abused her power within her movement, but he clashed repeatedly with Peabody over the humorist's willingness to take many of the claims of Christian Scientists seriously. In a letter from December 1902, Peabody expressed his disappointment thus: "Your adoption of the Christian Scientist claim as to the extent of their influence . . . and the actuality of their cures, will be hailed by them with rejoicing, but cannot but be regarded by those who are combating the harmful influence . . . as unfortunate."[12] He concluded this particular letter with the hope that he and Clemens were of one mind in their "wish for the domination of sanity, not the sanity of your article, but absolute sanity in the affairs of men."[13]

They were not. The word "sanity" comes up repeatedly in Peabody's letters, but Clemens apparently had little interest in it: "Making fun of that shameless old swindler, Mother Eddy, is the only thing about it I take any interest in. At bottom I suppose I take a private delight in seeing the human race making an ass of itself again—which it has always done whenever it had the chance."[14] Twain appears to have been more interested in Eddy as a "type" than as a person or even a religious leader. She was an example of human fallibility and hubris, a symptom of certain troubling qualities in human nature. As he wrote to Unitarian minister Dr. Edward Everett Hale, in his early attempts to write something on Christian Science, "I was trying to prove that men are born crazy, and that that, by help of some other circumstances, secures perpetuity and a wide dominion for the new fad."[15]

This is the source of the disconnect: contemporary skeptics were, essentially, hoping that Mark Twain would help them wage an information war against Christian Science and "correct" the views of the public. They were committed to a restitution narrative in which the problem or "sickness" that Christian Science represented was an intellectual problem that could be corrected by reason. Clemens was not committed to such a narrative and was, at times, even openly contemptuous of it. Though critical of religion, he remained unconvinced by what Tracy Fessenden calls "the emancipatory power of unbelief."[16] For him, the problem of Christian Science was to be traced directly to human nature, and his assessment of Mary Baker Eddy and her religion is of a piece with his broader rejection of progress narratives—amply in evidence in his other writings from the period—whether generated by the likes of Eddy *or* her skeptical detractors.

OF SCIENTIFIC REVOLUTIONS

In April 1903, Frederick Peabody forwarded a letter from disenchanted New York Christian Scientist Henry Case to Clemens: "'Science and Health' says 'Error uncovered is two thirds destroyed.' The old lady must be pretty afar gone."[17] Case's appropriation of Eddy's concept of "error" is emblematic of the ways that both Christian Science and its skeptics competed over claims to the progress narratives of modernity. Each shared a supreme confidence in the ability of transcendent truths, whether obtained from empirical observation or divine revelation, to drive out untruth.

Such a tendency can also be observed in the widespread coverage that medical journals gave to the Woodbury trial. In November 1899, the *Illinois Medical Journal* published the following notice:

> The part of the trial that will interest the people more generally is, that complainant's counsel, a leading member of the Boston bar, proposes to examine the doctrine of Christian Science from beginning to end and to scrutinize closely the career of Mrs. Eddy and the leaders of her church, and to submit its spiritual claims to cold judicial investigation. As this is the first time that this new doctrine has been submitted to the courts, it will prove of great interest to the public to have determined the question if a judge on a bench can skillfully dissect and understand the peculiar conglomeration of sentences and reversed reiterations of the repeating paragraphs of the "Bible Annex." We apprehend that a discerning legal mind will not be influenced while judicially considering the case by the "Can't you see?"[18]

There are a number of noteworthy things about the way these medical professionals undertook their championship of Woodbury, including the decision to support a woman who claimed to have conceived a son through parthenogenesis. We have also the assertion—rejected by the court—that the question of libel somehow necessitated the full elucidation and careful examination of Eddy's entire religio-medical system. What did onlookers hope to gain from subjecting the "spiritual claims" of Christian Science to "cold judicial investigation?" What hopes were riding on the possibility that a "judge on the bench" would be able to "skillfully dissect and understand the peculiar conglomeration of sentences and reversed reiterations" of *Science and Health*? Awarding damages to Woodbury would not have undone Christian Science.

Rather, writers for medical journals appeared to hope that the sensationalism of it all would lead to a withdrawal of public support or that a judge's ruling on the validity of Christian Science's claims would simply make people stop believing in them. A notice in *Gaillard's Medical Journal* pays close attention to the strangeness of the beliefs attributed to Eddy:

> Outsiders will be interested principally in the revelation which this suit makes of the marvelous—almost incredible—assumption by this new apostle [Eddy], of a sort of divinity in her own person—founded on passages from the Book of Revelation. Not content with claiming to be the glorified woman referred to in the 12th chapter of Revelation as: "Clothed with the sun" and "with the sun and moon under her feet," &c.—she undertakes to destroy Mrs. Woodbury's character (against whom she had conceived a violent prejudice) by declaring in a public lecture that Mrs. Woodbury was the realization and fulfillment of the description given in the 17th chapter of the same book, of the "Scarlet Woman," the "Mother of Harlots," etc. It will be interesting to see just how this ecclesiastico-legal fight will terminate, although we are free to express the opinion that the majority of people outside will bet on the "Scarlet Woman," and will rejoice should the courts decide to give her the damages.[19]

While Eddy frequently spoke of her movement in millennial terms, it is not at all clear that she herself believed in any of this. Gillian Gill convincingly argues that the claim that Eddy was somehow the fulfillment of biblical prophecy originated with her followers: "There is overwhelming evidence that certain individuals and groups in the movement liked to give Mrs. Eddy an exalted religious role—Ira Knapp and his son Bliss, for example, identified her as the woman crowned with stars named in Revelation. The evidence is equally strong, however, that Mary Baker

Eddy herself was quick to see and to censure any attempt to make her or any of her works into what she liked to call a Dagon, a false image."[20] In the meantime, *Gaillard's* endorsed a woman who not only never stopped believing in Christian Science but was known to have made even more extravagant claims for herself. This is likely because Woodbury's story fit a set of tropes about women being seduced by alien religions. Stories about young women escaping from convents or Mormon settlements were, by this time, a staple of popular culture. In newspaper interviews, Woodbury portrayed herself as an innocent who was manipulated and controlled by Eddy: "I was being fed on Eddy pap for a constant diet. We were taught that the message of God as sent through 'Mother Mary' and set forth in 'Science and Health,' should receive all our attention and devotion. . . . I worked hard for the cause in which I had put all my hopes, all my enthusiasm. It was a dreadful shock when the awakening came."[21]

Woodbury's use of the word "awakening" along with the *Illinois Medical Journal's* "Can't you see?" is once again suggestive of the ways in which both Eddy and her critics drew from a shared set of tropes and metaphors—awakenings, conversions, and yes, healings—in order to describe the move from incorrect ways of thinking to more correct ones. The similarities don't stop there. Just as Peabody and his supporters hoped that a judge would somehow be able to determine the merit of a set of religious claims (though the standard to be used, theological or scientific, isn't at all clear), Eddy also invoked disputation, testimony, and justice when telling her students how to combat the errors of Mortal Mind: "When the first symptoms of disease appear, dispute the testimony of the material senses with divine Science. Let your higher sense of justice destroy the false process of mortal opinions which you name law, and then you will not be confined to a sick-room."[22] And while Eddy claimed to be able to heal illnesses that doctors could not, doctors frequently used the language of disease and epidemic to describe the threat that Christian Science posed to society. The *Illinois Medical Journal*, for example, referred to an "epidemic of 'fads'" competing with the regular medical profession for patients.[23] Another writer for the *Journal of the Kansas Medical Society* bemoaned the "sporadic and sometimes almost epidemic, hysteria of the people for patent nostrums, and such delusions as vitopathy, osteopathy, Christian Science, etc."[24]

Extending the metaphor, Dr. Victor C. Vaughan, writing for the *Brooklyn Medical Journal*, bemusedly regarded

> The present widespread belief in pseudo-science as a form of atavism, a tendency to reversion to that state in which man read his destiny in the stars and regarded disease as a visitation from heaven. Please permit me to say that I am not a pessimist and that I do not believe that this pathological condition is going to spread to the great mass of thinking people in this country. I have no fear of this, but as a mental epidemic it offers an interesting study. Its etiology, pathology, treatment, both prophylactic and curative, are proper matters for scientific inquiry.[25]

Those viewed as most vulnerable to this "epidemic," as with all epidemics, were the poor and uneducated, along with racial and religious others. Dr. Vaughan attributed the success of Christian Science to the "half-educated classes," suggesting that while "the majority of the people in this land are neither mental nor moral degenerates.... It must be admitted, however, that there are many degenerates among us and they are by no means confined to the humbler walks of life."[26] His prescription for combating this epidemic of derangement was, of course, more widespread scientific education and tighter regulations on medical practice. The *Interstate Medical Journal* led its story on the trial with the headline "An Attempt to Expose Christian Science" and attributed to Peabody the claim that "the libel, embracing the whole Christian Science, cannot be made intelligible to a jury without bringing into court the most extravagant of Mrs. Eddy's teachings. It is to be hoped that such an exposure will effectually dispose of this cult."[27]

Christian Science was the centerpiece of a restitution narrative that doctors and other professionals were attempting to enact, positing themselves and their rational, secular expertise as the remedy to the sickness of backward beliefs. This is a line of thinking for which Mark Twain had very little patience. In the book version of *Christian Science*, which updated the previously published articles, the author responds directly to the claim that Christian Science appealed only to the socially marginal and poorly educated:

> Four years ago I wrote the preceding chapters. I was assured by the wise that Christian Science was a fleeting craze and would soon perish. This prompt and all-competent stripe of prophet is always to be had in the market at ground-floor rates. He does not stop to load, or consider, or take

aim, but lets fly just as he stands. Facts are nothing to him, he has no use for such things; he works wholly by inspiration. And so, when he is asked why he considers a new movement a passing fad and quickly perishable, he finds himself unprepared with a reason and is more or less embarrassed. For a moment. Only for a moment. Then he waylays the first spectre of a reason that goes flitting through the desert places of his mind, and is at once serene again and ready for conflict. Serene and confident. Yet he should not be so, since he has had no chance to examine his catch, and cannot know whether it is going to help his contention or damage it.

The impromptu reason furnished by the early prophets of whom I have spoken was this: "There is nothing *to* Christian Science; there is nothing about it that appeals to the intellect; its market will be restricted to the unintelligent, the mentally inferior, the people who do not think." They called that a reason why the cult would not flourish and endure. It seems the equivalent of saying: "There is no money in tinware; there is nothing about it that appeals to the rich; its market will be restricted to the poor." It is like bringing forward the best reason in the world why Christian Science should flourish and live, and then blandly offering it as a reason why it should sicken and die.[28]

It is not clear whether Twain accepted at face value the claim that the constituency for Christian Science was uneducated, which also was not true. But it is clear that Twain was far more skeptical of the power of reason than any of the men who wished him to rally to their side in combating Mary Baker Eddy. Note, too, that Twain here is accusing the skeptic of being a "prophet," of making claims based on "inspiration" rather than fact, suggesting that such hopes are as rooted in fantasy as any religious belief. "Reason," at the end of the first paragraph, can be spectral.

"Environment," Twain argues, is a far more powerful force than enlightenment in that it supersedes rational assessment in the dissemination of religious or political ideas: "It is not the ability to reason that makes the Presbyterian, or the Baptist, or the Methodist, or the Catholic, or the Mohammedan, or the Buddhist, or the Mormon; it is *environment*." The evidence for the primacy of environment, he argues, is seen in the tendency of religious groups to pass on beliefs to the children born into them:

If religions were got by reasoning, we should have the extraordinary spectacle of an American family with a Presbyterian in it, and a Baptist, and a Methodist, a Catholic, a Mohammedan, a Buddhist, and a Mormon.

> A Presbyterian family does not produce Catholic families or other reli-
> gious brands, it produces its own kind; and not by intellectual processes,
> but by association.

The success of Christian Science, therefore, must depend not on its ability to make a logical appeal but to establish an environment. And in that
regard, he argues, Christian Science does succeed: "There are families of
Christian Scientists in every community in America, and each family is a
factory; each family turns out a Christian Science product at the custom-
ary intervals, and contributes it to the Cause in the only way in which
contributions of recruits to Churches are ever made on a large scale—by
the puissant forces of personal contact and association."[29]

Both Eddy and her critics were engaging in what Bruno Latour calls
"the modern type of debunking." Styling themselves as the unveilers of
truths previously kept hidden by illegitimate authorities or human ignorance, both Christian Science and conventional science revolted from
prior forms of religion and experienced this break as a revolution in the
name of truth. As Latour says of the Enlightenment thinkers and first
natural scientists,

> The obscurity of the olden days, which illegitimately blended together
> social needs and natural reality, meanings and mechanisms, signs and
> things, gave way to a luminous dawn that cleanly separated material
> causality from human fantasy. The natural sciences at last defined what
> Nature was, and each new emerging scientific discipline was experienced
> as a total revolution by means of which it was finally liberated from its
> prescientific past, from its Old Regime.[30]

Recall from chapter 1 how physician A. S. Coe blamed the backwardness of medicine on "the vague speculations of philosophers and meta-
physicians and the mysticisms of the priesthood" and called for the
emancipation of medicine from "their dogmatic spirit by rejecting all
hypotheses and returning to the unbiased study of natural processes as
shown in health and disease."[31] Tracing the history of medical absurdities from Galen to his present, Coe also identified Christian Science as
a pernicious example of an attempt to restore the Old Regime and once
again combine medicine with theology and metaphysics, which had, "until
within a comparatively recent period, absorbed and misguided all efforts
to advance rational medicine and place it on a scientific basis."[32] Christian

Science was a problem for Coe because it threatened to reverse the course of the revolution, to take us back, as Vaughan says, to "that state in which man read his destiny in the stars and regarded disease as a visitation from heaven."[33] However, for Mary Baker Eddy, Christian Science needed to be preserved because it represented the *true* revolution.

Both stories pivoted on a historical rupture between what came before and what came after, a moment of crisis conversion in which truth was revealed and error set aside. Twain satirizes this narrative in the short story fragment "The Secret History of Eddypus," which is set one thousand years in the future after Christian Science has become the dominant world religion and controls all governments. Referring to the stories the denizens of this dystopia tell about their past, the narrator says:

> We are in the habit of speaking of the 'dawn' of our era. It is a misleading expression inherited from the ancients. It conveys a false impression, for it places before the mind's vision a picture of brooding darkness, with a pearly light rising soft and rich in the east to dispel it and conquer it. In the interest of fact let us seek a more truthful figure wherewith to picture the advent of Christian Science (as it was originally called) as a political force.[34]

Twain seemed to fully recognize how Christian Scientists had borrowed the rhetoric of scientific revolutions. But in making fun of the apocalyptic way Christian Scientists often spoke of the dawning of their era—one of the themes of the Communion Address that triggered the Woodbury suit—Twain also implicates the millennialism at the core of all narratives of modernity and modernization. Twain was not committed to any progressive historical narrative. History, for him, was not characterized by a rupture between the epochs of the benighted and the enlightened. As Andrew Levy notes, Twain saw history as continuous:

> "Story up history," he once jotted in his notebook; it was a kind of mission. Sometimes, he thought that he saw progress everywhere, but more often he did not. In his essays, he frequently found ways to argue that the sins and virtues of one era or country reinvent themselves in others. And as he was writing the last chapters of *Huck Finn*, he devised a history game called "Mark Twain's Memory-Builder": "The board represents *any* century," Twain told its players. "Also, it represents *all* centuries. . . . If you choose, you can throw your game open to all history and all centuries." It was exactly the game one might invent if one had concluded that history *was* a game—the same thing over and over.[35]

As Twain told Peabody, he could foresee a future in which Christian Science would "supplant all the other religions & boss all the governments."[36] And that future would be perfectly consistent with the way human beings had behaved in every era before.

THE LAW OF PERIODICAL REPETITION

Twain's cynical view of history emerges most vividly in *A Connecticut Yankee in King Arthur's Court* but also appears in some of the stranger parts of his published and unpublished short fiction. This segment of Twain's work, which is the focus of the remainder of this chapter, travels back and forth in time in order to examine grand historical processes and the limited self-awareness of the individuals involved in them. Some of these stories reach far back into the past and attempt to create continuities between modern human societies and their more primitive forebears. Among these are *Connecticut Yankee* itself, Twain's sprawling novel about a late-nineteenth-century American who finds himself magically transported back to medieval times. It also includes a collection of stories set in the time of Genesis and told from the perspective of various biblical characters, including Adam and Eve, Shem, Methuselah, and certain pure products of Twain's imagination. Collectively, I refer to these stories as "the antediluvian diaries." "The Secret History of Eddypus," on the other hand, imagines a dystopian future with its roots in Twain's present. In that story, the society that the narrator calls "The Great Civilization" has died out, and in its place is a theocracy ruled by the descendants of Mary Baker Eddy, all of whom, regardless of gender, call themselves "Mary Baker Eddy."[37]

The unifying thesis of this part of Twain's work is that human history is continuous and recursive, constantly folding back in on itself and repeating the same moments, the same mistakes, again and again rather than unfolding in a series of revolutions or total breaks with the past. In the antediluvian diaries, Twain imagines this as a cycle with various stages of progress, decadence, destruction, and rebirth, a cycle described by the narrator of one fragment, the Mad Philosopher, as the Law of Periodical Repetition. This is why the civilization of Genesis looks, in these stories, very much like the late-nineteenth-century United States. It is a modern, industrialized society with the direct descendants of the "First Family"—Adam, Eve, and their children—at the top of its social hierarchy. Slavery, social stratification, exploitation, and religious hypocrisy appear as elements in these accounts of a civilization that is about to bring down God's watery wrath.

Science and technology also play a particularly dark role in presaging this world's impending doom. Twain was neither an early techno-utopian nor a Luddite, but his uncertainty and ambivalence about the progressive narratives of science are registered in his depiction of scientific curiosity as both an inborn gift and a potential source of humankind's destruction. The "Autobiography of Eve" portrays the prelapsarian mother of the species as a naturally gifted scientist who shares with Adam a passion for "studying, learning, inquiring into the cause and nature and purpose of everything we came across . . . this research filled our days with brilliant and absorbing interest. Adam was by constitution and proclivity a scientist; I may justly say I was the same, and we loved to call ourselves by that name."[38] In fact, their ardor for discovery brings about their fall from grace. As Twain revised the project that began as Eve's autobiography into the much broader "Diaries Antedating the Flood," he inserted an excerpt from Satan's diary, which shows Satan persuading Eve to eat the apple not by appealing to her vanity, as Milton's Satan does, but by exploiting her desire to understand concepts rendered meaningless to her without a Moral Sense. Here, as in "Letters from the Earth," another epistolary story written in the voice of Satan, Twain adopts the Promethean trope of the devil as truth-teller and enlightener. The Fall is presented here neither as a regrettable loss of innocence nor as unalloyed intellectual liberation. It is merely the first step toward producing a modern human civilization.

This first civilization, founded by Adam and Eve, reaches a level of technological achievement on par with the United States in the early twentieth century. But their achievements have negative consequences, and in a section of Eve's diary called "Extracts from Article in 'The Radical,' Jan., 916," the narrator bemoans the scourge of overpopulation. Thanks to the extraordinarily long lives of Old Testament humans, improvements in sanitation, and the discovery of microbes, the global population swells to sixty billion and threatens to overwhelm planetary resources. At the end of this piece, the author of the diary looks to the depredations of war as the potential savior of human civilization, saying, "Honor to whom honor is due: the physician failed us, war has saved us. Not that the killed and wounded amount to anything as a relief, for they do not; but the poverty and desolation caused by war sweep myriads away and make space for immigrants. War is a rude friend, but a kind one. It keeps us down to 60,000,000,000 and saves the hard-grubbing world alive. It is all that the globe can support." As the beginning of the preceding quote suggests, the medical profession has its own role to play in combating overpopulation. Taking a jab at nineteenth-century doctors and their "heroic" treatments (bloodletting, calomel dosing, etc.), the narrator refers to physicians as a boon: "In the past fifty years science has reduced the doctor's effectiveness by half. He uses but one deadly drug now, where formerly he used ten."[39]

Elsewhere, these stories make eerily prescient pronouncements about weapons of mass destruction and a rapidly accumulating technology for waging war. In a fragment titled, "From the Diary of a Lady of the Blood, Third Grade," an obscure scientist discovers "a means whereby he could sweep a whole army out of existence in an instant" but refuses to reveal the secret "since war was already terrible enough and he would not be party to the augmentation of its destructiveness." When presented with this argument, the tyrannical shoemaker-emperor who rules this world declares him a fool and, stating that this "invention would abolish war altogether," creates the weapon, setting out "alone against the sovereigns of the eastern world, with it in his pocket. Only one army ever came against him. It formed itself in battle array in a great plain, and at a distance of twelve miles he blew it into the air, leaving no vestige of it behind but a few rags and buttons."[40]

This is a society trapped in an exceedingly grim cycle: scientific discovery and innovation make extending and improving life possible but also increase competition for resources and thus necessitate the invention of life-destroying technologies in order to restore balance. But the narrative voices of these stories also suggest that none of this would be possible without the involvement of financial interests to incentivize this sort of innovation. The voice of the Mad Philosopher calls his own civilization "wonderful, in certain spectacular and meretricious ways; wonderful in scientific marvels and inventive miracles, wonderful in material inflation, which it calls advancement, progress, and other pet names; wonderful in spying-out the deep secrets of Nature—and its vanquishment of her stubborn laws; wonderful in its extraordinary financial and commercial achievements." The greatest of these achievements is "ORGANIZATION, the latest and most potent creation and miracle worker of the commercialized intellect." In Twain's usage, "organization" is the machine—propagated by modern science—that creates marvels of industry and commerce, that allows human beings to engage in collective efforts in ways heretofore unimagined, but it is also the machine that precipitates the end of that civilization by inducing "the money-fever, sordid ideals, vulgar ambitions, and the sleep which does not refresh; it has invented a thousand useless luxuries, and turned them into necessities, it has created a thousand vicious appetites and satisfies none of them; it has dethroned God and set up a shekel in His place."[41]

Organization is a concept that also emerges in *Christian Science*, wherein Twain suggests that Eddy's genius was not in her Great Idea—metaphysical healing—but in her ability to turn the Great Idea into an organization and a salable commodity. At various points, he compares Christian Science to Standard Oil and the Klondike, suggesting that Eddy's true accomplishment was in the creation of a commercial monopoly. This is, indeed, part of the thrust behind such comments as the following:

> We have seen what her methods were after she passed the stage where her divine ambassadorship was granted its exequatur in the hearts and minds of her followers; we have seen how steady and fearless and calculated and orderly was her march thenceforth from conquest to conquest; we have seen her strike dead, without hesitancy, any hostile or questionable force that rose in her path: first, the horde of pretenders that sprang up and tried to take her Science and its market away from her—she crushed them, she obliterated them: when her own National Christian Science Association became great in numbers and influence, and loosely and dangerously garrulous, and began to expound the doctrines according to its own uninspired notions, she took up her sponge without a tremor of fear and wiped the Association out; when she perceived that the preachers in her pulpits were becoming afflicted with doctrine-tinkering, she recognized the danger of it, and did not hesitate nor temporize, but promptly dismissed the whole of them in a day, and abolished their office permanently; we

have seen that, as fast as her power grew, she was competent to take the measure of it, and that as fast as its expansion suggested to her gradually awakening native ambition a higher step she took it; and so, by this evolutionary process, we have seen the gross money-lust relegated to second place, and the lust of empire and glory rise above it. A splendid dream; and by force of the qualities born in her she is making it come true.[42]

Here we see Twain's concerns about Mary Baker Eddy folded into a much broader antimonopolistic and anti-imperialist animus.[43] The Woodbury case, which brought into public view Eddy's tendency to suppress innovation and dissent within her movement, raised questions about what such organizational patterns, the "lust of empire and glory," might mean if applied on a mass scale.

Christian Science does, in fact, appear in the antediluvian diaries. When the Mad Philosopher describes his Law of Periodical Repetition, he includes Christian Science in his panoply of phenomena that reemerge in each cycle of human history:

> Did not the Science of Health rise, in the old time, and did it not pass into oblivion, and has it not latterly come again and brought with it its forgotten name? Will it perish once more? Many times, I think, as the ages drift on; and still come again and again. And the forgotten book, Science and Health, With Key to Scriptures—is it not with us once more, revised, corrected, and its orgies of style and construction tamed by an educated disciple? Will it not yet die, once, twice, a dozen times, and still at vast intervals rise again and successfully challenge the mind of man to understand it? We may not doubt it. By the Law of Periodical Repetition it must happen.[44]

Much of this paragraph is making fun of Eddy's incoherent writing style, but Twain also saw in Eddy a symptom of democracy's decline. As John S. Tuckey states, "Civilization, he believed, was due to perish and be followed by a new Dark Age." As Twain himself stated in his Autobiographical Dictation of January 15, 1907,

> Republics have lived long, but monarchy lives forever. By our teaching, we learn that vast material prosperity always brings in its train conditions which debase the morals and enervate the manhood of a nation—then the country's liberties come into the market and are bought, sold, squandered, thrown away, and a popular idol is carried to the throne upon shields or shoulders of the worshiping people, and planted there in permanency.[45]

The theme of civilizational collapse emerges just as hyperbolically in "The Secret History of Eddypus," which replicates many of the same narrative devices as the antediluvian diaries. The story is written as a series of letters between an unnamed scholar and his secret correspondent. In these letters, the narrator attempts to relate the "true history" of the calamity (a millennium past) that brought about the death of Western civilization at the beginning of the twentieth century and the rise of a world empire led by Christian Science. As the narrator tells his interlocutor: "Warn your friend that he is getting Christian Science history mixed up with *history*. There is a difference between the two. If you are sure he is a safe person and not in the clandestine service of the Holy Office, you may whisper to him certain of the facts—but on your life put nothing on paper!"[46]

As with the antediluvian diaries, "The Secret History of Eddypus" uses time travel to project the concerns of the author's historical moment onto different points in history. The "true history" of Eddypus is really a burlesque history of the United States. It is a hyperbolic critique of Twain's milieu, but its many hilarious inaccuracies call the perspicacity of the "scholar" who provides it into serious question. I deal with the implications of the story's reflexivity and tendency to sow doubt about its narrator in the next section. But for the moment, let us read the story's critique of the United States more or less straight. The scholar-narrator's invective against the West is summarized thus:

> Civilization is an elusive and baffling term. It is not easy to get at the precise meaning attached to it in those far distant times. In America and Europe it seems to have meant benevolence, gentleness, godliness, magnanimity, purity, love, and we gather that men considered it a duty to confer it as a blessing upon all lowly and harmless peoples of remote regions; but as soon as it was transplanted it became a blight, a pestilence, an awful terror, and they whom it was sent to benefit fled from its presence imploring their pagan gods with tears and lamentations to save them from it. The strength of such evidence as has come down to us seems to indicate that it was a sham at home and only laid off its disguise when abroad.[47]

In other words, the hypocrisy of the United States was revealed through its imperialistic ventures. "George Wishington," the narrator says, objected to the Declaration of Independence because "he could not tell a lie." The declaration announced that the democracy it was founding would be "the friend of all oppressed weak people, never their oppressor; it was never to steal a weak land nor its liberties; it was never to crush or betray struggling republics, but aid and encourage them with its sympathies," but "Wishington" recognized that "such a Declaration would prove a lie; that human nature was human nature, and that such a Declaration could not long survive in purity; that as soon as the Democracy was strong enough it would wipe its feet upon the Declaration and look around for something to steal." There are excellent reasons to read authorial sincerity into this polemic, knowing Twain's criticism of US involvement in the Philippines, Guam, Cuba, Hawaii, and Puerto Rico. These trespasses upon the sovereignty of other peoples "endeared it to the monarchies and despotisms, and admitted it to their society as a World Power. It lost its self-respect, but after a little ceased to be troubled by this detail."[48]

Such imperialistic ventures, the narrator argues, are the foundation of society's march of so-called Progress. And this march precipitated the Christian Science "eclipse":

> Christian Science did not create this eclipse unaided; it had abundant help—from natural and unavoidable evolutionary developments of the disease called Civilization. Within certain bounds and limits Civilization was a blessing; but the very forces which had brought it to that point were bound to carry it over the frontier sooner or later, and that is what happened. The law of its being was Progress, Advancement, and there was no power that could stop its march or even slacken its pace. With its own hands it opened the road and prepared the way for its destroyer.[49]

Christian Science, the narrator argues, achieved imperialistic dominance not because it stood athwart the tide of scientific progress but because it helped advance it. Here the scholar-narrator implicates basically the whole Enlightenment in the creation of Christian Science and its reign of terror. Proceeding through his tour of history, he places Joseph Priestly, Isaac Newton, and Charles Lyell on the same list as Cornelius Vanderbilt and Thomas Edison. Robert Bunsen, Alexander Graham Bell, and Louis Pasteur are presented alongside Andrew Carnegie and John D. Rockefeller, and the narrator states that "these relays wrought day and night at the Great Civilization and perfected it."[50] Once again, as in the antediluvian diaries, the collusion between science and the moneyed interests creates the real threat. Speaking of "Isaak Walton" and his discovery of gravitation, the narrator says that it, "proved to be valuable" and led to the formation of the first corporate trust,

> the Heavenly Trust, for the exploring of the skies for new products, and placed in the hands of an experienced explorer, Henry M. Stanley. It was granted monopolistic powers: whenever it discovered a new product in the skies it could claim and hold the like product when found in the earth, no matter who found it nor upon whose premises it was discovered. The parent company worked the Milky Way personally, but sublet the outlying constellations to minor companies on a royalty. The profits were prodigious, and in ten years the small group of original incorporators came to be described by a word which was as new as anything they had found in the stars—billionaires.[51]

This history of the Heavenly Trust (an allegory for Standard Oil and US Steel) overlaps with one of Twain's other critiques of Eddy: that she had made a fortune by copyrighting something that was originally the property of no one.[52] Though Twain rejected the claim that Eddy had plagiarized *Science and Health* from Phineas Quimby, he saw her central accomplishment as her conversion of extant ideas about mental healing, ideas that had simply been "in the atmosphere," into something that could be packaged, copyrighted, and sold at a profit: "Whether she took it or invented it, it was—materially—a sawdust mine when she got it, and she has turned it into a Klondike."[53]

But the "Eddypus" narrator isn't only a conspiracist. Through his true history, he isn't only seeking to implicate bad actors but to demonstrate a set of historical interactions that contribute to the creation of what he calls "circumstances," circumstances that accumulate like a snowball rolling down a hill: "Every new thing begets another one; every new thing that is done moves many many minds to take up that thing and examine it, expand it, improve it, add to it, exploit it, perfect it. Each result of each effort breeds other efforts of other minds, and the original idea goes on growing, spreading, ramifying, and by small and hardly noticed degrees changing *conditions*." The Scientific Revolution liberated the human mind: "The chains of thought lay broken; for the first time in the history of the race, men were free to think their own thoughts instead of other people's, and utter their conclusions without peril to body or estate." However, many of the products of that revolution merely contributed to more oppression.

The key example of that irony at work is the history of technology and American slavery: "For instance, at a certain time wise men were prophesying the early extinction of slavery in America and were forecasting the very date, with confidence. And they had their reasons, which were logically sound and mathematically sure: for slavery had ceased to pay." The invention of techniques for processing cotton for clothing, improvements to the steam engine, and finally the creation of the cotton gin reinvigorated the slave trade by strengthening its economic incentives:

> America had long ago been turning her cotton fields into cornfields because cotton was unprofitable; it was profitable, now, and she resumed its culture.... Slavery got a new impulse; the slave's price rose higher and higher, the demand for him grew more and more pressing; men began to *breed* him for the market, other men (pirates under the law) began to kidnap him in Africa and smuggle him into the country.

And, most abominably of all, the narrator reports, American religion and society rose up to celebrate and justify this new development: "Slavery was gratefully recognized by press, pulpit and people, all over the land, as God's best gift to man, and the Prophecy which had once been so logically sound and mathematically sure drew the frayed remnants of its drapery about it and in sorrow lay down and died." Nineteenth-century slavery serves as that consummate example of religion, culture, science, technology, and commerce working together in the propagation of oppression and suffering on an unimaginable scale.[54]

The voice of "Eddypus," like the voice of the antediluvian diaries, suffers no illusion that human history is a story of evolutionary progress or that Mary Baker Eddy and Christian Science represent a throwback to some earlier stage of human development. It is profoundly uninvested in a restitution narrative, arguing instead that human history is not the product of "thought-out plan and purpose" but "logical and blind evolution . . . a tidal wave of accumulated accidents."[55] Human beings are not working together toward greater levels of enlightenment and freedom, even when they think that they are. Rather, the contingencies of history and the inability of people to reason their way out of the accumulation of circumstances contribute to a human society that is doomed to shortsightedness and prone to depicting evolutionary accident as the inevitable and desirable culmination of progress. Instead of a throwback, Christian

Science was merely a recurring player in the never-ending cycles of human folly.

ENVIRONMENT AND THE HISTORICAL OBSERVER

As I stated earlier, "Eddypus" tends to sow doubt about the seriousness of its apocalyptic pronouncements and the reliability of the characters who make them. To read this story the way one might read *1984* would probably be a mistake. Twain is likely quite sincere in his many indictments of American hypocrisy and imperialistic greed, but at the center of this vision of history as "a tidal wave of accumulated accidents" is the idea that none of us really know what we are doing, that none of us are capable of judging the historical ramifications of our actions. And Twain included himself in that evaluation, as he would essentially have had to do in order to remain consistent. The device of projecting the problems of the nineteenth century into the distant past and future *could* be seen as a way of seeking enough distance to get perspective on them. But using characters like Adam and Eve and the anonymous narrator of "Eddypus"— all commenting on their own historical moment—simply collapses that distance and obliterates any perspective one might get, as the author remains committed to having each character speak from his or her own quite blinkered vantage point. At the moment when Twain was writing about Christian Science, Twain was also clearly preoccupied not only with his worries about imperialism and demagoguery but with doubt about the individual's ability to accurately assess or solve the true problems of his or her historical moment. In fact, the stories suggest that even "progressive" innovations could wind up being the sources of humanity's annihilation.

Twain was deeply pessimistic about the progressive potential of "reason" and was far more convinced that "environment" was the critical force in shaping human decisions. "Environment" in *Christian Science* is similar to what Hank Morgan, protagonist of *A Connecticut Yankee in King Arthur's Court*, describes as "training":

> Training—training is everything; training is all there is *to* a person. We speak of nature; it is folly; there is no such thing as nature; what we call by that misleading name is merely heredity and training. We have no

thoughts of our own, no opinions of our own; they are transmitted to us, trained into us. All that is original in us, and therefore fairly creditable or discreditable to us, can be covered up and hidden by the point of a cambric needle, all the rest being atoms contributed by, and inherited from, a procession of ancestors that stretches back a billion years to the Adam-clan or grasshopper or monkey from whom our race has been so tediously and ostentatiously and unprofitably developed.[56]

This preceding disquisition on the burdens of "training" is delivered from the dungeons of Morgan le Fay, where the protagonist bears witness to her arbitrary cruelty. He believes ignorance and "training" to be the source of not only her moral blindness but that of her entire society. Morgan, who, once again, has been transported from nineteenth-century Connecticut to Arthurian England, aspires to be one of those few who transcends his training and enters the world with a mind unfettered, a truly rational actor in a world plagued with superstition. And he believes that he can accomplish this at least partly because, as a time-traveler, he has knowledge of the future as well as knowledge of modern science. In one of the novel's opening episodes, he saves himself from execution by predicting a solar eclipse and presenting it as evidence of his magical abilities. Feats such as these enable him to win over King Arthur and discredit Merlin and the Catholic Church.

Were he content to remain a satirical observer, Hank Morgan's values need never substantially conflict with those of the world he inhabits. But he is presented as a man of action who cannot remain idle in the face of the dirt, superstition, and wanton abuse that he witnesses all around him. His remedy is to turn medieval England into a replica of the nineteenth century, and he becomes "The Boss," King Arthur's right-hand man, specifically in order to do so. This doesn't work out well. After a string of successes in establishing schools, Protestant churches, factories, newspapers, and a telephone system, the Catholic Church launches a counter-revolution that restores the status quo. The end of the novel sees Hank and his tiny band of followers defending themselves with modern weaponry against mounted knights with shields and swords. Though they succeed in annihilating their enemy, they pile up so many bodies in the process that they are unable to escape their own fortifications. Hank Morgan himself is ultimately saved by a deus ex machina in the form of Merlin, who performs a *genuine* act of magic by returning the Yankee to his own time. The calamity Morgan creates doesn't stem from his desire to alleviate suffering and combat cruelty but from his belief that the nineteenth-century civilization he uses for a model is adequate to the task. The grotesque consequences of trying to turn Camelot into an industrial, commercial center—which Morgan calls his "Man Factory"—is every bit as much a product of Morgan's "training" as of the counterrevolutionary threat posed by the nobility and the church.

Similarly, the narrator of "Eddypus" purports to be the holder of the "true history" of his civilization, a lone heretic, bearer of the truths that threaten to overturn the global despotism of Christian Science. Responding to his interlocutor, who asks him to write a history of Eddypus, the narrator says, "You mean a real history, of course? Not the ruck of pious romances which the Government calls history and compels the nations to buy—every family has a set, along with Science and Health." Yet almost instantaneously, we are shown that the "true history" he possesses is monstrously and hilariously inaccurate, a nearly incoherent hodgepodge based on half-remembered facts and complete misunderstandings. On the first page, the narrator informs his friend that this secret history was gotten from "a paper by one Mark Twain, (A.D. 1898 = A.M. 30) a revered priest of the earlier faith, sometime Bishop of New Jersey, hanged in A.D. 1912 = A.M. 47."[57] In this history, Uncle Remus is "celebrated as a daring voyager and explorer of in his time. He was with Columbus in the Mayflower and assisted him in discovering America and Livingston." Livingston, he informs us, "was an island." Yellow journalism was invented by Ralph Waldo Edison, and Sir Walter Raleigh "settled Plymouth Rock, but was driven away by the Puritans and other Indians; after which he discarded armed force, and honorably bought a great tract of land and named it Pennsylvania, after himself." In other words, throughout this narrator's incisive pronouncements about the state of the world at the turn of the twentieth century, we are reminded that his historical perspective is contaminated, limited by the availability of information, distortions in the record, and his own prejudices.[58]

Therefore, in a very real way, this narrator is guilty—though unknowingly so—of the same sins of omission and revision that he accuses the church of deliberately committing. The text tells us, in fact, that his history is a creative work, a fabrication. Though he accuses the regime of supplying "pious romances" instead of history, he describes his own project in artistic terms, saying that "in my clandestine trade of antiquary and student of history I am like an artist who paints beautiful pictures and hungers for the happiness of showing them, but lives among the blind."[59] Thus, history becomes artifice even as it undertakes the responsibility of conveying truth to people incapable of perceiving it, just as in *Connecticut Yankee*, the science that Hank Morgan uses to combat the superstitions of King Arthur's Court becomes, in the words of Michael Davitt Bell, another form of "magic, a matter of deceptive and spellbinding effects."[60] The more one tries to deny the effects of one's own training and environment, the more one becomes like Merlin, "an old numbskull, a magician who believed his own magic; and no magician can thrive who is handicapped like that."[61]

Through the unreliable narrators in *Connecticut Yankee* and "The Secret History of Eddypus," Twain reveals that his mistrust of human subjectivity extends even to himself. As Christopher Morris says of *Connecticut Yankee*, "It does not take Paul de Man to understand Twain's work as allegorizing hermeneutic self-deception in reading and writing."[62] At various points in "Eddypus," Twain satirizes himself by having the narrator mock his own writing just as Twain so gleefully did to the work of others, including Mary Baker Eddy. There is a remarkable point when the fabulist historian takes the Bishop Mark Twain to task for lacking a sense of humor. He dissects the absurdities of his aphorisms, all the while offering suggestions as to how the author might have expressed his points better. The scholar claims that the improvements he makes to Twain's prose prove "that the little book has merit, and that my labors in relieving that merit of its obscuring and obstructing cloud of defects were worth the fatigue those labors imposed upon me."[63] This is what Twain does in a section of *Christian Science*, taking apart Mary Baker Eddy's texts (*Science and Health* was often referred to as "the little book") and putting them back together again in order to liberate the "merit" of her essential ideas from the obfuscation of her prose.

In these writings, Twain seems to be reflecting on the limited ability of any author to control the way in which he or she is received, a poignant reflection for a man who was thinking about his autobiography and contemplating his own legacy (and, perhaps, a concession to the woman whose work he was busy tearing to pieces). That autobiography, and his scheme for delaying its publication a century after his death, also appears in "Eddypus." The narrator declares that this plan, which was meant to protect the sensibilities of Twain's friends and family, "made his [Twain's] pen the freest that ever wrote. As a result, his friends stand before us absolutely naked. They had not a grace that does not appear, they had not a deformity that is not present to the eye." The autobiographer, however, "was intending to wear clothes himself, and as constantly as he could he did; but many and many is the time that they slipped and fell in a pile on the floor when he was not noticing." The narrator claims that through these unintentional slippages, we can "know him better than he knew himself," a statement that rings both true and false, since the "Eddypus" narrator is so egregiously wrong about the facts of Twain's life and work. Twain appears to be contemplating the fact that though historical distance may protect the immediate subjects of a work, the trade-off is loss of comprehension. The narrator tells us that "[Twain] thought he would put off publication a thousand years, but he gave up that idea because he wanted his book to be readable by the common people without necessity of translation. 'The epic of Beowulf is twelve hundred years old,' he says; 'it is English, but I cannot read a line of it, so great is the change our tongue has undergone.'" Thus, "Eddypus" turns from a restitution narrative that seeks to reform the present by "recovering" a "true" history into a black comedic look at the inadequacies of cultural memory and the limits of narrative to help us understand the past.[64]

Let us return for a moment to *Christian Science*, which begins with a burlesque of Christian Science cure. The narrator, a stand-in for the author, tells a story in which he falls from a precipice in Switzerland, breaking every bone in his body. A Christian Science healer is sent for, and she and "Twain" argue at some length over many of the central principles of her religion. The healer quotes liberally from *Science and Health*, and every sentence she utters is held up for ridicule. The healer—and Eddy herself— appear to be the butt of the joke, except for one thing: the treatment works, though our hero feels obliged to seek the help of a "horse doctor" for his stomachache and head cold. Even after the Christian Science healer has knitted his broken bones, he does not trust her to treat his other ailments, figuring that she would have done so already if she could. The horse doctor, for his part, prescribes heroic treatments that involve turning the stomachache and head cold into symptoms of something far, far worse.

One can read in this story Twain's equal-opportunity contempt for quacks (even the ones with accredited degrees) as well as his belief, given voice by Hank Morgan in *Connecticut Yankee*, that "any mummery will cure if the patient's faith is strong in it."[65] But taken alongside all of the other evidence, it can also be viewed as an example of the author's willingness to embrace Christian Science's fundamental challenge to commonsense realism. "*Science and Health* may contain a lot of nonsense," Twain seems to be saying, "but who cares as long as it seems to help some people?" Worry instead about the internal politics of the church, the way it deals with dissent and treats its members. "Eddypus," like *Connecticut Yankee*, is rooted in epistemic doubt and pessimism about the ways in which we attempt to engineer society based on what we think we know. Thus, it is Eddy's undemocratic leadership style and apparent refusal to tolerate dissent, not really her stated beliefs, that the author finds horrifying and dangerous. He is more offended by her dogmatism than her strangeness. But this quality, his work suggests, is shared by many who also lay claim to narratives of progress and use them in order to transform societies against their will. This linking of concerns about how we perceive and know with doubts about any effort to advance a progressive civilization—about the restitution narrative itself, in other words—has implications that will carry over into the next chapter, where journalists and literary realists based their calls for social reform on the existence of a world of facts simply waiting to be made public.

NOTES

1. Gill, *Mary Baker Eddy*, 421, 426.

2. The full transcript of the trial is preserved among Georgine Milmine's research materials at the Mary Baker Eddy Library. "Court Transcript: Woodbury v. Eddy," 1899 (typescript, Georgine Milmine Collection, Mary Baker Eddy Library for the Betterment of Humanity, Boston).

3. Woodbury was motivated by a desire for revenge against the perceived insult, and Peabody, as Gillian Gill argues, was motivated by a personal animus for Mrs. Eddy, the source of which we may never really know. Desire for fame and a ferocious antifeminism may have been contributing factors. Certain aspects of Peabody's biography suggest a desire for social status and a predilection for seeking revenge against women he felt had wronged him. In 1912, Peabody sued his ex-wife for libel, and the ensuing trial revealed that Peabody had lied to his

fiancée and her family about his financial viability, that he had married her for her modest wealth, and that he had proceeded to embezzle said fortune away from her. Anna Peabody eventually left him, taking their two daughters, when her husband drove the family into crushing debt. Peabody sued his wife three times between 1901 and 1908 and finally obtained a divorce in 1908. The 1912 libel case was also part of an attempt to renegotiate visitation rights. According to Gill, "Judge Almy, who heard the case, gave a crushing indictment of Peabody's faults." Gill, *Mary Baker Eddy*, 438.

4. Robert Peel, *Mary Baker Eddy: Years of Authority*, 156.

5. See Frederick Peabody, *Complete Exposure of Eddyism or Christian Science: The Plain Truth in Plain Terms Regarding Mary Baker Eddy* (Boston: Author, 1904), for the paradigmatic example of Peabody's work.

6. See, for example, chap. 4 of *The Cambridge History of American Literature, Vol. III: Prose Writing, 1860–1920*, ed. Sacvan Bercovitch (Cambridge: Cambridge University Press, 2005).

7. Laura E. Skandera-Trombley, *Mark Twain in the Company of Women* (Philadelphia: University of Pennsylvania Press, 1994), 172.

8. Peel, *Mary Baker Eddy: Years of Authority*, 204.

9. Problematically, given the nature of Susy's illness, Hamlin Hill declares that her interest in Christian Science was "perhaps fatal" in the afterword to the Oxford edition of *Christian Science*. For more on the Clemens family's history with alternative healing movements, see K. Patrick Ober, *Mark Twain and Medicine: "Any Mummery Will Cure"* (St. Louis: University of Missouri Press, 2003).

10. Samuel Clemens, Letter to Joe Twichell, 4 April 1903 (Mark Twain File, Mary Baker Eddy Library for the Betterment of Humanity, Boston).

11. Clemens's correspondence with Woodbury is notable for its professionalism, especially when laid alongside the correspondence with Peabody. There is something delightful about the straightforward, businesslike way in which Woodbury invites the most famous man of his generation to make an appointment with her: "If you wish to be posted as to where and how to find the 'meatiest' paragraphs—'changes' etc etc., and will make an appointment, I will give you my aid. When you say. I have Thursday free, also Sat this week. Sincerely, J. Woodbury. P.S. If you phone me tomorrow [illegible] before eleven as to which books you would like I'll express them immediately." Josephine Woodbury, Letter to Samuel Clemens, 3 February 1902 (Mark Twain Project, University of California at Berkeley). William McCracken, however, did not believe that Mrs. Woodbury's influence was benign. As Peel reports, McCracken suspected that Clemens was writing under her hypnotic influence. See Peel, *Mary Baker Eddy, Years of Authority*, 602.

12. Frederick Peabody, Letter to Samuel Clemens, 2 December 1902 (Mark Twain Project, University of California at Berkeley).

13. Ibid.

14. Samuel Clemens, Letter to Frederick Peabody, 5 December 1902 (Mark Twain Project, University of California at Berkeley).

15. Samuel Clemens, Letter to Dr. Hale, 1 November 1899 (Mark Twain File, Mary Baker Eddy Library for the Betterment of Humanity, Boston). In this letter, Clemens intimates that Livy Clemens, his wife, "suppressed" some of these writings because of his outlandish claims about Christian Science's potential for world dominance. "Mrs. Clemens despises prophets," he says, "but no matter. I shall smuggle those suppressed chapters into a book next spring. For when I am engaged in a good work I have no principles."

16. Tracy Fessenden, *Culture and Redemption*, 179.

17. Henry L. Case, Letter to Frederick Peabody, 5 April 1903 (Mark Twain Project, University of California at Berkeley).

18. "Woodbury vs. Eddy," *Illinois Medical Journal* 49, no. 5 (November 1899): 223–24. The "Bible Annex" is a reference to *Science and Health*. Twain also frequently called it this.

19. "Snap Shots at Current Events," *Gaillard's Medical Journal* 71, no. 5 (November 1899): 725–26.

20. Gill, *Mary Baker Eddy*, 413.

21. "Declares Christian Science All a Fraud," *Sioux City Daily Tribune*, 1899 (newspaper clipping, Alfred Farlow Scrapbooks, Mary Baker Eddy Library for the Betterment of Humanity, Boston).

22. Eddy, *Science and Health*, 390.

23. "Woodbury v. Eddy," 534.

24. J. Dillon, "Medical Organization," *Journal of the Kansas Medical Society* 6, no. 8 (August 1906): 311–16.

25. Victor C. Vaughan, "An Address before the Alumni Association of the Long Island College Hospital," *Brooklyn Medical Journal* 15, no. 3 (March 1901): 134.

26. Ibid., 136.

27. "New York Letter," *Interstate Medical Journal* 11, no. 10 (October 1899): 534–35.

28. Mark Twain, *Christian Science*, 93.

29. Ibid., 93–95.

30. Bruno Latour, *We Have Never Been Modern*, translated by Catherine Porter (Boston: Harvard University Press, 1993), 43, 35.

31. Coe, "Modern Medical Science," 406.

32. Ibid.

33. Vaughan, "An Address," 134.

34. Mark Twain, *Mark Twain's Fables of Man*, ed. John S. Tuckey (Berkeley: University of California Press, 1972), 333.

35. Andrew Levy, *Huck Finn's America: Mark Twain and the Era That Shaped His Masterpiece* (New York: Simon and Schuster, 2014), 27.

36. Samuel Clemens, Letter to Frederick Peabody, 5 December 1902.

37. The editors of *The Bible according to Mark Twain* indicate that the similarities between "Eddypus" and the Old Testament sketches are more than simply thematic. Rather, "Working notes and other details" indicate that the two projects were linked in Twain's mind. Mark Twain, *The Bible according to Mark Twain*, edited by Howard G. Baetzhold and Joseph B. McCullough (New York: Touchstone, 1995), 36.

38. Twain, *The Bible*, 54.

39. Ibid., 70–72.

40. Ibid., 70–75.

41. Ibid., 76.

42. Twain, *Christian Science*, 274–75.

43. Filtered, of course, through misogyny and anti-Catholicism. See Cynthia Schrager, "Mark Twain and Mary Baker Eddy: Gendering the Transpersonal Subject," *American Literature* 70, 1 (March 1998): 29–62.

44. Twain, *The Bible*, 79.

45. Twain, *Fables of Man*, 316.

46. Ibid., 315–16, 318.

47. Ibid., 327.

48. Ibid., 329.

49. Ibid., 333–34.

50. Ibid., 357.

51. Ibid., 365.

52. This may very well have also been a backhanded compliment. Samuel Clemens was, in fact, on spectacularly good terms with Standard Oil. He declined to publish Henry Demarest Lloyd's scathing exposé of the trust because of his friendship with Standard Oil executive Henry Rogers (Lloyd later found a patron in William Dean Howells). He visited 26 Broadway to have lunch with John Rockefeller Jr. and "later blamed the muckrakers and Teddy Roosevelt for Standard Oil's infamy. That the trust had scarcely had a strike in more than four decades proved to him that 'the Standard Oil chiefs cannot be altogether bad or they would oppress their sixty-five thousand employees from habit and instinct, if they are so constituted that it is instinctive with them to oppress everybody else.'" See Ron Chernow, *The Life of John D. Rockefeller, Sr.* (New York: Vintage, 2004), Kindle edition, loc. 8692.

53. Twain, *Christian Science*, 102.

54. Twain, *Fables of Man*, 379–82.

55. Ibid., 382.

56. Mark Twain, *A Connecticut Yankee in King Arthur's Court* (New York: Barnes and Noble, 2005), 177.

57. *Anno Mundi*, "Year of the World," the reckoning of time that begins with the discovery of Christian Science.

58. Mark Twain, *Fables of Man*, 318–19, 327.

59. Ibid., 322.

60. Bell argues that through this central irony, "Twain brilliantly (however unwittingly and unconsciously) dramatizes what is already a fundamental instability in William Dean Howells's version of literary realism. For what is Howellsian realism, after all, but a lie that claims to be truthful, a form of literature that claims *not* to be 'literary,' a deployment of style that claims to *avoid* 'style'"—a species of magic, in short, that justifies itself as a righteous battle *against* magic." Michael Davitt Bell, *The Problem of American Realism: Studies in the Cultural History of a Literary Idea* (Chicago: University of Chicago Press, 1993), 66.

61. Twain, *Connecticut Yankee*, 224.

62. Christopher D. Morris, "The Deconstruction of the Enlightenment in Mark Twain's *A Connecticut Yankee in King Arthur's Court*," *JNT: Journal of Narrative Theory* 39, no. 2 (Summer 2009): 160.

63. Twain, *Fables of Man*, 341.

64. Ibid., 340–42.

65. Twain, *Connecticut Yankee*, 273.

4

All the News Worth Reading

Literary Journalism and the *Christian Science Monitor*

In 1904, Georgine Milmine, a native Canadian and staff writer for the *Auburn Citizen*, approached Ida Tarbell, then an editor at *McClure's*, the famous muckraking and literary magazine, with a manuscript and a voluminous stack of notes on the subject of Mary Baker Eddy. Tarbell was fresh off the success of her landmark series *The History of the Standard Oil Company*, which was released as a book that same year. One wonders if she recognized the other journalist's likely conscious attempt to emulate her narrative of exposure. Milmine had spent months interviewing the residents of every place that Eddy had lived, seeking to reconstruct her dramatic career in a factual but gripping manner. What Tarbell did with this project beyond inspiring its writer and purchasing her materials is unknown; by the time *The Life of Mary Baker G. Eddy and the History of Christian Science* began its serial run in 1907, Tarbell had departed *McClure's* along with many of its most celebrated writers and editors to found the *American Magazine* and disentangle themselves from the magazine's increasingly autocratic owner. When the series was completed in August 1908, it had passed through the hands of some of the most famous names in the field of early-twentieth-century American letters—not only Tarbell's, but those of Burton Hendrick, Mark Sullivan, Willa Cather, and, of course, S. S. McClure himself.

It was hardly the only attempt to expose the inner workings of Eddy's organization in the press, and it certainly was not the only biographical treatment of Eddy herself. *McClure's* published its series contemporaneously with Sibyl Wilbur's hagiography in *Human Life*. But for a variety of reasons, the *McClure's* version played the most significant role in shaping public opinion about Christian Science. And the *McClure's* version— released as a book in 1908—became the baseline for almost all subsequent attempts to write Eddy's biography by people unaffiliated with the church. One of the major reasons why is encapsulated in one of the advertisements for the series:

> One of the most important, certainly the most interesting contributions to McClure's in 1907 will be the first life of Mrs. Mary Baker Glover Eddy, head of the Christian Science Church. She is the richest woman in the United States, who got her money by her own efforts; the most powerful American woman by all odds, easily the most famous; yet no one has ever before written the true story of her life. She is eighty-five years old, has been three times married; at fifty-five she was unknown and a dependent, and yet she has worked up a fortune which no one has been able quite to estimate, but which must be more than $3,000,000. She is the most absolute church head in the world, not even excepting the Pope.
>
> The whole story of her life is a romance. McClure's Magazine is going to tell the story for the first time. Never was a series of articles in any magazine more carefully prepared than this. Georgine Milmine, the author, has worked on it steadily for more than two years, gathering data, and five of the members of the McClure's staff have helped to confirm and fill out her results.
>
> It will be a great historical series, as great, perhaps, as the history of the Standard Oil, and to most people more interesting. It is not an attack on Christian Science, as most magazine articles have been. It is the history of a remarkable woman and a remarkable movement.[1]

In its framing of the project, the editors traded on the magazine's established reputation as a purveyor of provocative long-form journalism, referring explicitly to the Rockefeller series, which remains the magazine's most famous achievement. The ad also appeals to the values of impartiality, asserting that it is "not an attack" and describing the efforts that went into the collection and verification of information. Yet in that same paragraph, Eddy's life is described as a "romance," as, essentially, a literary construct. And the biography's literary pedigree ensured its continued impact on public opinion and future historiography.

In March 1908, a few months before the *McClure's* series completed its run, a *Boston Globe* reporter and Christian Scientist named John L. Wright wrote to Mary Baker Eddy about the necessity of creating

> a general newspaper owned by Christian Scientists and conducted by experienced newspaper men who are Christian Scientists; so presenting news more as Christian Scientists would like it presented than any newspaper now presents it. I have heard a number of Scientists express a desire for, or the expectation of such a paper as perhaps the next thing to result from the Christian Science movement.[2]

Embedded in his call for a Christian Science newspaper was a broader critique of journalism that was shared by many of Wright's contemporaries. Referring to the perceived dominance of sensational news sources over more informational ones, he decried "the disappearance so largely of the more stable, sane patriotic newspaper, the usurpation of the newspaper field in great centres by commercial and political monopolists, and the commercialization of newspapers." Eddy replied, in a note scribbled on the back of Wright's letter, that "I have had this newspaper scheme in my thought for quite a while and herein send my name for our daily newspaper The Christian Science Monitor."[3] In November of that year, just before Thanksgiving, the first issue of the *Christian Science Monitor* appeared in print.

Just as the *McClure's* biography of Mary Baker Eddy is the most enduring biographical portrait of the Christian Science leader, so the *Monitor* is arguably the most enduring part of her legacy. Though its daily form is now digital-only and its print form is a weekly newsmagazine, the *Monitor* has been a mainstay of American journalism for more than a century, lauded for its reliability and attentiveness to world affairs. During the 1937 Chicago Exhibition, the *Monitor* staged an exhibit celebrating its first three decades in print and featuring letters of appreciation from major figures in US political and intellectual life and popular culture. These letters—some solicited specifically for the occasion and some collected from the paper's archives—uniformly attested to the daily's high standards of journalistic objectivity. As University of California President Robert Sproul stated, "I have been struck by the discrimination with which it eliminates from the news of the day those items which cater to pathological emotionalism, and by the thoroughness with which it reports matters of serious and lasting import." Reflecting on its merits relative to other news outlets, he added, "These comparisons have led me to wish that the spirit of intellectualism which guides the editorial policy of the Monitor might be more widely adopted in journalism."[4] This reputation for fairness and a judicious avoidance of sensationalism followed the paper throughout its history, becoming a central feature of its brand. In 1970, a survey by Seminar magazine (a quarterly publication for newspaper reporters published by Copley Newspapers) ranked the Christian Science Monitor as the "fairest" newspaper in the United States, with 32 percent of respondents believing it had a liberal bias and 41 percent a conservative one.[5] Second place went to the Wall Street Journal, which survey respondents overwhelmingly said had a conservative bias (72 percent). That same year, Walter Cronkite wrote to Monitor editor Erwin Canham, describing the Monitor as "representative of the finest in independent, courageous and unbiased American journalism."[6] In 2005, on the occasion of its move to digital, the Boston Globe praised it for its "distinctive brand of nonhysterical journalism."[7]

The creation of the Monitor can be seen as a direct response to the beating that Christian Science took in the press throughout the 1890s and 1900s. The McClure's biography was merely one particularly distressing symptom of a trend that had been progressing for some time, including the coverage of the Josephine Woodbury lawsuit, the trials of Christian Science practitioners for manslaughter, and the Next Friends Suit, a 1907 media spectacle that was both instigated and extensively covered by Joseph Pulitzer's New York World.[8] It is remarkable that in creating a newspaper of her own, Mary Baker Eddy and her publishing society never set out to create a propaganda organ or even to "correct" the record. Rather, they saw the negative coverage of Christian Science as part of a much bigger problem in professional journalism. And in that assessment, they were in very good company.

The Monitor was birthed into the world during a period of change and even turmoil in the journalistic profession, which had, in the previous three decades, sought to redefine itself as a true profession based on rising educational standards and its commitment to the common ethos of fact-mindedness. This commitment, shot through with progressive idealism, was to depict reality as faithfully as possible for the edification of the reading public. What this pursuit of the real and the factual looked like depended on the journalistic outlet. The infamous "yellows" like Joseph Pulitzer's *World* and William Randolph Hearst's *Journal* (though Pulitzer long lamented the public association of his paper with Hearst's extremism) sought to inform and entertain their readers with engaging and often sensational stories written for a primarily working-class readership. Muckrakers in the tradition of Ida Tarbell, Lincoln Steffens, and Ray Stannard Baker represented the journalistic vanguard of the Progressive movement, a largely middle-class effort toward the radical refashioning of American society. In their narratives of exposure, revealing a corrupt core at the heart of American business and politics, they also frequently married novelistic storytelling techniques to the emerging methods of investigative journalism. However, in the first decade of the twentieth century, the profession began turning toward more conservative values, rejecting the "story" model for the "information" model epitomized by the *New York Times* as the best possible method for dispensing salutary facts to the reading public. This more conservative turn involved not only a rejection of the perceived stylistic excesses of the yellows but a change in priorities that shifted away from disclosing the darker, more corrupt side of human dealings. Both models were, in their own way, producing restitution narratives, identifying social ills—whether business corruption or sensationalism—that could be treated by experts wielding the rhetoric of science.

Thus, the journalists and editors who helped bring the *Monitor* to life not only saw themselves as doing something good for their religion but, in a very real way, healing their profession. When Wright appealed to Eddy in his letter, he cited as symptoms of journalism's sickness not the negative coverage of Christian Science but "the pictures and glaring and detailed descriptions of crime, death and other depressing representations that daily confront one at first glance at almost any newspaper." The antidote Wright prescribed is "a paper that takes less notice of crime, etc., and gives attention especially to the positive side of life, to the activities that work for the good of man and to the things really worth knowing."[9] One of the early (discarded) mottos of the *Monitor* was "All the News Worth Reading," signaling its desire to emulate the *Times* rather than the likes of the *World*. Like the classic *Times* motto, "All the News That's Fit to Print," this early draft denotes comprehensiveness—"all the news"—and discretion, the determination to filter out for the reader all that is superfluous or offensive.

This move toward what Michael Schudson calls the "information" model of journalism also had the effect, for better or for worse, of purging the profession of some of the more literary impulses that are on grand display in *The Life of Mary Baker G. Eddy*. Using that biography as an example, in this chapter, I show how the *Monitor* came to define itself—in terms of aesthetics as well as content—against a particular *style* of journalism and not just against anti–Christian Science reporting. This stylistic revolt centered on debates over how best to represent the "real," a driving concern for both the journalists and the literary writers of the day (who were often the same people).

FACTS, REALISM, AND THE PROFESSIONALIZATION OF JOURNALISM

Like medicine, which was discussed in chapter 1, journalism underwent a process of professionalization during the late nineteenth century, a process that granted its members authority and social status based on their special competence and adherence to a set of professional values. As the biographer of Lincoln Steffens, one of this period's most celebrated muckrakers, indicates, this was a period when the "old-style city reporter, colorful, tough, unschooled, socially marginal—'drunkards, deadbeats and bummers,' according to President Charles W. Eliot of Harvard—was giving way to a new school of professionals."[10] And like physicians, these reporters linked their credibility not only to their college degrees but to their commitment to the act of discovering and unveiling facts in the manner of a scientist, "more 'realistically' than anyone had done before."[11] That act of unveiling was linked to the new reporter's aesthetic and social agendas. No longer was newspaper or magazine work just a job. It was a professional calling imbued with a set of sacred values that elevated it above mere remunerative employment. Muckrakers, for example, "practiced the literature of exposure because they hoped it would bring about the moral regeneration of a corrupt, overly materialistic American society" and shared "a sweeping ideological vision of reform."[12] Many of them also looked to journalism as the jumping-off point for their literary careers, and in the biographies of Ambrose Bierce, Bret Harte, Richard Harding Davis, William Dean Howells, Henry James, Theodore Dreiser, Frank Norris, and many others, professional journalism became intertwined in the development of literary realism.

Steffens, in fact, linked these literary, social, and scientific callings without seeing any inherent contradictions among them: "What reporters know and don't report is news, not from the newspapers' point of view, but from the sociologists' and the novelists'."[13] And in their endeavors to portray life as it was lived as accurately as possible, journalists and literary men and women helped produce what Thomas Connery calls "a paradigm of actuality":

> One that is defined by a focus on the actual and real, on people, events, and details that are verifiable and based on observation and experience. It includes common things and common people, but also can deal with daily concerns, experiences, and relationships, both cultural and personal, of the emerging middle and commercial class. This paradigm stands in contrast to the more romantic one—previously overwhelmingly dominant—that focused on the ideal, one whose depictions were ideational and weakly representational and at the same time mostly unrecognizable in the rapidly changing American social and demographic landscape.[14]

Karen Roggenkamp terms it "the cult of the real thing . . . a common appreciation of 'the real' over 'the imaginary'" that "nourished both new journalism and American literary realism."[15]

Realism was *not* the same thing as journalistic objectivity, a value that gained importance much later on. Realism contained nowhere in its formulations the distrust of individual subjectivity espoused by later advocates of objectivity in journalism.[16] The commitment to the actual and the real was influenced by the growth of the empirical sciences and the desire to appropriate its ethos of detachment, but as a journalistic and literary movement, it represented an attempt to transform observations about reality into stories that people would be interested in reading, stories that might also influence social change. As Schudson indicates, "In their desire to tell stories, reporters were less interested in facts than in creating personally distinctive and popular styles of writing."[17] For many writers of both fiction and journalism, this meant that though their writing might be rooted in facts and "reality," it should also carry the dramatic and moral weight of romance. As Frank Norris—journalist, novelist, and proponent of naturalism—said in "A Plea for Romantic Fiction," romance is the form of storytelling that searches for the truth that lies beyond mere surfaces:

> [Romance] would be off upstairs with you, prying, peeking, peering into the closets of the bedrooms, into the nursery, into the sitting-room; yes, and into that little iron box screwed to the lower shelf of the closet in the library; and into those compartments and pigeonholes of the *secretaire* in the study. She would find a heartache (maybe) between the pillows of the mistress's bed, and a memory carefully secreted in the master's deedbox. She would come upon a great hope amid the books and papers of the study table of the young man's room, and—perhaps—who knows—an affair, or, great heavens, an intrigue, in the scented ribbons and gloves and hairpins of the young lady's bureau. And she would pick here a little and there a little, making up a bag of hopes and fears, and a package of joys and sorrows—great ones, mind you—and then come down to the front door, and stepping out into the street, hand you the bags and package, and say to you—"That is Life!"[18]

With that same voyeuristic pleasure and zeal for uncovering the true nature of experience, S. S. McClure, owner of the magazine that bore his name, sought out, in the words of Steffens, "facts, startling facts." Likewise, Ray Stannard Baker described the editor's obsession with "the excitement and interest and sensation of uncovering a world of unrecognized evils— shocking people."[19] Pulitzer, throughout his life as a publisher, harangued his editors and writers on the need for accuracy, which "is the first and most urgent, the most constant demand I have made upon them."[20] The need for accuracy, however, was always in tension with the newspaper's desire to shock, provoke, and entertain: "For Pulitzer a news story was always a *story*. He pushed his writers to think like Dickens, who wove fiction from the sad tales of urban Victorian London, to create compelling entertainment from the drama of the modern city. To the upper classes, it was sensationalism. To the lower and working classes, it was their life."[21]

With his or her power to both shock and inform, these young, newly professionalized reporters saw themselves as engaged in an endeavor that would better the community, the nation, and the world. According to

Michael McGerr, "Twentieth-century American reform depended on a confrontation with the facts: cold statistics of child labor or corporate oligopoly; Jacob Riis's hard-edged photographs of urban poverty; muckraking revelations from Samuel Hopkins Adams and David Graham; realist fictions by Hamlin Garland and Upton Sinclair."[22] They were animated by a new mandate not to act as the mouthpiece for a political party but to provide information to the public for the purpose of contributing to a better democracy. For some, this enterprise was nonideological, while for others, it was informed by a commitment to progressive values in exposing and thereby combating the influence of monopolies, trusts, and special interests wherever they operated, to "transform other Americans, to remake the nation's feuding, polyglot population in their own middle-class image."[23]

It was entirely predictable, then, that Christian Science should have captured the interest of journalists of this era. Stories about the rising sect had all the drama of life and death, the epic struggle between science and religion. Mary Baker Eddy and many of her most famous acolytes—like Josephine Woodbury and Augusta Stetson—were larger-than-life personalities, ripe for investigation by reporters who were interested in uncovering the scandal and corruption that unfolded behind the staid façades of the Mother Church in Boston or its sister churches in New York and Chicago. And as a rather wealthy religious organization, Christian Science also provoked the muckraker's suspicion of monopolies and the accumulation of private wealth. Indeed, this was not the only church to come under criticism. After its series on Christian Science, McClure's published a series on the Latter-day Saints. Meanwhile, in 1908, Charles Edward Russell muckraked New York's Trinity Church in the pages of Everybody's. Upton Sinclair included Christian Science in his book The Profits of Religion, voicing the widely espoused critique that Christian Science was an unusually money-driven faith: "It is a strict religion—strictly cash. The heads of the cult do not issue cheap editions of 'Science and Health, With Key to Scriptures,' to relieve the suffering of the proletariat." Sinclair likewise condemned the Christian Scientists for their lack of charitable activity and said of its system of church governance, "the Roman Catholic hierarchy is a Bolshevik democracy in comparison."[24]

LITERARY JOURNALISM AND *THE LIFE*
OF MARY BAKER G. EDDY

McClure's magazine was founded in 1894 by Samuel McClure and became, by the end of the century, the foremost purveyor of the *respectable* sort of muckraking. As historian Harold Wilson notes, when Theodore Roosevelt coined that term of opprobrium, he "was careful to inform the leading muckrakers at *McClure's* that they were excluded from the odium of the phrase."[25] The magazine was pathbreaking in its reconfiguration of the relationship between the editor and his writers, Sam McClure being foremost among a "new generation of business-minded, entrepreneurial editors whose own biographies were patterned by the Horatio Alger novels" and who "proceeded to reinvent the American magazine and redefine its editor-publisher."[26] The staff that McClure drew to himself was modeled on that of the *London Times*, and the picture that Wilson paints of the editorial offices evokes the adventure and romance of magazine journalism at its height: "Well-educated, literate young men were slowly added to the staff, men who often conferred with McClure on one of his hasty proprietary tours of the editorial offices, then race away on one of the zesty editor's assignments." *McClure's* published literature and original reporting, and in the latter effort, its leader sought to maximize "the magazine's principal advantage over the daily newspaper: the ability to analyze events and reconstruct them in perspective."[27] The magazine's most lauded pieces of long-form journalism combined judicious fact-finding with gripping narrative and nuanced analysis, all of which reflected the editorial room's antimonopolistic politics.

The most famous of these was, of course, Tarbell's *The History of Standard Oil*. Combining a biographical portrait of John Rockefeller with a probing investigation into the trust he famously founded, Tarbell's work shaped public opinion, influenced policy, and became a seminal text in the history of investigative journalism. Yet as the Standard Oil series shows, the magazine was not immune to the impulse to polemicize, and as much as McClure and his writers "revered sociology and science," as Justin Kaplan notes, "their stance and rhetoric were moralistic, evangelical, millennial, and echoed the pulpit as much as the laboratory, the lecture hall and the soapbox." *McClure's* was valued for its reliability, but its writers were charged with righteous zeal and a commitment to particular aesthetic goals in their storytelling: "What opportunities were there, in the age of McKinley and Roosevelt any more than in the age of Ulysses Grant, for the creative interplay of art, intellect and reality? The *McClure's* group of 1903 saw the answer in a concept of literature as truthtelling, as a way of applying science to experience. In their work a vagrant strain of grass-roots dissent and suspicion of authority fused with a definition of naturalism as a life force in literature and advocacy as a life force in journalism."[28]

Tarbell's articles on Rockefeller and Standard Oil were painstakingly researched and backed with hundreds of pages of appendices referencing court transcripts, business records, and sworn affidavits. They also make for a great story. As Cecilia Tichi notes, "The picturesque and the dramatic, Ida Tarbell knew, were prime components of her expose of Standard Oil, not flourishes but integers."[29] The tools of storytelling produced a document of immense persuasive value due to its ability to thoroughly immerse the reader in the world that it presented, a world that was *supposed* to be as close to the absolute truth as its writer could make it. But storytelling enables the writer to smooth out inconsistencies, leap over gaps, and provide a clear, continuous chain of causality. A story's impossible seamlessness paradoxically makes its version of events feel all the more plausible. In the case of *The History of Standard Oil*, the events surrounding the creation of the great oil trust are shown to proceed directly from Rockefeller's singularly pathological personality, the history of his company reading something like the biography of the devil himself. Indeed, Tarbell quotes one Ohio journalist who called the magnate the "Mephistopheles of the Cleveland company."[30]

The History of Standard Oil layers historical events and character study in the way that one might expect of any biography. But there are moments of authorial omniscience in which the author projects thoughts, ambitions, values, and priorities onto her subject that make this portrayal of Rockefeller feel more like that of a character in a novel than a historical personage whose inner life and motivations are being reconstructed piecemeal through the available evidence. Take, for example, this description of Rockefeller from the second installment:

> With such a set of associates, with his organization complete from
> his buyers on the creek to his exporting agent in New York, with the

transportation advantages which none of his competitors had had the daring or the persuasive power to get, certainly Mr. Rockefeller should have been satisfied in 1870. But Mr. Rockefeller was far from satisfied. He was a brooding, cautious, secretive man, seeing all the possible dangers as well as all the possible opportunities in the thing, and he studied, as a player at chess, all the possible combinations which might imperil his supremacy.[31]

This is emblematic of how Tarbell combined impressions gathered from her sources (Rockefeller was known as a "brooding, cautious, and secretive man"), outright conjecture about his mental state ("far from satisfied . . . seeing all the possible dangers"), and moral evaluation of both his actions and the mental states that supposedly drove them ("Mr. Rockefeller certainly should have been satisfied").

There is a stark, almost Calvinist morality at work in this story. Tarbell characterizes the early conflict between independent oil refiners and Rockefeller's combination as a standoff not between different business approaches but between moral systems, and she clearly gives the advantage to one over the other: "On one hand there was an exaggerated sense of personal independence, on the other a firm belief in combination; on one hand a determination to root out the vicious system of rebates practiced by the railway, on the other a determination to keep it alive and profit by it." Rockefeller, Tarbell argues, was indifferent to the commonsense fairness of the former system:

> This lack of comprehension by many men of what seems to other men to be the most obvious principles of justice is not rare. Many men who are widely known as good, share it. Mr. Rockefeller was "good." There was no more faithful Baptist in Cleveland than he. Every enterprise of that church he had supported liberally from his youth. He gave to its poor. He visited its sick. He wept with its suffering. Moreover, he gave unostentatiously to many outside charities of whose worthiness he was satisfied. He was simple and frugal in his habits. He never went to the theatre, never drank wine. He gave much time to the training of his children, seeking to develop in them his own habits of economy and of charity. Yet he was willing to strain every nerve to obtain for himself special and unjust privileges from the railroads which were bound to ruin every man in the oil business not sharing them with him. He was willing to array himself against the combined better sentiment of a whole industry, to oppose a popular movement aimed at righting an injustice, so revolting to one's sense of fair play as that of railroad discriminations. Religious emotion and sentiments of

charity, propriety and self-denial seem to have taken the place in him of notions of justice and regard for the rights of others.[32]

Rockefeller's modern biographers have done a great deal to illuminate how his revivalist, Baptist upbringing and commitment to a rigid moral system influenced the way he saw business. What's more, these studies have revealed how promiscuously idealism and entrepreneurialism mixed in mid-nineteenth-century America. Ron Chernow, for example, reads Rockefeller as "a finely tuned instrument of the zeitgeist, the purest embodiment of the dynamic, acquisitive spirit of the postwar era. Like other Gilded Age moguls, he was shaped by his faith in economic progress, the beneficial application of science to industry, and America's destiny as an economic leader."[33] But for Tarbell, what happened with Standard Oil is not attributable to culture but to a single nefarious individual.

Ultimately, Rockefeller and Tarbell represented different restitution narratives about American progress. The former "saw petroleum as the basis of an enduring economic revolution" and saw combinations in business as the only means of saving an industry that was wracked by ruinous price fluctuations.[34] For the muckraking journalist of a magazine like *McClure's*, progress lay in protecting the consumer who ultimately paid a price for such collusion. In the late nineteenth and early twentieth centuries, there was little room for compromise between these narratives, and thus, in the story provided by Tarbell, Rockefeller could only ever have been a villain.

As we have seen, the advertisements for the Eddy series linked it to *The History of Standard Oil*, and comparisons of Christian Science to big business were widespread. Journalists who referenced Eddy's business acumen were rarely complimentary, though I suppose it is possible that some *McClure's* editor thought the following line from Part VI of the biographical series reflected balance and impartiality: "It is an interesting fact that, however incoherent Mrs. Eddy became in other matters, she was never so in business. Through hysteria and frantic distress of mind, her shrewd business sense remained alert and keen."[35] This characterization was not exactly singular. Upton Sinclair's *The Profits of Religion*, as the title suggests, resorts to the profit motive as an explanation for virtually every religion in existence, including Christian Science. Twain described God's personal interest in Mrs. Eddy as "a warm, palpitating, Standard-Oil interest."[36] This preoccupation with the financial aspects of Christian Science reflects the muckraker's broader social agenda (and how facile their explanations for social ills could sometimes be).

But *The Life of Mary Baker Eddy* also patterns itself on the Rockefeller series through its use of psychology to explain the unusual career of its subject, weaving its assiduously researched facts with conjecture about Eddy's motives into a highly compelling portrait of improbable coherence. But while *The History of Standard Oil* was primarily a historical account of the American oil industry from the late 1860s forward and only secondarily a study of Rockefeller's character, *The Life of Mary Baker G. Eddy* is a biography proper, taking as its primary object the development of the personality of the leader of Christian Science. The "Editorial Announcement" that appeared in the December 1906 issue states clearly that *"McClure's* will take no stand upon the assertion of Christian Science that it cures disease. This is to be a history, not a treatise. Until Christian Science submits its cures to the examination of men of science, working with the exact knowledge of the laboratory, this assertion cannot be proved or disproved with the scientific accuracy which will satisfy the unbeliever.... This is to be only a history—the story of a romantic life and of a great human movement."[37] This strategy is notable for how it differed from the tack taken by much of the medical profession. Choosing to remain agnostic on the question of whether Christian Science did what its proponents said it did, *McClure's* absolved itself of the odious task of disputing individual healing cases or intervening in the sad circumstances of those that went to court. Notably, at the end of the project, Samuel McClure brought in Emmanuel Movement leader Richard Cabot to offer a perspective on what these healings actually meant in the context of psychotherapeutics.

By declining to take a stand, the magazine got to claim a degree of neutrality on the most inflammatory questions surrounding the movement. Instead, it discredited Christian Science by attempting to dismantle the mythos surrounding its founder, arguing that the religion was false because it was the product of a disordered personality. The announcement describes Eddy's character thus:

> These are only the main facets in a character which shines with all the angles of genius. She has other traits, more subtle. There is the mystic quality

which shows in her obscure writings and still more in the genuine fears of "mental influence," which haunted her nights during the period when she and her leading student had their historic quarrel. There are feminine hesitations and inconsistencies at variance with her real strength, unaccountable attachments, strong aversions. Above all this, there seems to reign a kind of megalomania—a thirst for great achievements and for great glory.[38]

As with Tarbell's portrayal of Rockefeller, there is an implausible smoothness to the arc of Eddy's personal development. The traits it gives her in this paragraph are the traits she still has by the story's end, only in a state of greater development. In the first installment, Eddy is depicted as an hysterical, attention-seeking child and young woman whose need to control those around her groomed her for domineering leadership: "It had been a hard life, sordid in many of its experiences, petty in many of its details, revolving in small circles and around small people. No one knows how much the narrow, Puritanical atmosphere of Mark Baker's farm cramped and warped her hysterical and somewhat abnormal nature.... She had her peculiarities, her flaws of conduct; yet, so far as her world could judge her, these might have been only the shadows of a dominant character."[39] These traits carry through the story, shaping the author's depiction of her career as a spiritual innovator and a religious leader. When not a tyrant, Eddy is always a somewhat pitiable victim of both her unkind circumstances and her own whims. *McClure's* describes her years of itinerancy following the death of Quimby and the departure of Daniel Patterson thus: "There was, indeed, a cruel hardness in Mrs. Glover's position. A proud, self-willed woman, imperious of temper, inordinately vain, and with an insatiable craving for admiration, she was forced to go from house to house and village to village, almost destitute and dependent upon others."[40]

Though the *McClure's* biography of Eddy was the brainchild of Georgine Milmine, it passed through the hands of many editors, including those of Willa Cather. The documentary evidence available makes it difficult to discern who was responsible for what, though that has not stopped numerous people from claiming this as an early Cather work and suggesting that the intricate psychology of this portrayal is attributable to her.[41] Certainly, working on this biography may have helped inform the psychological richness of characters like Thea Kronberg, the protagonist of *Song of the*

Lark, but *The Life of Mary Baker G. Eddy* is cast in the mold provided by Ida Tarbell, and Milmine's early drafts, likely produced before Cather arrived at *McClure's,* suggest that this character study was part of Milmine's plan from the beginning. Long sections from the "Religion and Neurology" chapter in James's *The Varieties of Religious Experience* are transcribed word for word in her notes. The notes and drafts show that from early on, Milmine was persuaded by the plagiarism allegations of the Dressers and other New Thought proponents and wanted to use the biography to, at least partially, offer a possible explanation for Eddy's appropriation of Quimby's work.

Two early drafts of the biography are preserved in the Milmine Collection at the Mary Baker Eddy Library, and the introduction to the longer (and likely later) of the two announces that the author was concerned with "that strength which often goes hand in hand with weakness, which makes no account of means if the desire is obtained."[42] These drafts are notable for how much more sympathetic they are to their subject. "That strength which often goes hand in hand with weakness" is several degrees less heated than the editorial announcement, which would have been edited (if not actually written) by Burton Hendrick, who was replaced by Willa Cather after the January 1907 installment. Cather herself was somewhat disdainful of the segments edited by her predecessor, telling her friend Edwin Anderson that the January piece, which describes Eddy's life to age forty, "frankly deals with legend—with what envious people and jealous relatives remember of Mrs. Eddy's early youth. It was given for what it was worth, but I always consider such sources dubious."[43]

Cather's account of Hendrick's tenure calls into question S. S. McClure's own editorial ethos. Amy Ahearn indicates that at least some of the installments of the Eddy biography were subject to his final approval. McClure, she says, shaped Cather's prose style in the later issues, based on his belief that "'plain facts' were most persuasive to readers," discouraging "his reporters from engaging in 'literary' styles."[44] But this assertion simply does not wash if you compare the early drafts from the Milmine files to the final product. Milmine was clearly not a great writer, but her problem wasn't "literariness." Rather, it was the lack of it. Milmine's style was spare and unadorned. Her drafts contain bare recitation of fact and long, tedious passages of uninterrupted quotation from the affidavits and from *Science and Health* itself. The analysis is measured. Subsequent editorial interventions, if anything, *embellished* her prior work, embroidering this rather dull history into a work approaching the literary standards of the magazine.

These interventions also altered Milmine's argument. The drafts and final published versions are all preoccupied—but with varying emphases—with Mary Baker Eddy's temperament, with reports of her hysterical fits as a child and a young woman, her prolonged bouts of neurasthenia, and her difficulties with her early followers. In her draft, Milmine advances the argument that Eddy's exceptional sensitivity was part of her psychological makeup as a religious "genius." At certain points, she even considers credible the notion that Mary Baker Eddy may have been, from a very early age, a psychic. In her autobiography, Eddy reported receiving a spiritual calling as a very young girl similar to the calling that the Old Testament prophet Samuel received as a boy. Eddy also later reported that she "took on" the sufferings of the individuals she healed and was sensitive to the thoughts of others, thoughts that she believed had the power to harm or even kill her if directed at her with malicious intent. Milmine also takes these claims seriously, suggesting that "in this peculiar 'sixth sense' may lie the physiological reason for her outbreaks of passion as a child, for her over-fine nerves, and for all or many of the traits which rendered her a peculiar child, a disagreeable girl and a difficult woman." She goes on to express sympathy for the emotional burden such a sensitivity must have presented, which "suggests that Mary Morse Baker may never have been understood by her family, her neighbors, or associates, or even by herself, but may have been in a large measure at the mercy of ~~her~~ <a> peculiar, complex organism."[45]

Milmine also attempted to provide a psychological explanation for how Eddy could have appropriated the work of Quimby and claimed that she was the true originator of Christian Science without being a rank deceiver. The analysis that appears in the drafts differs rather substantially from what appeared in the articles themselves. In the long draft, she writes:

> From this time on, Mrs. Glover gradually ~~and perhaps naturally, to a woman with her pronounced desire to dominate and control,~~ ceased to proclaim Dr. Quimby as her physician and teacher, or as the discoverer of mental cure. She talked less and less of him and finally even said to one of her students that Dr. Quimby had been a hindrance to her instead of

a help ... doing away with head rubbing was the first deviation she had
made from the letter of the Quimby instructions. It, no doubt, profoundly
impressed Mrs. Glover and gave her a strong feeling of proprietorship
in the system, since she must have felt that it was an improvement over
the Quimby method, and a step in advance. She was looked up to, also,
by her students, as the only interpreter and expounder of the new idea
<"science">. This attitude of her pupils, all of whom were much younger
than Mrs. Glover, very likely helped to hasten to a conclusion the idea,
slowly forming in her own mind, that she herself was more responsible for
Dr. Quimby's "science" than Dr. Quimby himself.[46]

She negotiates her way through the moral complexities of the problem,
indicating that it is not her intention

> to excuse Mrs. Glover's weakness in appropriating Dr. Quimby's ideas,
> but merely to point out that this false step, which has been unreservedly
> condemned by all who know the facts, may have been only the yielding
> <surrender> to a natural temptation to take advantage of a situation which
> seemed to suggest <to her> at every point that she had reason to be recog-
> nized as the "founder" of Christian Science, and to that extent it was prob-
> ably not a deliberate, premeditated, steal <appropriation of Dr. Quimby's
> ideas> as has been charged.[47]

She does, however, indict Eddy for shoddy attempts to cover her tracks
once the appearance of dishonesty was uncovered:

> The part of the transaction on Mrs. Eddy's side for which no good word
> can be said is her subsequent attitude. Failing ~~of~~ the strength of char-
> acter to acknowledge her human weakness in substituting herself for
> Dr. Quimby as the originator of ~~the application of~~ the <mental system of>
> healing ~~principle~~<,> Mrs. Glover, when the word was finally spoken pro-
> claiming herself to be the author and discoverer of Christian Science, and
> finding that this aroused the resentment of Dr. Quimby's friends and pa-
> tients, <to a degree which she could not have foreseen>, felt herself obliged
> to defend her position, and <she> has kept at it constantly since, ~~at the ex-
> pense of truth~~ <in the face of> all the ~~easily obtained~~ evidence of her own
> making which shows her to have been an ardent disciple of Dr. Quimby
> and to have ~~acknowledged~~ <proclaimed> him as the <apostle> of ~~the~~ <a>
> new truth which <she thought> was to revolutionize the world.[48]

This paragraph seems to be the basis for the following paragraph from the
final articles:

From the history of this controversy, it is evident that, for Mrs. Eddy, there have existed two Phineas P. Quimbys: one the Quimby who was her physician and teacher, who roused her from the fretful discontent of middle-age, and who gave her purpose and aspiration; the other Quimby who, after the publication of "Science and Health," became, in a sense her rival—whom she saw as an antagonist threatening to invalidate her claims. If she has been a loser through this controversy, it is not because of what she borrowed from Quimby, but because of her later unwillingness to admit her obligation to him. Had she observed that etiquette common enough in what she terms the "profane sciences," where personal ambition is subsidiary to a desire for truth, and where discoverers and investigators are scrupulous to acknowledge the sources from which they have obtained help, it would have strengthened rather than weakened her position.[49]

According to Milmine's draft, Mary Baker Eddy came to believe herself to be the originator of Christian Science through a process of self-deception. In the published articles, Eddy's motives are rather darker. While never questioning her genuine commitment to the idea, the final versions portray her as a person with primarily venal motives, pursuing her all-consuming interest in metaphysical healing but always out of a desire for money and attention:

> While she certainly cherished a vague, half-formulated plan to go out into the world some day and teach the Quimby doctrine, her imperative need was to control the immediate situation; to be the commanding figure in the lodge, the sewing-circle, the family gathering. The one thing she could not endure was to be thought like other people. She must be something besides plain Mrs. Glover,—invalid, poetess, healer, propagandist, guest; she must be exceptional at any cost.[50]

In other words, the development of her theology proceeded not out of her absorption of and innovation upon extant theories but as a result of making things up whenever her control started to slip or her privileged position among those who would otherwise be her equals was beginning to erode: "She added to her philosophy from time to time, to meet this or that emergency, very much as a householder adds an ell or a wing to accommodate a growing family. Christian Science as it stands to-day is a kind of autobiography in cryptogram; its form was determined by a temperament, and it retains all the convolutions of the curiously duplex personality about which it grew."[51]

Just as the Rockefeller series concludes with a chapter on "The Legitimate Greatness of Standard Oil," the final installment of the Eddy series suggests that the leader of Christian Science was in possession of a powerful, transformative idea, even though it proceeded from a misshapen mind:

> New movements are usually launched and old ideas are revivified, not through the efforts of a group of people, but through one person. These dynamic personalities have not always conformed to our highest ideals; their effectiveness has not always been associated with a large intelligence or with nobility of character. Not infrequently it has been true of them—as it seems to be true of Mrs. Eddy—that their power was generated in the ferment of an inharmonious and violent nature. But, for practical purposes, it is only fair to measure them by their actual accomplishment and by the machinery they have set in motion.[52]

This is a highly pragmatic assessment. If, as William James argued, religions are to be judged by their effects and not their origins, then *McClure's* could certainly claim that these revelations about Mary Baker Eddy would do no violence to Christian Science itself. But this is also a rather convenient rationalization. The team that assembled this biography was guilty of embroidering the facts that were there and of relying on questionable sources.

According to Lyman Powell, a Protestant minister who later wrote his own biography of Eddy and consulted personally with Milmine, Cather, and other writers from the magazine, Milmine's research method was essentially to establish herself in one of the small towns that Eddy had lived in and to talk with whomever was willing: "Her method of work, as she described it to me, was to stay long enough in a place to get naturally reticent New England people to talk freely to her, and then with her trained newspaper mind she put what she learned from them often into the form of affidavits, to which in most cases those she met readily subscribed."[53] Powell, however, casts suspicion on the reliability of the accounts this method produced. One of the principal towns Milmine visited was Eddy's childhood home of Tilton, Massachusetts. Mary Baker Eddy was in her eighties when this research was performed, and most of the people who had any knowledge of her were deceased or had been children at the time that the future founder of Christian Science had walked among them. Hannah

Sanborn Philbrook, who had attended the same school as Mary Baker but admittedly did not know her very well, was one of Milmine's most prolific correspondents on the subject of Eddy's past, and as Gillian Gill suggests, she had very little to say that wasn't self-serving: "We can all imagine how we would feel as worthy octogenarians to find that in researching our youth reporters were quoting only the girls who hated us most at school!"[54] As Powell indicates, "Three years ago Mr. Perkins of Tilton confirmed this affidavit story, and told me in some detail how, as Notary Public, he went around with Georgine Milmine and took the affidavits of many people in his part of the country, though his estimate of their value—knowing many of the people—was not as high as Georgine Milmine's."[55] The same problems of memory and bias plague the chapters on Eddy's life during the 1870s and 1880s. Frank Sprague was not merely being paranoid when he wrote feverishly to fellow Christian Scientist Alfred Farlow that "various opponents of Mrs. Eddy have used the opportunity to give her [Milmine] such statistics and information as would aid in making an effective presentation; and she has had ample opportunity to collect whatever material could be gathered from all hostile sources."[56] Milmine's research notes reveal that many of the affidavits on Mrs. Eddy's life during this period were provided by none other than Frederick Peabody, who, as we saw in chapter 3, was also Mark Twain's principal informant.[57]

The Rockefeller and Eddy series were highly accomplished works of investigative journalism, but they are also examples of a particular literary-journalistic genre. They demonstrate the commitment of *McClure's* to exposing the wealthy and the powerful and protecting the public. But they also suggest a preoccupation with what they took to be abnormal personalities.[58] Christian Scientists had reason to object to not only criticism of Mary Baker Eddy by *McClure's* but journalistic fixation on the negative aspects of human nature, exemplified by the series' almost prurient interest in the weirder aspects of Eddy's story. *The Life of Mary Baker G. Eddy* spends an inordinate amount of time on malicious animal magnetism, which it takes to be the signal manifestation of Eddy's psychopathology. However, while MAM is one of the important distinguishing features between Christian Science and New Thought, for Eddy it was always linked to dwelling on negative, harmful, evil thoughts outside the reality of God's goodness. As we shall see, emphasizing that reality and promoting the positive potential for human development (even if it was as yet unrealized) was the most noticeable way in which Christian Scientists joined with other critics of the New Journalism in order to revise the narratives of corruption produced by magazines like *McClure's* and newspapers like the *World* and the *Journal*.

CLEAN JOURNALISM AND THE GROWTH OF THE *MONITOR*

In the summer of 1908, Mary Baker Eddy instructed the Christian Science Publishing Society to create a daily newspaper. Paul Deland, an editor who was involved from the beginning, described the enterprise as motivated by "the realization of the need for a newspaper that would spread confidence instead of fear, the desire and provision to have it ably edited and the establishment of a helpful, hopeful guide for all time."[59] The first issue appeared the day before Thanksgiving in 1908, just nine weeks after Eddy gave the order. Like Deland, many of the original staff members describe their conviction that the newspaper would be a boon not only to Christian Science but to the public and the journalistic profession. Contrary to expectation, the editors saw more advantage for the movement in downplaying the daily's religious character rather than merely using it as a tool for deflecting hostile press. Indeed, they seem to have had the long game in mind, exercising perhaps a kind of soft influence that might eventually place the name "Christian Science" in the mainstream of American intellectual life rather than on its fringes. The paper published "one brief metaphysical article daily," but otherwise, the only evidence of its religious character was "the rigid exclusion of matters repugnant to the religious convictions of its readers, whatever their church or creed."[60]

How exactly the editors attempted to avoid offending *anybody* and *everybody's* religious sensibilities (an impossible feat, to be sure) is unclear. But the paper tended to reflect the philosophical and theological orientation of Christian Scientists through its "rigid exclusion" of anything that gave credence to "mortal mind." This meant eschewing the "bizarre, the grotesque, the freakish," and the sensational.[61] In other words, the founding mandate of the *Monitor* was to avoid what the yellows and the muckrakers were often accused of dwelling on. It sought to avoid controversy for controversy's sake, to celebrate human progress rather than expose human corruption, to "inform" rather than advocate. It was a church-owned newspaper that showed no real desire to preach, unless it was its "doctrine of clean journalism." And that is fitting, perhaps, given that sermons had at this point been banned from Christian Science services, replaced by readings from the Bible and *Science and Health*, presented to the congregation without mediation or interpretation. If muckraking, as some scholars have argued, was a fundamentally evangelical enterprise, the *Monitor* was underwritten by a religion without hellfire or brimstone.[62]

Because of the paper's commitment to unmediated "facts" or "truth" and its lack of an explicit political or commercial agenda, the *Monitor* editors adopted the rhetoric of objectivity and impartiality, asserting that the paper was "burdened by no financial and commercial ties" and therefore "is free to give an accurate report of a meeting, an impartial account of an event and to present all sides of the case." And in articulating this objective stance, editors like Deland reflected the Christian Science belief in the discoverability and efficacy of Truth, which Eddy taught had the power to drive out the Error of human suffering. As Deland stated, "*Monitor* editors work upon the idea that the most original story is the one that comes nearest to 'the truth, the whole truth, and nothing but the truth'" and trained their reporters to "make *Monitor* stories absolutely accurate in the light of fundamental truth."[63]

The editors of the *Monitor* also saw themselves participating in something entirely new and heroic in the field of journalism. Two weeks before the publication of the first issue, Alexander Dodds informed his compatriots that "they were to turn traditional newspaper practice upside down."[64] Deland, who was present at that meeting, qualified that "it wasn't long before we found that we were not turning things upside down. We were turning things right side up. It was the other newspapers that were upside down."[65] Erwin Canham, who served the paper for forty-nine years, half of them as its editor, states in his book-length history of the paper,

> In its early years, the *Monitor* preached the doctrine of "clean journalism"
> almost as much as it practiced it. Part of its articulate missionary work
> was to sell itself to an increasing readership. Part of it was to remind
> other newspapers of their duties, by word as well as by deed. As time
> went on, the word became less necessary than the deed. The *Monitor's*

position became better known, its editors and staff members took a more active role in newspaper organizations dedicated to the betterment of newspapers.[66]

"Clean journalism" became the byword for the *Monitor* throughout its earliest phase. "Clean" for these reporters meant presenting salutary, non-sensational facts in a pure and unembroidered form, in contrast to the unseemly scandal-mongering that saturated the yellows. Deland spoke of how they vigorously sought out "new sources, standards and treatments of news" and described how "the reporters of the old school are redirected and young reporters trained on radically different lines from those long established."[67]

In defining themselves against the "old school," they were certainly not alone. They weren't even all that original. The *Monitor*, indeed, was decidedly within the tradition of Horace Greeley, Charles Dana, and the *New York Times*. By 1908, a conservative backlash against "story journalism" was well under way, setting its sights on not only the suspect practices of the yellows (which had become infamous at the end of the previous decade) but the advocacy of the muckrakers. This represented a movement within the profession away from the populist crusading of Pulitzer and the storytelling of McClure toward what sociologists of the profession call the "information" model of journalism. And in some cases, those calling for a return to sanity were the remorseful (or self-protective) former exponents of new journalism's excesses. This turn was marked by Theodore Roosevelt's speech "The Man with the Muckrake," in which he referenced (and made a hash of) Bunyan's *Pilgrim's Progress* in order to condemn "the man who in this life consistently refuses to see aught that is lofty, and fixes his eyes with solemn intentness only on that which is vile and debasing." To look upon the filth, he admits, is sometimes necessary—"there are times and places where this service is the most needed of all the services performed"—but the man who sees nothing else, "who never thinks or speaks or writes save of his feats with the muckrake, speedily becomes, not a help to society, not an incitement to good, but one of the most potent forces of evil."[68] And when the disenchanted writers of *McClure's* left to establish their own magazine, what they had in mind was "a magazine of joyous reading" that would emphasize the positive, upward progress of humanity in "a happy, struggling, fighting world, in which, we believe, good people are coming out on top." In Steffens's words, "Every man in this whole country who is for better things is with us."[69] Christian Science, with its assertion that the good things that proceed from God constitute the primary reality of the universe, had found its moment and its audience. A demand existed for restitution narratives that emphasized the inevitability of the cure rather than dwelling on the nature of the disease itself.

This shift in editorial practice was aided by journalism's continuing path toward professionalization, toward the codification and entrenchment of various institutions and standards that would separate the "real journalists" from the amateurs and pretenders. New schools of journalism introduced "an educational curriculum that imposed desirable professional standards on young reporters and upheld a rigid line between literature (or 'invention') and journalism (or 'fact')." In 1904, Pulitzer supplied the initial endowment for the Columbia School of Journalism, which opened in 1913. When told that such a school would create class distinctions within the profession, "Pulitzer answered that this was exactly what it should do—establish a distinction between the fit and the unfit."[70] Determined to see journalism become "one of the great and intellectual professions," he "proposed that journalists receive training on a par with that given to lawyers and doctors."[71]

David Mindich characterizes the confrontation between these two models of journalism as a "moral war" in which the participants saw themselves as fighting not only for business models but for the health of society.[72] Critics of the excesses of the yellows "were outraged by new journalism's tendency to fictionalize and invent, practices they considered morally and epistemologically dangerous. Newspapers functioned as a form of public record. If the facticity of these public documents was only a veil, how could one finally determine what was real?"[73] Class interests and a certain hierarchy of tastes at least partially informed this debate. Noting that story journalism tended to be preferred by the working classes and information journalism by the middle and upper classes, Schudson demands that we consider that "in the critical decades from 1883 to the first years of this [the twentieth] century, when at the same moment yellow journalism was at its height and the *New York Times* established itself as the most reliable and respected newspaper in the country, why did wealthier people in New York read the *Times* and less wealthy people read the *World*?"[74] Indeed, he dates the emergence of professional crisis to the moment when "the educated middle class . . . no longer recognized in 'public opinion' what it took to be its own voice, the voice of reason."[75] As Roggenkamp notes, "Some critics, often the same ones who criticized the democratic gestures of realism in literature, openly assailed the equalizing tendencies of new journalism, fearing that it would 'drive out the ideas and serious discussion' seemingly inherent in more elite papers and fiction, and fretting that 'these new papers' provided a vulgar immigrant audience with 'frightening political power.'"[76] At the height of the circulation war between the *World* and the *Journal* at the turn of the century, the Young Men's Christian Association Library in Brooklyn boycotted both papers, declaring that they "brought into our rooms a very undesirable class of readers."[77]

Through "clean journalism," the *Christian Science Monitor* adapted itself to this informational model wholly and self-consciously, regularly voicing its repudiation of anything that might be deemed sensationalistic. As a general rule, this meant that the paper tended to emphasize any news that might be construed as positive or pointing to mankind's trajectory toward enlightenment, peace, and prosperity. When it was necessary to cover a war or a disaster, the early *Monitor* tended to stick to a bare outline of the facts, refusing to dwell on the details of violence or the material suffering of human beings. Where possible, reporters emphasized whatever was being done to provide humanitarian aid, demonstrating how the good in humanity could be revealed in times of trouble. As Willis Abbot informed the members of the professional journalistic fraternity Sigma Delta Chi,

> Writers for *The Christian Science Monitor* are instructed to avoid reporting crimes, disasters, epidemics, deaths, or trifling gossip. There are qualifications to each clause in these instructions. A crime or a death by which the course of history might be affected would be reported—the assassination of a ruler, for example, or the death of a man whose passing would end some notable service to mankind. The disaster such as the Japanese earthquake would be reported in the expectation that *Monitor* readers would eagerly avail themselves of the opportunity to extend charitable aid—as indeed in that particular instance they did with notable liberality. But in neither case would anything more than a dispassionate statement of the facts be published.[78]

In the aftermath of the devastating 1909 earthquake in Italy, the *Monitor* offered a rehearsal of the facts along with the following qualification: "It is quite unnecessary to dwell on the appalling details of the disaster. True charity is born of the desire to fulfill one's duty toward one's neighbors, and not emotional heart-burnings. John Ruskin, speaking of charity, once said that he gave because he realized that it was his duty to give. This should always be so; they should give because they realize it is their duty and privilege to give, and not because Pelion has been piled on Ossa in the shape of sensational details."[79] Withholding whatever might be shocking here has both moral and aesthetic dimensions. Fellow-feeling for the suffering of another person and the good deeds that might inspire, it suggests, ought to come from a rational contemplation of one's "duty" rather than the pure pathos provoked by the horrifying nature of that suffering.

The invocation of Ruskin also distinguishes the *Monitor's* style as not only a reportorial or a moral choice but an aesthetic one. And indeed, this commitment to reason and a certain kind of spiritual and intellectual elevation informed what Abbot went on to describe as the positive aspects of the paper's editorial policy: "*Monitor* correspondents are instructed to report fully all advances made in education methods, notable discoveries in science, great public benefactions, incidents of social or political progress, conferences of religious, educational, reformatory, or economic associations, and indeed every event, material, intellectual, or spiritual, which has its bearing upon the ascent of man."[80]

In its coverage of literature, the *Monitor* often challenged the prevailing dogmas of the realist and naturalist genres by portraying the positive side of human nature as fundamentally more "real" than the corruption and depravity that certain men and women of letters tended to dwell on. One brief item in the "Home Forum" section praises a story by Richard Harding Davis—one of New Journalism's more famous practitioners—called "A Charmed Life," which appeared in the November 1910 issue of *Scribner's*. The story centers on a young couple separated by the man's military conscription during the Cuban War. Though all odds are against them, the man manages to survive the conflict uninjured. He encounters more danger on the trip back across the gulf, but each time, he is saved by some seemingly miraculous force. When the couple is reunited, the woman tells him that she had sensed he was in peril and prayed to God to protect him.

That this story should have appealed to Christian Science readers is not at all surprising, but the terms the Home Forum uses to praise the story indicate the ways that the aesthetics of optimism (we might even call it sentimentality) were linked to a loose concept of realism, of truth-telling: "The incidents are all delightfully natural in their working out." The article also praises Davis, "a contemporary writer of light literature of often a rather bravado type" for writing "this pretty idyll to stand for the power of love and prayer to protect the absent friend."[81]

But the *Monitor* did not rely only on the purity of its content for its ethos. Visual aesthetics, down to precise font specifications, were important for projecting the paper's credibility and distinguishing it from those that were corrupted. According to Abbot, "the news pages of many papers have deteriorated in proportion as the advertising pages have been improved. Glaring black type which in the best papers has disappeared from the advertising pages, now appears in headlines on the first page and too much of the news published is as offensive in character as were the detailed symptoms of loathsome diseases which formerly were given space in those columns, which were sold for a price."[82] Deland states, "Use of very heavy type, solid black effects and dark backgrounds is not permitted, neither is freakish typography. Position is sold only on the picture page. The pyramid form of make-up is employed, except for the financial and hotel-travel pages, on which the make-up is from the top of the page downward." Furthermore, "In preparing copy for *The Christian Science Monitor* writers are required to write concisely and to the point but not to be handicapped by the modern fallacy of inadequate brevity that merely records an occurrence. The tendency is to revert in a measure to the journalism of Greeley, Dana and Bennett, to give the interpretation necessary in presenting stories of important developments and actions."[83] Praise for the paper tended to highlight these very qualities. The editors of the *Granite State Free Press* lauded the paper's discretion in content, layout aesthetics, and advertising all at once: "We see that it is neat, newsy, clean, in good large, legible print, wholesome in tone and that only about one-sixteenth of it, or a little more, is given to advertising; of course, no patent medicine ads."[84]

Monitor editors and reporters saw themselves involved in an enterprise with the potential for global impact. It is no accident that of the accolades the paper has garnered over its century-long history, the most notable have been for international reporting. In 1950, *Monitor* correspondent Edmund Stevens won the Pulitzer Prize for his forty-three-part series "This is Russia Uncensored," based on a three-year stint in Moscow at the height of the Soviet era. John R. Hughes won in 1967 for his reporting on Indonesia's "Transition to the New Order" and David Rohde in 1996 for his work on the Srebrenica genocide. According to the paper's announcement about this award, Rohde was "the first Western journalist to visit the sites of suspected mass graves . . . uncovering grim and convincing evidence that Bosnian Serb forces had executed Muslim prisoners in Europe's worst massacre since the Holocaust."[85] Rohde's pictures of the mass burial sites—which he discovered after interviewing refugees in holding camps and obtaining location data from Western intelligence sources—got him arrested by Bosnian Serb soldiers. He was held for ten days under threat of imprisonment or death and eventually released under pressure from US officials, journalists, and NGOs.

The nature of this reporting indicates that at least in the present day, *Monitor* reporters don't exactly shy away from violence or from documenting human suffering on a grand scale. And despite its desire to appear neutral, the *Monitor*'s commitment to reporting the major news of the world has been consistent almost since its inception, though different editors disagreed about how exactly such news should be covered. In describing the newspaper's policy of avoiding sensationalism, Deland insisted that "[the *Monitor*] does not ignore conditions and always hastens to lend a helping hand. Instead of trying to make its readers squirm by making suffering, damage and death the motive as do so many newspapers in their frantic sensationalism, the *Monitor* endeavors to bring out the thoughts of relief as the dominant idea."[86] Similarly, Canham asserted that

> it does not leave out news just because it is unpleasant, nor seek to throw a rosy glow over a world that is far from rosy. To describe the *Monitor* as a "clean" newspaper is correct but incomplete. It also strives to expose whatever needs to be uncovered in order to be removed or remedied. It seeks to put the news in a sound perspective, giving greatest emphasis to what is important and reducing the merely sensational to its place in an accurate system of values. It seeks also to amuse and entertain, but in wholesome and socially desirable terms.[87]

Indeed, the foreign affairs side of the paper flourished under Canham.[88] He characterized the *Monitor*'s approach to internationalism as "strictly of the sort expressed by Mrs. Eddy in her phrase 'to bless all mankind.'"[89]

One way the paper saw itself dispensing this blessing was by connecting the rather small flock of Christian Scientists to a broader cosmopolitan community. According to Canham, "It is dedicated to the enlightenment of all whom it can reach. Its audience is global."[90] Indeed, the publishing society saw it as the duty of a Christian Scientist to subscribe to and read the *Monitor* not only in order to support the church financially but also to become a more enlightened global citizen:

> As we observe our Leader's request that we subscribe for and read the *Monitor*, our mental horizon is broadened, for thereby we break the hampering bonds of local, selfish views and interests, and we become citizens of the world in the true sense. Consistent and intelligent reading of the *Monitor* lifts us out of the narrow valley of local considerations to a higher and better point of view where we gain a more universal and sympathetic survey of the problems confronting mankind. Of course, the recognition by Christian Scientists of these problems calls forth the right metaphysical work which is needed to neutralize and nothingize the erroneous beliefs and practices which tend to debase and enslave men. Thus the reading of the *Monitor* helps to awaken us to the unlimited possibilities for unselfish service to others and for spiritual growth and enlarged understanding with ourselves.[91]

Without a doubt, the *Monitor*'s unique viewpoint resulted in some idiosyncrasies. The paper did not print obituaries and tended to shy away from medical news, reporting only on "medical news that effects the general community, such as legislative actions or sanitary and hygienic decisions" and rarely—if ever—on medical research or discoveries.[92] Mary Baker Eddy rarely gave instructions on how the paper was supposed to be run or what it was supposed to print. But when she did, she tended to focus on tellingly minute issues. She insisted, for example, that reports on the weather emphasize their status as "predictions" rather than certainties. According to Canham, this was so that

> they need not bind or impair man, responsive to God's law. Here once more, in addition to a position of religious principle, was another highly

practical point. What the Weather Bureau announces is, after all, strictly
a prediction, and how often does it turn out to be wrong! It is the height of
journalistic accuracy to make this point, though with sufficient subtlety to
not offend the hard-working meteorologists of the Weather Bureau.[93]

And in January 1909, Mary Baker Eddy wrote to then editor Archibald
McClellan not to report too extensively on automobile accidents. Curiously, she did not express any concern that doing so would give credence
to "mortal mind" but made the request so as "not to make those who have
interest in the automobiles our enemies."[94]

Even Canham admits that these proscriptions frequently hampered
the paper's ability to be effective. Of the first decade, he says that what
began as a bold experiment in journalism gave way to "a varying and in-
determinate set of taboos which had a considerable effect on *Monitor* style
and did not begin to melt away until the mid-1920s. The nature and extent
of these taboos should not be exaggerated." He attempts to downplay the
impact of the editorial desk's byzantine list of prohibitions as "largely
stylistic" but admits that "they produced in the community and the world
at large an impression, not altogether unjustified as far as style went, that
the *Monitor* was 'odd.'"[95] Keith S. Collins, a former writer for the paper,
paints a less rosy picture, suggesting that "clean journalism" effectively
meant "sanitized news":

> Despite the similarity in appearance to other papers, the *Monitor* was
> clearly different in tone. All stories of suffering had happy endings but one,
> and that one—a report of the burning of the cruise ship Sardinia, when
> "many lives . . . were lost"—bore the headline "Sardinia Beached Because
> of Fire," as if the ship had simply run aground with no further problems.
> The dominant theme came through clearly in the lead story on the Charles
> River dam: Don't worry; despite what you may hear and see, mankind is
> making progress![96]

In other cases, the *Monitor* failed to sufficiently cover stories on which
the public needed to be informed. In the case of the lynching of three
black men in Tennessee, the paper "merely sketched its outlines, trying
to minimize the fear of it," while the *Times* managed to offer context and
a moral outlook that the *Monitor* might have also been uniquely equipped
to provide had it not shied away from the task.[97]

Collins also suggests that in its pursuit of an anomalous concept of "accuracy," the *Monitor* frequently became a mouthpiece for the powerful, even going so far as to let "public figures revise what they said for publication." And unlike the crusaders who wrote for *McClure's*, the *Monitor* did not make speaking truth to power a priority. Of the paper's leadership under Willis Abbot in the 1920s, he says, "There was no recognition of underlying errors in the world that did not, in fact, make war improbable and capital-labor disputes susceptible to easy moralizing. There was no attempt to probe festering evils and identify ways to eliminate them."[98] In other words, through its kid-gloves handling of the "facts" and its judicious avoidance of obvious bias, the paper failed to illuminate systemic abuses of power or to present the perspectives of people who might have had a grievance. The *Monitor* remained a conservative paper, a defender—through omission if not through direct action—of the status quo.

To be fair, some comparable criticisms were also leveled against the muckrakers, who have been accused of naïveté in their use of facts and incoherence in their ideology.[99] And as Kaplan says of *McClure's*, "The implicit achievement of muckraking, as Steffens later suggested, was actually to strengthen the system by alerting it to its own vulnerabilities. According to this view, muckraking was a fundamentally middle-class, loyalist strategy, despite dramatic appearances to the contrary; and its net effect was comparable to that of administering underdoses of antibiotics: warned and inured, the hostile organism becomes stronger than ever."[100] Failure to effectively perform the "watchdog" role of the press is also a problem associated with the model of information journalism that proceeded out of the early twentieth century. This critique continues to be leveled against mainstream reporters, who are often accused of serving as stenographers for government interests in Washington. According to Schudson, the news during the rise of the information model "appeared to become less the reporting of events in the world than the reprinting of those facts in the universe of facts which appealed to special interests who could afford to hire public relations counsel."[101] The papers that became the new elite earnestly desired to present themselves as the reasonable, respectable alternative to the gossip and gore of the yellows, which were "deviant, unmanly, and uncivilized."[102] And thus "the professions developed a proprietary attitude toward 'reason' and a paternalistic attitude toward the public."[103] The rapid social changes that defined the turn of the century—industrialization, urbanization, and the expansion of the franchise—placed urban professionals in contact with "new categories of persons," who had "often been conceived of as passional beings, incapable of sustained rationality."[104]

As Mindich argues, journalists of this era came to associate the concept of "objectivity" with civilization, which they presumably had while the masses did not: "Charles Dana, for example, wanted his reporters to know Greek and Latin, to read Shakespeare, the Bible, and other 'great' literary works. For Dana, the paradigm for news gathering represented another Western tradition, the tradition of an industrialized and stratified society, one that gains its wealth from the service of others."[105] Tellingly, the *Times* not only advertised itself as "all the news that's fit to print" but claimed it would "not soil the breakfast cloth," depicting their ideal reader as the type of person who ate at a table draped with white linen. According to Roggenkamp, "Not incidentally, the information "fit to print" was most often suitable for business interests and conservative politics."[106] And "fit to print" quite often meant excluding news that ought to have been of interest to the public. Despite the ethos of authenticity, Mindich argues, "the truth about lynching or even a reasonable facsimile of the truth, was not conveyed by the mainstream media."[107]

In the *Monitor* files is an undated[108] proof containing a "Word of Appreciation" from a reader who states that he read "the Herald, World and Times" and saw "about 20 columns of murders, wife beaters and drunken and depraved boys killing their fathers and mothers and how three thieves strangled Mrs. Vanderbilt and stole her pearl necklace, and how citizens of Texas burned 10 negroes." Then he describes being handed a copy of the *Monitor* and finding "all the pure news of the world without a single blood-curdling crime."[109] While in this proof, "Eli Perkins" appears representative of the type of reader who became exhausted with the tawdry voyeurism of the other papers, the response of much of the respectable and enlightened segment of society to the problems of their communities was likely to simply avoid reading about them. Thus, a turn toward internationalism could also mean looking away from corruption and human suffering closer to home.

When *McClure's* initially announced its series on Eddy, it stated that the history would be followed by an article on Christian Science by a neurologist and a rebuttal by a Christian Scientist. Richard Cabot's article appeared in the summer of 1908, but no Christian Science answer was printed. On behalf of the church, John V. Dittemore attempted to negotiate with S. S. McClure and Willa Cather directly, naming Edward Kimball, who had rebutted Mark Twain in the pages of *Cosmopolitan*, as a possible contributor.[110] Ultimately, his suggestion was rejected. According to Dittemore, "They even had the effrontery to voice the argument that they doubted whether the literary merit of the article was up to their standard, but this was met by reminding them of your Cosmopolitan article and others, and they seemed to perceive that they were arguing against something that had not even been inspected."[111] Ultimately, no article by Kimball was published. Dittemore eventually lost faith in Christian Science and went on to write his own scathing biography of Mary Baker Eddy, which the church, to its discredit, suppressed by buying the copyright and the plates.[112]

This was not the only incident in which Christian Scientists attempted to intervene with the press when they felt maligned, nor was Dittemore's the only book the church attempted to remove from the hands of the public. Under mysterious circumstances, the Doubleday edition of *The Life of Mary Baker G. Eddy* disappeared from circulation soon after it was released. In many cases, these efforts were unsuccessful and only worsened public perception. Therefore, the establishment of the *Monitor* may be a case study in the virtues of joining them when you can't beat them. *McClure's* printed its last number in 1929. The *Monitor* endures, not because it attempted to accomplish through propaganda what it couldn't through censorship but because it joined an ongoing effort to reform the journalistic profession from within. It was a revolt in style as well as in content. Loathed by the medical profession, Christian Science managed to place itself squarely in the mainstream, appealing to a middle class that had become exhausted with sensation, that demanded "information" detached from its visceral embodied implications.

NOTES

Major sections of this chapter originally appeared in revised form in L. Ashley Squires, "All the News Worth Reading: *The Christian Science Monitor* and the Professionalization of Journalism," *Book History* (2015): 235–72.

1. "The Life of Mrs. Eddy," *McClure's* (clipped magazine advertisement, Milmine Collection, Mary Baker Eddy Library for the Betterment of Humanity, Boston).

2. John L. Wright, Letter to Mary Baker Eddy, 12 March 1908 (Incoming Correspondence File, Mary Baker Eddy Library for the Betterment of Humanity, Boston).

3. Ibid.

4. Robert G. Sproul, Letter to Wilbur P. Robinson, 31 October 1939 (Christian Science Monitor Subject File, Mary Baker Eddy Library for the Betterment of Humanity, Boston).

5. "Monitor Judged 'Fairest' Survey Ranks U.S. Publications," *Christian Science Monitor*, 28 August 1970.

6. Walter Cronkite, Letter to Erwin Canham, 30 April 1970 (Christian Science Monitor Subject File, Mary Baker Eddy Library for the Betterment of Humanity, Boston).

7. Alex Beam, "Appealing to a Higher Authority," *Boston Globe*, 9 June 2005.

8. The lawsuit was the product of a rumor that Mary Baker Eddy was senile and incapable of managing her own affairs, a rumor that the *World* did much to propagate. The paper eventually hired former senator William Chandler to file suit against the leaders of the church board on behalf of her son and nephew (her "next friends"), arguing that the powerful men who surrounded the leader of Christian Science had illegitimately seized control of her financial affairs, which she was mentally incompetent to manage. See chap. 1 of Gottschalk, *Rolling Away the Stone*.

9. Wright to Eddy, 16 March 1908.

10. Justin Kaplan, *Lincoln Steffens: Portrait of a Great American Journalist* (New York: Simon and Schuster, 1974), 63.

11. Michael Schudson, *Discovering the News: A Social History of American Newspapers* (New York: Basic Books, 1967), 62.

12. Howard S. Good, "Epilogue: Muckraking and the Ethic of Caring," in *The Muckrakers: Evangelical Crusaders*, edited by Robert Miraldi (London: Praeger, 2000), 157–58.

13. Lincoln Steffens, *The Autobiography of Lincoln Steffens, Vol. I* (New York: Harcourt, 1931), 223.

14. Thomas Connery, *Journalism and Realism: Rendering American Life* (Chicago: Northwestern University Press, 2011), 14–15.

15. Karen Roggenkamp, *Narrating the News: New Journalism and Literary Genre in Late Nineteenth-Century American Newspapers and Fiction* (Kent, OH: Kent State University Press, 2005), 21.

16. As Michael Schudson argues, "It would be a mistake to read contemporary views of objectivity into the fact-mindedness of the 1890s. Objectivity is an ideology of the distrust of the self, something Richard Harding Davis and his colleagues did not feel. The Progressives' belief in facts was different from a modern conviction of objectivity." Schudson, *Discovering the News*, 62.

17. Ibid., 63.

18. Frank Norris, "A Plea for Romantic Fiction," in *The Norton Anthology of American Literature*, 8th ed., Vol C, edited by Nina Baym and Jerome Klinkowitz (New York: Norton, 2007), 915.

19. Harold S. Wilson, *McClure's Magazine and the Muckrakers* (Princeton, NJ: Princeton University Press, 1970), 190.

20. Qtd. in James McGrath Morris, *Pulitzer: A Life in Politics, Print, and Power* (New York: HarperCollins, 2010), 234.

21. Morris, *Pulitzer*, 233.

22. Michael McGerr, *A Fierce Discontent: The Rise and Fall of the Progressive Movement in America* (New York: Oxford University Press, 2005), 268.

23. Ibid., 7.

24. Upton Sinclair, *The Profits of Religion: An Essay in Economic Interpretation* (Pasadena: Author, 1918), 259–60. A socialist himself writing from the vantage point of the Russian Revolution's early days, Sinclair would likely have seen nothing ironic in this comparison.

25. Wilson, *McClure's Magazine and the Muckrakers*, v.

26. Cecilia Tichi, *Exposés and Excess: Muckraking in America 1900–2000* (Philadelphia: University of Pennsylvania Press, 2004), 86.

27. Wilson, *McClure's Magazine and the Muckrakers*, 81.

28. Kaplan, *Lincoln Steffens*, 124–25, 130.

29. Tichi, *Exposés and Excess*, 25. See also Steve Weinburg, *Taking on the Trust: The Epic Battle of Ida Tarbell and John D. Rockefeller* (New York: Norton, 2008).

30. Ida Tarbell, *The History of the Standard Oil Company* (New York: McClure, Phillips, 1905), 97.

31. Ibid., 51.

32. Ibid., 102.

33. Chernow, *Titan*, Kindle edition, loc. 2389.

34. Ibid., loc. 2446.

35. Georgine Milmine, "The Life of Mary Baker G. Eddy and the History of Christian Science," Part VI, *McClure's* 29, no. 3 (July 1907), 336.

36. Twain, *Christian Science*, 137.

37. "Editorial Announcement," *McClure's* 28, no. 2 (December 1906), 216.

38. Ibid., 215.

39. Georgine Milmine, "The Life of Mary Baker G. Eddy and the History of Christian Science," Part I, *McClure's* 28, no. 3 (January 1907), 242. I deliberately quote from the magazine itself in this chapter. The 1908 book version published by Doubleday and reissued by Nebraska University Press in 1993 differs substantially in structure from the original articles. See Willa Cather and Georgine Milmine, *The Life of Mary Baker G. Eddy and the History of Christian Science*, edited by David Stouck (Lincoln: University of Nebraska Press, 1993).

40. Georgine Milmine, "The Life of Mary Baker G. Eddy and the History of Christian Science," Part IV, *McClure's* 28, no. 5 (April 1907), 619.

41. For examples, see David Stouck's introduction to the Nebraska edition of the biography as well as David Porter, *On the Divide: The Many Lives of Willa Cather* (Lincoln: University of Nebraska Press, 2008). For a full assessment of the authorship question, see Squires, "The Standard Oil Treatment."

42. Georgine Milmine, *The Life of Mary Baker G. Eddy*, long draft, 1905? (typescript, Milmine Collection, Mary Baker Eddy Library for the Betterment of Humanity, Boston), 4.

43. Willa Cather, Letter to Edwin Anderson, 24 November 1922, Letter 0649 of *A Calendar of Letters of Willa Cather: An Expanded, Digital Edition*, edited by Andrew Jewell and Janis P. Stout, 2007–2010, The Willa Cather Archive, http://cather.unl.edu.

44. Amy Ahearn, "Engaging with the Political: Willa Cather, *McClure's Magazine*, and the Production of National Rhetoric" (dissertation, University of Nebraska, 2008), 22.

45. Milmine, long draft, 69. The drafts preserved in the collection include handwritten insertions and deletions. I have preserved these notations to the best of my ability here, indicating stricken portions with a strike-through and additions with angle brackets.

46. Ibid., 105.

47. Ibid., 118–19.

48. Ibid., 119.

49. Georgine Milmine, "The Life of Mary Baker G. Eddy and the History of Christian Science," Part III, *McClure's* 28, no. 5 (March 1907), 524.

50. Georgine Milmine, 28, no. 5, 619.

51. Georgine Milmine, "The Life of Mary Baker G. Eddy and the History of Christian Science," Part VI, *McClure's* 29, no. 3 (July 1907), 336.

52. Georgine Milmine, "The Life of Mary Baker G. Eddy and the History of Christian Science," Part XIV, *McClure's* 31, no. 2 (June 1908), 189.

53. Lyman Powell, Letter to Lucia Warren, 13 January 1933 (typescript, Milmine Collection, Mary Baker Eddy Library for the Betterment of Humanity, Boston).

54. Gill, *Mary Baker Eddy*, 38.

55. Ibid., 38.

56. Frank Sprague, Letter to Alfred Farlow, 15 July 1905 (typescript, *McClure's* File, Mary Baker Eddy Library for the Betterment of Humanity, Boston).

57. The finding aid for the Milmine Collection in the Mary Baker Eddy Library indicates that certain documents, including interview notes, are in Peabody's hand, and a handwritten note by Milmine indicates that Peabody supplied the affidavits from Horace T. Wentworth, Catherine Isabel Clapp, Lucy Holmes, and Charles Wentworth, all critical informants for the section on Eddy's early years as a teacher of Christian Science.

58. According to David Zimmerman, escalation had indeed become a real problem in the journalism field by 1906: "Fueled by popular demand, sustained by editors' need to outsell competitors, and propelled by a sense that corruption could be found wherever one looked for it, exposés had become more sensational, less concerned with analyzing social ills and aimed more at unveiling an underworld of vice and fraud." See David Zimmerman, *Panic! Markets, Crises, and Crowds in American Fiction* (Chapel Hill: University of North Carolina Press, 2006), Kindle edition, loc. 1136.

59. Paul Deland, "Helpfulness—Keynote of Christian Science Monitor," reprint from *The Quill*, 1925 (clipping, CSM Subject File, Mary Baker Eddy Library for the Betterment of Humanity, Boston).

60. Willis J. Abbot, "A Force for Clean Journalism," reprint from *The Quill*, 1933 (clipping, Christian Science Monitor Subject File, Mary Baker Eddy Library for the Betterment of Humanity, Boston).

61. Ibid.

62. See Good, "Epilogue."

63. Deland, "Helpfulness."

64. Erwin Canham, *Commitment to Freedom: The Story of the Christian Science Monitor* (Boston, Houghton Mifflin, 1958), 52.

65. Qtd. in Canham, *Commitment to Freedom*, 52.

66. Ibid., xxii.

67. Deland, "Helpfulness."

68. Qtd. in Kaplan, *Lincoln Steffens*, 162.

69. Ibid., 168.

70. Roggenkamp, *Narrating the News*, 264.

71. Morris, *Pulitzer*, 411. Critics at the time frequently accused Pulitzer of merely attempting to polish his legacy and redeem himself from a career of indulging some of New Journalism's worst impulses, but the image that Morris presents is far more nuanced.

72. David Mindich, *Just the Facts: How "Objectivity" Came to Define American Journalism* (New York: New York University Press, 2000), 129.

73. Roggenkamp, *Narrating the News*, 119.

74. Schudson, *Discovering the News*, 79.

75. Ibid., 109.

76. Roggenkamp, *Narrating the News*, 120.

77. Morris, *Pulitzer*, 360.

78. Abbot, "A Force for Clean Journalism."

79. "The Distress in Italy," *Christian Science Monitor*, 1 January 1909, p. 1.

80. Abbott, "A Force for Clean Journalism."

81. "New Note in Fiction," *Christian Science Monitor*, 7 January 1910, p. 13.

82. Abbott, "A Force for Clean Journalism."

83. Deland, "Helpfulness."

84. Notice from the *Granite State Free Press* (clipping, Christian Science Monitor Subject File, Mary Baker Eddy Library for the Betterment of Humanity, Boston).

85. Peter Grier, "Monitor Correspondent Wins Pulitzer," *Christian Science Monitor*, 10 April 1966.

86. Deland, "Helpfulness."

87. Canham, *Commitment to Freedom*, xvi.

88. William Dicke, "Erwin Canham, Longtime Editor of the Christian Science Monitor, Dies," *New York Times*, 4 January 1982.

89. Canham, *Commitment to Freedom*, xviii.

90. Canham, *Commitment to Freedom*, xviii.

91. "A Message from the Trustees of the Christian Science Publishing Society," 16 March 1936 (memorandum, Christian Science Monitor Subject File, Mary Baker Eddy Library for the Betterment of Humanity, Boston).

92. Canham, *Commitment to Freedom*, 124.

93. Ibid., 96.

94. Mary Baker Eddy, Letter to Archibald McClellan, 22 January 1909 (Outgoing Correspondence File, Mary Baker Eddy Library for the Betterment of Humanity, Boston).

95. Canham, *Commitment to Freedom*, 119.

96. Keith S. Collins, *The Christian Science Monitor: Its History, Mission, and People* (Lebanon, NH: Nebbadoon Press, 2012), 28.

97. Ibid., 50.

98. Ibid., 91.

99. See Gregory Kolko, *The Triumph of Conservatism: A Reinterpretation of American History, 1900–1916* (New York: Free Press, 1963), 160.

100. Kaplan, *Lincoln Steffens*, 129.

101. Schudson, *Discovering the News*, 117.

102. Mindich, *Just the Facts*, 142.

103. Schudson, *Discovering the News*, 111.

104. Ibid.

105. Mindich, *Just the Facts*, 131.

106. Roggenkamp, *Narrating the News*, 123.

107. Mindich, *Just the Facts*, 144.

108. The proof contains a brief response from Eddy, so this was clearly from the paper's first couple of years.

109. Eli Perkins, "A Word of Appreciation" (undated proof, Christian Science Monitor Subject File, Mary Baker Eddy Library for the Betterment of Humanity, Boston).

110. John V. Dittemore, Letter to S. S. McClure, 14 November 1908 (typescript, Mary Baker Eddy Library for the Betterment of Humanity, Boston).

111. John V. Dittemore, Letter to Edward Kimball, 31 October 1908 (typescript, Mary Baker Eddy Library for the Betterment of Humanity, Boston).

112. John V. Dittemore and Ernest Sutherland Bates, *Mary Baker Eddy: The Truth and the Tradition* (New York: Knopf, 1932); Charles S. Braden, *Christian Science Today: Power, Policy, Practice* (Dallas: Southern Methodist University Press, 1958), 384–85.

5

The Tragedy of Desire

Social Justice, Gender Politics, and
Theodore Dreiser's The "Genius"

In 1918, a decade after the publication of the *McClure's* series and the founding of the *Christian Science Monitor*, eight years after the death of both Mary Baker Eddy and Mark Twain, Upton Sinclair published *The Profits of Religion* at his own expense. This book included Christian Science in a long list of religions that, according to its author, were fleecing a gullible public. A few months after its appearance, Stephen Alison, a socialist and editor of the *Christian Scientist*, an unofficial (meaning unsanctioned) Christian Science periodical, printed an open letter to Sinclair, deputizing another famous author into his argument:

> I suppose that you do read sometimes the novels of other novelists, and
> it is by no means unlikely that you have read "The Genius," by Theodore
> Dreiser, a great novel which has been ruthlessly suppressed by a tyrannical
> Mrs. Grundyism[1] that tolerates so much infamous trash; but it is quite
> obvious that Dreiser's work was suppressed because he saw so completely
> through the conventional lies of our civilization and did not bow down
> to nor adore them. Several chapters toward the end of "The Genius" deal
> with Eugene Witla's experiences in connection with the application of
> Christian Science to the problems of his existence; and Dreiser has at least
> endeavored to honestly comprehend the message of Christian Science. He
> does not make the mistake of confusing it with hypnotism or the opera-
> tion of the "sub-conscious mind." In case you do not care to read more
> carefully the volume of "Science and Health" which you purchased,—to
> get "The Genius" cost me twice as much—if you have Dreiser's novel or
> can borrow it from someone who has it, for, of course, it is not to be found

in the libraries,—it would be well for you to review the chapters in it
dealing with Christian Science. I do not say that they are perfect, but they
show a sympathetic and intelligent understanding and he discerns the
difference between the spiritual and metaphysical conception of God and
Infinite Mind, and the feeble counterfeit belief in the operation of human
will-power, as manifested in connection with the human mind. Dreiser
may be more of a realist than an artist in words, but he is at least desirous
of getting his facts straight and takes pains to do so.[2]

Though Dreiser himself never converted to Christian Science as his sisters
and first wife did, Alison had ample reason to believe that he had found
in the famous author a fellow traveler, or, at the very least, an interlocutor between Christian Scientists and the world of skeptical elites. The
final sixty pages of The "Genius"—derisively called "the Christian Science
fugue" by Dreiser's friend Edward H. Smith—contain a thorough exploration of Mary Baker Eddy's writings and place them in conversation with
the other metaphysical and scientific theories that preoccupied Dreiser
at the time. The novel fictionalizes the author's own nervous breakdown
following the commercial failure of Sister Carrie, the collapse of his marriage to Sara "Jug" White, and his abortive affair with Thelma Cudlipp, the
young daughter of a family friend. During that crisis, "Dreiser and Jug had
consulted with [Christian Science] practitioners in the manner of contemporary couples visiting a marriage counselor," according to biographer
Richard Lingemann.[3] The author's interest in Christian Science turns up
at various points in both his fictional and autobiographical writings but
especially in this final section of The "Genius."

Dreiser's fascination with Christian Science has been difficult for many
of his readers to square with the other things that we know about him,
particularly his commitment to naturalism and his inclination toward
socialism. Naturalism, the literary movement with which Dreiser is usually identified, offers, like socialism, a fundamentally materialist account
of the world and of human experience, which seems incompatible with
Christian Science's denial of the reality of matter. What's more, both in
his life and in his novels, Dreiser was famous for challenging the Victorian
moral norms that Mary Baker Eddy and the official Church of Christ,
Scientist (fairly or unfairly) were perceived as upholding. Indeed, one of
the great ironies here is the fact that the novel that contains the author's

deep dive into Mary Baker Eddy's antimaterialist theology was itself suppressed for being too sensual, thanks to its frank depiction of its protagonist's sexual misadventures. The "Genius" ran afoul of the Comstock Law prohibiting the circulation of obscene material, a ruling that was eventually overturned, allowing for the novel's republication several years later. Dreiser's victory was considered a landmark case in the history of censorship and the slow transition of American culture away from Victorian norms. According to Jerome Loving, the novel's reappearance "marked the general demise of puritanical censorship in literary America. In a way, this novel did for American literature what *Sister Carrie* had done— loosened the stranglehold of American moralists."[4] Though it was neither a critical nor popular success, as Rachel Bowlby indicates, "such sales as it did have were inflated by the notoriety that followed from suppression through the influence of a society for moral reform, and subsequent republication a decade later."[5]

More recent scholarship has suggested that despite this legacy, *The "Genius"* is riddled with evidence of sexual conservatism, sentimentality, and ambivalence.[6] Indeed, ambivalence may be the novel's most pervasive quality. Like Dreiser himself, Eugene Witla is constantly torn between opposing ideas and forces: between the conventionality of Angela Blue (the fictional surrogate for Dreiser's first wife) and the sexual liberalism of his other lovers, between the world of art and the world of commerce, and finally between Mary Baker Eddy's metaphysical account of experience and a materialist one. Such ambivalence may even be said to be characteristic of Dreiser's work as a whole. The degree to which Dreiser is either critical of or enamored with consumer capitalism has been the subject of scholarly debate for the past few decades. Dreiser's later affiliation with socialist and communist causes points in one direction. However, looking to novels like *Sister Carrie* and *The Financier*, critics have noted how his novels refuse to condemn or punish their protagonists' consumeristic desires.[7] Such a tension also shows up in Dreiser's diary from his trip to the Soviet Union in 1927, where he vacillates between a commitment to capitalist individualism and sympathy with the collectivist ethos of early Stalinism.[8] Michael David-Fox suggests that "Dreiser's peculiar mix of Social Darwinism and progressive social conscience, determinism and rugged individualism formed a layered mélange that, as is often the case, was neither fully 'Left' or 'Right' politically."[9]

The seemingly (and frustratingly) contradictory nature of Dreiser's thinking is, perhaps, rooted in a tendency to latch onto ideas that were appealing and useful to him at any given time. This is not to say that he was an opportunist or incapable of committing himself ideologically. Though deeply unsettled by some of the things he saw in Stalinist Russia, Dreiser committed himself to socialist causes later in life, becoming a passionate labor advocate and antilynching activist. He joined the Communist Party of America as a largely symbolic gesture just months before he died in 1945. He also attended a Church of Christ, Scientist with his long-term partner Helen Richardson as he lived out his final days in California.[10] But Dreiser's interest in Christian Science, along with other movements outside the religious mainstream, wasn't necessarily incompatible with his socialist commitments. As this chapter shall demonstrate, anticapitalists in the 1910s found much to like about Christian Science. Mary Baker Eddy's rejection of the material world provided a natural rationale for rejecting the money consciousness that underpinned Western capitalism. But this mix of metaphysical and political interests may have exacerbated the ambivalence that Clare Eby observes in The "Genius" toward sex and the fulfillment of sexual desire.[11] As this chapter will also show, desire in the early twentieth century was seen as an economic force as well as an interpersonal one. Desire, in the work of Spencer and other social theorists, was the force that drove the capitalist engine. Viewed as something that men have and women do not, desire was also a concept that many progressives during this period interrogated and critiqued. And the account of embodied experience as fundamentally a product of mind, provided by Christian Science, enabled progressives to challenge the gendered concepts of desire that underpinned the prevailing economic and social order. Dreiser's exploration of Christian Science in The "Genius" is a means of sorting through desire's unsettling implications.

CHRISTIAN SCIENCE IN THE LIFE OF THEODORE DREISER

The appearance of Christian Science in other parts of Dreiser's writing suggests that throughout his life, he viewed it as both an intriguing metaphysical idea and a pragmatic tool for coping with life's troubles. As early as 1901, Dreiser mentioned Christian Science in his *Harper's* profile of the artist William Louis Sonntag, Jr., later anthologized in *Twelve Men*: "He had a fine mind, philosophically and logically considered. He could reason upon all things, from the latest mathematical theorem to Christian Science. Naturally, being so much of an individualist, he was drifting toward a firm belief in the latter, and was never weary of discussing the power of the mind—its wondrous ramifications and influences."[12] He references the illusory nature of aging and death in Lester Kane's deathbed scenes in *Jennie Gerhardt* (1911), asserting that "man, even under his mortal illusion, is organically built to last five times the period of his maturity and would last as long as the spirit that is in him if he but knew that it is spirit which persists, that age is an illusion, that there is no death."[13] In *A Traveler at Forty* (1913), he records an instance in which he recommends Christian Science to a friend and her family:

> On the way home, I remember, we discussed Christian Science and its relative physical merits in a world where all creeds and doctrines blow, apparently, so aimlessly about. Like all sojourners in this fitful fever of existence, Mrs. Grant Allen and her daughter and son, the cheerful Jerrard Grant Allen, were not without their troubles, so much so that being the intelligent woman that she was and quite aware of the subtleties and uncertainties of religious dogma, she was nevertheless eager to find something upon which she could lean, spiritually speaking—the strong arm, let us say, of an Almighty, no less, who would perchance heal her of her griefs and ills. . . . I think I established the metaphysical basis of life quite ably, for myself, and urged Mrs. Grant Allen to take up Christian Science.[14]

A few years later, in *A Hoosier Holiday* (1916), he speaks of discussing the central principle of Christian Science with a friend who had recently converted:

> Then Franklin and I sat back in the cushions and began to discuss [automobile] blowouts in general and the mystic power of the mind to control such matters—the esoteric or metaphysical knowledge that there can be no such thing as evil and that blowouts really cannot occur. This brings me again to Christian Science, which somehow hung over this whole tour, not so much as a religious irritant as a pleasant safeguard. It wasn't religious or obtrusive at all. Franklin, as I have said, is inclined to believe that there is no evil, though he is perfectly willing to admit that material appearances seem all against that assumption at the time.[15]

Much later, in a July 1940 letter to Dorothy Payne Davis, he placed Eddy
at the level of Gautama: "Buddha and Mary Baker Eddy affirmed an *over*
or *one* universal soul," he wrote, "itself *being* and so *containing* all wisdom
and all creative power." Dreiser clearly regarded Christian Science as a
balm for the suffering soul, a spiritual recourse that was free from many
of the trappings and limitations of the major organized religions. It was
a form of spirituality that even the educated and skeptical, those "aware
of the subtleties and uncertainties of religious dogma" could lean on in a
time of trouble.[16]

As with Frances Hodgson Burnett, Dreiser's fascination with Christian
Science grew in the context of his interest in other unorthodox forms
of spirituality. He was fascinated by spiritualism, a subject to which he
devoted a six-part series in *The Delineator* called "Are the Dead Alive?"[17]
He was also quite superstitious. The Christian Science passage from *A
Hoosier Holiday* occurs just after Dreiser and his friend have had an intense discussion about luck signs. For Dreiser, however, these curiosities
were not incompatible with his interests in modern science. His readings
in *Science and Health,* his visits with psychics, and his fascination with
theoretical physics, biology, and Social Darwinism were all of a piece,
all part of his interest in the hidden workings of the universe. As Louis
Zanine argues, Dreiser remained fascinated but ultimately dissatisfied
with the modern scientific establishment "as he realized that scientists did
not share his interest in the supernatural. He eventually grew impatient
because they refused to investigate the mysterious, occult phenomena
that so fascinated him."[18]

In *The "Genius,"* Eugene Witla, Dreiser's fictional alter ego, first encounters Christian Science during the collapse of his relationship with both
his wife, Angela, and his would-be lover, Suzanne Dale. His life falling
to pieces all around him, Witla seeks a remedy for his existential despair:

> He was one of those men who are metaphysically inclined. All his life
> he had been speculating on the subtleties of mortal existence, reading
> Spencer, Kant, Spinoza, at odd moments, and particularly such men as
> Darwin, Huxley, Tyndall, Lord Avebury, Alfred Russel Wallace, and lat-
> terly Sir Oliver Lodge and Sir William Crookes, trying to find out by the
> inductive, naturalistic method just what life was.[19]

He brings Mary Baker Eddy's theories together with "chemistry and physics" to try to explain the problem of morality, of where the moral laws
that govern society come from. He finds confluences between *Science and
Health* and Carlyle, who "had once said that 'matter itself—the outer world
of matter, was either nothing, or else a product due to man's mind.'"[20] He
also compares Christian Science to theories about cell biology and physics, quoting at length from Edgar Lucien Larkin on the nature of invisible
particles and Alfred Russel Wallace on the hidden processes that govern
the workings of the human body and the universe:

> This [Wallace's] very peculiar and apparently progressive statement in
> regard to the conclusion which naturalistic science had revealed in regard
> to the universe struck Eugene as pretty fair confirmation of Mrs. Eddy's
> contention that all was mind and its infinite variety and that the only
> difference between her and the British scientific naturalists was that they
> contended for an ordered hierarchy which could only rule and manifest
> itself according to its own ordered or self-imposed laws, which they could
> perceive or detect, whereas, she contended for a governing spirit which
> was everywhere and would act through ordered laws and powers of its
> own arrangement.[21]

While Dreiser (and Eugene) ultimately rejected Christian Science's "denial of the existence of evil in the universe, he agreed completely with
Eddy's assertion that 'there is no life, truth, intelligence, nor substance
in matter. All is infinite Mind and its infinite manifestation, for God is
All-in-All.'"[22]

Dreiser's religious eccentricity distressed his friends and colleagues,
who saw in these flights of fancy the last remaining traces of the Indiana
rube in this enlightened visionary. H. L. Mencken was horrified to find
Christian Science magazines in the home of Theodore and Sara (the author's first wife) when he visited them in 1911, assuming that Sara was "a de-
luded believer. To him, Mary Baker Eddyism was the worst kind of pious
snake oil." For this reason, "Dreiser apparently hadn't told Mencken of his
own interest in Christian Science, or else passed it off as mere scientific curiosity, knowing the other's violent dislike of any sort of 'spiritualism.'"[23]
Mencken panned *The "Genius"* in his review for *The Smart Set*, an event
that marked the beginning of a hostile period in his relationship with

Dreiser, but Mencken was hardly the only colleague who was perplexed by the novel and concerned about Dreiser's metaphysical bent.

In January 1921, Edward Smith, a former colleague from Dreiser's days as a journalist, confronted Dreiser about his religious and superstitious tendencies in a letter:

> I fear me, and with very deep concern, that Theodore Dreiser's mind turns ever a little more toward metaphysical symbols and signs. I shudder at your interest in that awful mess of a twaddle which Fort made into a book. I tremble at the Christian Science fugue in the end of *The "Genius."* Your plays of the supernatural rather appal [sic] me.[24] I find you playing more and more with metaphysical terms and ideas—perhaps unconsciously—in much of your later work).[25]

Dreiser was offended by his friend's insinuations. Smith takes a transparent stab at Dreiser's humble background, referring to his "religious parentage," the author's father having been a fanatically devout Catholic. "Men do not leap out of such trends in a single generation," says Smith.[26] In his response, Dreiser frames his interest as an academic one and suggests that the true value of religion is in soothing the aches of lesser minds:

> Religion is a bandage for sore brains. Morality, ditto. It is the same as a shell to a snail. The blistering glare of indefinable forces would destroy most, were it not for the protecting umbrella of illusion. That was what I meant when I said that Franklin Booth had been aided by Christian Science. He was looking for a blanket under which to crawl, and he found it. Eugene Witla was in the same position. I tried to show just how it was that he came to dabble with Christian Science, and why, in the long run it failed to hold him. Having recovered a part of his mental strength he shed it, as a snake does a skin. I have never been under any illusion in regard to religion, morality, metaphysical fiddle-faddle. I had my fill in my youth. Today I want facts but I am not to be denied the right to speculate in my own way and I have no fear that I shall be led into any religious or moralic bog. I am much too sane for that. If you see signs, kindly let me know.[27]

There's a sense here that Dreiser protests too much, but it does bolster the idea that he saw Christian Science as one among many pragmatic ways of addressing life's problems. The problem that Dreiser and his fictional surrogate use Christian Science to solve is both a physical and moral one. The crisis that leads Witla to read *Science and Health* is the consequence of desire, his waning desire for his wife no less than his overwhelming desire for the eighteen-year-old Suzanne Dale. Desire enables the hero of the novel to pursue beauty and create art, but desire's tendency to ebb serves as a reminder of contingency and mortality and endangers Witla's livelihood. In its economic dimensions, desire drives innovation and creates growth, but it also promotes greed and initiates the devastating boom and bust cycles of the market. Desire, as critics have long observed, is a theme that permeates the author's work. Dreiser called his three novels fictionalizing the life of financier Charles Yerkes *The Trilogy of Desire*, linking its protagonist's economic activity to his pursuit of romantic novelty, for an excellent reason. The economic as well as sexual implications of desire were, indeed, something that Dreiser's contemporaries were very concerned about, something that linked anticapitalist and feminist movements to new religions like Christian Science and New Thought, a set of complicated connections that I will unpack in the next section.

DESIRE AND GENDER IDEOLOGY AT THE TURN OF THE TWENTIETH CENTURY

The moral, social, and economic implications of desire preoccupied thinkers during a period marked by the rise of evolutionary theory, biological determinism, and Social Darwinism. Desire was seen as a force that had the power to shape society for good or ill in addition to shaping individual lives. This is a dimension of Victorian and Progressive Era culture that Beryl Satter explores extensively in her history of the New Thought movement. She writes that in the late nineteenth century, many white middle-class Americans were engaged in a debate over whether the key to Anglo-Saxon "race progress" was masculine desire or feminine spirituality, "whether manly 'desire' was the fuel of competition and hence progress, or whether it was the poisonous threat to civilization that must be contained by womanly altruism and spirituality." On one side of the debate were "prominent white male theorists," who "drew upon medical, anthropological, and evolutionary discourses to demonstrate 'scientifically' the ironclad linkages between male desire, female domesticity, industrial capitalist society, and the development of the Anglo-Saxon race."[28] One such theorist was Herbert Spencer, a hero of Dreiser's, who asserted that it is "criminal" to "deprive men, in any way, of liberty to pursue the objects they desire, when it was appointed to insure them that liberty."[29] On the other side were "white female activists" like Catherine Beecher and Charlotte Perkins Gilman, who "heralded themselves as the epitome of Anglo-Saxon racial development" and "claimed science as a womanly spiritual discourse, promoted cooperation over capitalism, and strategized toward the final eradication of devolutionary male desire."[30]

Part of the background for this debate is the culture's transition from gendered norms of restraint to the ideal of unfettered desire during the nineteenth century, as the white majority attempted to position itself in a rapidly changing and diversifying world by negotiating the lines of race, class, and gender. As Gail Bederman indicates, progressive men of the early twentieth century idealized "chest-thumping virility, vigorous outdoor athleticism."[31] This was a reaction to the antebellum ideal of manly restraint, in which men were meant to "embody rationality, will power, and self-control."[32] That earlier ideal was consistent with the mid-nineteenth-century understanding of human physiology as a "closed-energy" system that mandated "willed asceticism: like economic advancement or religious salvation, physical health was dependent upon mastering the body's wasteful impulses. Weakness, illness, madness, or even death would result if one allowed one's body to 'spend' its vital energies on debilitating sensual pleasures."[33] Manly restraint legitimized a man's authority "to protect and direct those weaker than himself: his wife, his children, or his employees."[34] Men were instructed to conserve their life force by avoiding masturbation and other forms of sexual profligacy.

Similar theories about the limited nature of the body's resources influenced the diagnosis and treatment of neurasthenia or "nervous exhaustion," the ailment that plagued both Frances Hodgson Burnett and Theodore Dreiser during the first decade of the twentieth century. In *American Nervousness* (1881), physician George Miller Beard defined neurasthenia as a "deficiency or lack of nerve-force," characterized by a variety of symptoms from chronic exhaustion to dyspepsia to headaches and sexual dysfunction.[35] Beard theorized that individuals had a limited amount of nervous energy, which tended to be too rapidly depleted by the forces of modern civilization and the performance of "brain work." Because the primary purpose of the civilized man was to engage in rational pursuits, "doctors warned men not to 'spend their seed' (i.e., the essence of their energy) recklessly, but to conserve themselves for the civilizing endeavors' they were embarked upon."[36] This regulation, even suppression of desire, had economic as well as physical consequences, prompting "young men to postpone marriage until they could support a family in proper middle-class style, to work hard and live abstemiously so that they could amass the capital to go into business for themselves."[37]

This "conservation of energy" paradigm held that women's physiological energies were dominated and therefore depleted by the reproductive system: "because reproduction was woman's grand purpose in life, doctors agreed that women ought to concentrate their physical energy internally, toward the womb. All other activity should be slowed down or stopped during the peak periods of sexual energy use."[38] Women were discouraged from getting an education and performing the sort of "brain work" reserved for men. Silas Weir Mitchell's "rest cure," a regimen of complete abstinence from any mentally taxing activity, was a paradigmatic treatment for female neurasthenics. Charlotte Perkins Gilman famously fictionalized her own disastrous experience with Mitchell's treatment in "The Yellow Wallpaper," in which isolation and lack of stimulation gradually drive the female protagonist insane.

Gender ideology and gendered conceptions of desire shifted in the post–Civil War era as "in a society of increasing economic complexity, white men found that hard work and self-discipline bore little relation to economic success."[39] The shifting demographics of the city and the entrance of white middle-class women into higher education and the professions also catalyzed the reconfiguration of white middle-class male identity as aggressive and desiring rather than rational and restrained: "The anthropological scenario depicted male desire—for money, off-spring, fame, or success—as the driving force behind progress and civilization."[40] The reorientation of middle-class attitudes toward desire also shaped (and was shaped by) a reconfiguration of middle-class life around leisure and consumption rather than labor and production.[41] Advertisers directed their efforts toward the creation of new desires rather than the fulfillment of basic needs. The white middle-class culture of restraint became a culture of entitlement, though that entitlement was mostly the purview of the white men whose sense of rightful authority and power had been challenged by women, immigrants, working-class whites, and ethnic minorities. Evolutionary biologists and sociologists like Spencer were convinced that the channeling of male desire toward productive economic pursuits was essential, not only to individual prosperity, but to the progression of the Anglo-Saxon race, which was deemed by white Victorians to be naturally superior to all others.

This valorization of male desire was accompanied by the reassignment of women to the domestic role of enabling but never emulating that desire and aggressiveness.[42] Many female activists rebelled against their subservient position, but they also tended to accept the prevailing notion that men were naturally aggressive and desiring while women were innately passionless and nurturing. Seeking an expanded role in public life, female activists argued that the advancement of civilization depended not on male desire and individualism but on feminine cooperation and altruism.[43] As Charlotte Perkins Gilman (then Stetson) argued in *Women and Economics* (1900), "Human progress lies in the perfecting of the social organization." She goes on to describe the myriad ways the trappings of civilization—"the linking of humanity together across ocean and mountain and desert plain by steam and electricity, in the establishment of such world-functions as the international postal service"—foster sympathy and cooperation among diverse peoples and nations.[44] Women, bceause of their superior morality and role as guardians of relationship, were, according to this theory, uniquely designed to be the ambassadors of middle-class Anglo-Saxon virtue.

These white feminists found common cause with various progressive and social justice movements and in many cases also found their way to New Thought and Christian Science. Woman movement leaders and social justice activists tended to view aggressive male desire as a social evil, responsible not only for such abominations as rape (including marital rape) and forced pregnancy,[45] but also the exploitation of the poor and the volatility of the market with its catastrophic boom and bust cycles. Male desire was linked not only to the sexual oppression of women but to the aggressive, predatory pursuit of individual wealth at all costs. The valorization of female desirelessness and cooperation was why the Knights of Labor, the Farmers' Alliance, and Bellamyite Nationalists not only encouraged women's participation in their ranks, but also supported temperance, women's suffrage, and social purity. These alliances were possible because by the last quarter of the nineteenth century reformers of all sorts began to understand the social chaos around them in heavily gendered terms. The Knights of Labor, the Grange, the Alliance and Populist movements, the Single-Taxers, and the Bellamyite Nationalists all hoped to implement politically the ideals of cooperation rather than conflict, harmonious sharing rather than cutthroat competition, and rational planning rather than unimpeded personal greed. As some woman movement leaders saw it, these were the values of refined womanhood, not lustful manhood.[46]

These arguments about both gender and social organization also tended to refer to shifting theories about the nature of the body and the mind. As both men and women came to accept the dichotomy of male carnality versus female spirituality, women and the movements they led became more closely allied to theories that subordinated the material world to the spiritual or, in the case of Christian Science, did away with the material world altogether.

As the more ecumenical and politically forward-looking of these related movements, New Thought is the one most closely associated with the woman movement[47] and with socialism.[48] Beryl Satter's history is concerned primarily with New Thought, but more "orthodox" Christian Scientists also felt an affinity between their religion and radical ideas about gender and society. In 1887, Reverend George B. Day preached a sermon for the First Church of Christ, Scientist in Chicago titled "Sheep, Shepherd, and Shepherdess" that sums up many Christian Scientists' radical theories about gender:

> Our masculine teachers declare that the day of miracles is passed. They smile at the unreasonable belief that Christ can or will save from disease and death. By their own declarations they stand condemned; and there is more than a suspicion, already awakened, that we are witnessing the transfer of the Gospel from male to female trust.
>
> You do well to note the signs of the times,—of a movement,— significant and already well defined,—which has assumed proportions which must impress you. Women no longer give a silent assent to the

theory that they are secondary and subordinate to men. Eighteen hundred years ago, Paul declared that man was the head of the woman; but now, in Science and Health, it is asserted that "woman is the highest form of man."[49]

Stephen Alison and Alice Boyd of the *Christian Scientist* also provide useful examples of how early feminism, socialism, and Christian Science found common cause. Though the periodical they published was not officially sanctioned by the church, its content is quite similar to that of the *Christian Science Journal* with the addition of European socialist thought. Mary Baker Eddy and the Bible are quoted extensively in every issue, as are other Christian Science luminaries like Edward Kimball. New Thought leaders such as Warren Felt Evans, Emma Curtis Hopkins, Ursula Gestefeld, Julius Dresser, and Phineas Quimby are conspicuously absent.[50] Articles take up the unreality of matter and the dangers of malicious animal magnetism at considerable length, points of doctrine that scholars like Gill, Voorhees, Albanese, and Gottschalk use to distinguish true Christian Science from its generic form as well as from New Thought. Alison saw Christian Science as the missing piece that completed the socialist ideal and at one point reflected ruefully that his fellow travelers in Great Britain were not influenced by the US-based Christian Science movement: "A better understanding of that form of teaching which Mary Baker Eddy has made familiar to many in 'Science and Health,' supplies an adequate solution [to the divisions between secular and Christian socialists], which, had it been known to Socialists and Secularists . . . would have given them both a common platform to stand on."[51]

Christian Science provided a rhetoric for critiquing capitalism by appealing to the material unreality of wealth. A letter attributed to "an early student of Mrs. Eddy" and published in the *Christian Scientist* advances the argument that "by handling money we handle every human belief of disease. We lust upon intellect, money, friends, home, etc., and what is the result? Death. The moment we begin to see that money as money does not exist, but that it is the idea that supports, strengthens, cares for and sustains us in every way, we are beginning at the foundation."[52] Alison similarly stated that "false theology, and cut-throat competition, causing ruthless rivalry among humans is a logical result of the belief in the material origin of man, that humans are children of men, instead of children of

God, and the concomitant belief in the 'good old rule—the simple plan, That they should take who have the power, And they should keep who can.'"[53] Those who advanced Christian Science and social justice together saw hope in a society structured by Love, a concept that Eddy returns to over and over again in *Science and Health*, an empathy engendered by the recognition that material possessions are unreal and human minds are interdependent. Christian Scientists echoed familiar arguments about the role of women as ambassadors of this superior model of social organization. As Eddy claimed in *Retrospection and Introspection*, "woman must give it birth," speaking of Christian Science and the spiritual revolution that it was supposed to engender. While men participated widely in the movement, many Christian Scientists believed that men must learn womanly virtues in order to be spiritually uplifted. As that same student of Eddy's wrote in the *Christian Scientist*, "Man is to be redeemed through the woman thought, and that visibly expressed, else it is not Science."[54]

Cooperation among Christian Scientists, woman movement leaders, and social justice advocates in a critique of aggressive desire as economic and sexual force was hardly universal. As Satter's history of New Thought demonstrates, many used the supremacy of mind over matter to justify the pursuit of personal success. Indeed, a generation of New Thought leaders in the early twentieth century began to recuperate female desire by insisting "that woman and man must equally learn to 'exalt' themselves, and that '[t]here isn't a greater, grander, more God-like thing to do than to *make money*."[55] One can follow this turn in the New Thought literature all the way to the beginnings of the modern-day prosperity gospel as well as the self-help segments of the New Age movement. But it horrified "older New Thought leaders" and Christian Scientists like Stephen Alison, who repudiated it in his letter to Upton Sinclair.[56] The ability of these metaphysical movements to provide religio-medical vocabularies to justify diametrically opposed ways of doing life and engaging in the world is interesting in the context of a study of Dreiser's attitudes toward them. The author was racked with ambivalence about desire and the correct approach to political economy. Ultimately, however, Dreiser's interpretation of Eddy is pretty clearly anti-desire. These are the terms in which he temporarily embraces her in this novel while ultimately keeping her ideas at arm's length.

DREISER'S AMBIVALENCE TOWARD DESIRE

Theodore Dreiser's life spanned the period we have been discussing, and his relationship to his body and sexuality were mediated at various points by internalized cultural norms that either mandated restraint or celebrated the expression of male desire, which helps explain the sexual ambivalence noted by Clare Eby and other critics. The author's biography reveals that as an adolescent, he was simultaneously sexually precocious and horrified by the immediacy of his own urges. Believing that his sexual thoughts were sinful, he confessed them to his priest, as he reports in *Dawn*:

> My thoughts were coming to be constantly on girls . . . and since I still deemed them wrong, I frequently confessed them to the Catholic priest. The latter, under the seal of the confessional, gravely warned me against them. . . . At the same time, as I have stated, I had this long time been find-ing decidedly heterodox references and counter-beliefs in almost all that I read. In such a mental state, and physically surrounded as I was, I was literally blazing physically."[57]

The "ridiculous and unsatisfactory practice of masturbation" also troubled him.[58] When he began noticing adverse physical symptoms, he was con-vinced, as a youth, that the habit was causing irreparable harm: "Theodore decided he was having a nervous breakdown, which was nature's way of restoring his system to 'parity.' He had been overtaxing his body, or, as he put it nearly fifty years later, 'paying out of one treasury by drawing too swiftly and heavily on others.' He retained the Victorian belief that emis-sions of semen represent a sort of overdraft on one's 'energy bank.' This was the prevailing opinion."[59]

Though he characterized these beliefs as superstitions from the per-spective of 1931, they plagued his early sexual experiences and emerged in his novels. While writing *The "Genius,"* he seems to have considered a connection between sexual restraint and artistic productivity. Eugene Witla, the novel's protagonist and Dreiser's alter ego, is a painter, not a writer, though like Dreiser he achieves early success that evaporates as quickly as it originally appeared. Just as Dreiser was unproductive for an entire decade following *Sister Carrie*, so Witla enters a period of profound depression and inability to work. However, instead of contextualizing this crisis in creative disappointment, the narrator of *The "Genius"* blames Witla's neurasthenic condition on overindulgence in the sexual act with his wife, Angela: "He had no knowledge of the effect of one's sexual life upon one's work, nor what such a life when badly arranged can do to a perfect art."[60] This assertion echoes George Miller Beard's theory that "indulgence of appetites and passions" was among the many causes of neurasthenia.[61] Eugene is instructed to abstain from such relations but has difficulty obeying: "He was continuing his passional relations with Angela, in spite of a growing judgment that they were in some way harmful to him. But it was not easy to refrain, and each failure to do so made it harder."[62] According to his biographer, this section of the novel accurately reflects Dreiser's own beliefs about his experience.[63]

Equally terrifying for the author was the less fantastical possibility of contracting a disease or impregnating his partner. Recounting his inaugural sexual experience in *Dawn*, Dreiser recalls fearing that she had given him "'the clap!' I remember that word as something menacing, something signifying a disease which one caught if one did not know with whom one was playing in this way."[64] He also observed the results of his sisters' sexual misadventures, two of them having become pregnant out of wedlock while Dreiser was a youth, bringing down his father's wrath and inviting social ignominy upon his family. His early relationships as a struggling journalist in Chicago were tainted by the fear that an unwanted pregnancy would tie him down and destroy his prospects. Richard Lingemann suggests that such fears were behind the performance issues that Dreiser reported in early drafts of *Newspaper Days*:

> It was a measure of how tightly the old bugaboos about masturbation gripped him that years later Dreiser thought of his precipitousness as "impotence." In a passage later expurgated from *Newspaper Days*, he writes "though I ejaculated copiously, I still imagined I was impotent due to youthful errors and bordering on senility." Inexperience and an inordinate fear of making Lois pregnant—not only because a child would tie him down to her but because of his memories of his sisters' experiences— probably go far in explaining his unsatisfactory performance. He considered "potency" equivalent to ejaculating inside a woman, which created the risk of impregnation. Dreiser's anxiety served as a psychic coitus interruptus. It induced a compulsion to withhold that was overridden by his strong desire, with the result that he "spent" uncontrollably. *Had* the affair

[with Lois] progressed, he would have felt obligated to "do right" by Lois even if they didn't have a child, and he didn't want to marry her.[65]

As his marriage to Sara, nicknamed "Jug," eventually soured, Dreiser was similarly worried that pregnancy would imprison him and destroy the object of desire and affection that he had so idealized: "Jug begged him to let her have a child, thinking that fatherhood would steady him. But he adamantly refused, as he had throughout their marriage. . . . He told her that giving birth would ruin her figure, the implication being that she would become unattractive to him. And, obviously, he disliked the idea of having a child because it would strengthen her hold over him."[66] The choice to have Angela contrive to get pregnant against Eugene's will in *The "Genius"* is, perhaps, a reflection of Dreiser's misogynistic fear that sexual relationships might tether him to a woman he no longer desired.

Like many men of his time, Dreiser tended to idealize female purity even as he rebelled against social and moral restraints regulating relations between men and women. Lingemann reports that "Dreiser's sexual nature was split: one part of him was drawn to women of experience who were openly sensual and took the lead in the affair ('made their way' with him). But another part sought an ideal, which meant fresh, young girls with petal-smooth faces and innocent eyes, like the nymph in the painting 'September Morn.'"[67] The split nature of the author's desire is reflected in his accounts of Eugene Witla's early affairs. As a young artist trying to make his way in New York City, Witla dallies with sexually experienced, sophisticated women with artistic careers of their own, women like Christina Channing (a brilliant contralto) and Miriam Finch (an accomplished sculptor and intellectual). He entertains himself with these women even as the conventional and conservative Angela Blue, to whom he is engaged, pines away in her father's house for him. Though he is drawn to more sexually liberated women, Eugene idealizes the pure, unsullied Angela and the example of clean Christian living that her family embodies: "They were written all over with Christian precept—not church dogma—but Christian precept, lightly and good naturedly applied. They obeyed the ten commandments in so far as possible and lived within the limits of what people considered sane and decent."[68]

This internal conflict reaches a crisis point when Eugene finally succeeds in pressuring Angela to have sex with him. Though he has gotten what he wanted, Eugene feels a profound sense of shame and loss. The consummation of their relationship serves to highlight the fact that purity was at the root of Eugene's attraction to Angela. However, he also feels guilty about betraying Jotham Blue, Angela's father:

> Eugene felt that Jotham believed him to be an honest man. He knew he had that appearance. He was frank, genial, considerate, not willing to condemn anyone—but this sex question—that was where he was weak. And was not the whole world keyed to that? Did not the decencies and the sanities of life depend on right moral conduct? Was not the world dependent on how the homes were run? How could anyone be good if his mother and father had not been good before him? How would the children of the world expect to be anything if people rushed here and there holding illicit relations? Take his sister Myrtle now—would he have wanted her rifled in this manner?[69]

After their tryst, the novel takes a dark turn in which Angela threatens to drown herself if Eugene tries to back out of their engagement: "Angela had thrown herself on his mercy and his sense of honor to begin with. She had extracted a promise of marriage—not urgently, and as one who sought to entrap him, but with the explanation that otherwise life must end in disaster for her."[70] Yet Dreiser makes it clear that Eugene does feel trapped and later resents both the forced promise and the social conventions that make her demand it. Lingemann, however, calls this reimagining of Dreiser and Jug's relationship "history soured by disillusionment. The truth was that Theodore's own desires trapped him, and his need for Sara was strong and more than just physical."[71]

Dreiser also blamed social norms—enforced monogamy, compulsory heterosexual marriage, wealth inequality—for the extreme consequences that consummated desire could produce. His later novel, *An American Tragedy*, might be accurately read as an extended argument for sex education and the accessibility of birth control as well as an indictment of the moral hypocrisy that made abortions available to the wealthy but not the poor. In the case of *The "Genius,"* Angela's conventionality—especially compared to the liberal Christina Channing, who has no marriage aspirations—forces Eugene into multiple untenable situations, pressuring him to marry her and later thwarting his affair with Suzanne Dale.

Dreiser's novels also reflect his concerns about the economic and social implications of desire. As stated earlier, the title of *The Trilogy of Desire* is a reference both to protagonist Frank Cowperwood's pursuit of beautiful women—in the form of Aileen Butler and Berenice Fleming—and his relentless pursuit of wealth. Cowperwood is a kind of Spencerian hero, one who accurately assesses the social order as a young man at the beginning of *The Financier*, seeing a lobster slowly feeding on a squid in a tank on the street, and applies this knowledge to his business dealings. While Cowperwood is undoubtedly idealized for his individualism, Dreiser also depicts the dark side of Cowperwood's predatory approach to finance: political scandal and personal catastrophe, not to mention the boom and bust cycles of the market.[72] According to Lingemann, Cowperwood "embodied a conflict within Dreiser. On the one hand he admired and envied the famous rogue builders of American capitalism, reflecting his own boyhood ambitions. . . . On the other, his acute sense of justice condemned them as exploiters of the common people."[73]

The "Genius" depicts just how temporary any sort of economic success can be, how readily society will throw away a formerly celebrated citizen. The first half of the novel traces Eugene's meteoric rise as an artist only to then depict his catastrophic fall as his neurasthenic condition prevents him from producing new paintings for a prolonged period of time. Physically weakened and deprived of his natural charisma, Witla is rejected by those who formerly sought to build him up, including the gallery manager who helped launch his career:

> Eugene's mental state, so depressed, so helpless, so fearsome—a rudderless boat in the dark, transmitted itself as an impression, a wireless message to all those who knew him or knew of him. His breakdown, which had first astonished M. Charles, depressed and then weakened the latter's interest in him. Like all other capable, successful men in the commercial world M. Charles was for strong men—men in the heyday of their success, the zenith of their ability. The least variation from this standard of force and interest was noticeable to him. If a man was going to fail—going to get sick and lose his interest in life or have his viewpoint affected, it might be very sad, but there was just one thing to do under such circumstances—get away from him. Failures of any kind were dangerous things to countenance.[74]

Once rejected by the cultural elites in Europe and New York City, Eugene is forced to walk from store to store attempting to sell his paintings for a fraction of what they would have brought at the peak of his fame. According to the novel's internal logic, Eugene's overindulgence in sex leads to the depletion of his resources, which weakens him as a man and makes him a less viable commodity. *The "Genius"* portrays capitalism as a thing that feeds on the desire and vitality of brilliant artistic minds, bleeds them dry, and then discards them.

Desire, its brief flame so easily extinguished, is also a reminder of human frailty and of the body's contingency. It is a sign of the temporality and futility of human pursuits. Eugene contemplates this problem throughout the novel. At a key moment in Eugene's and Angela's relationship, when Eugene is still pressuring her to have sex with him, he reflects on the frailty of that desire and the body itself, thinking, "'What is the human body? What produces passion? Here we are for a few years surging with a fever of longing and then we burn out and die.' He thought of some lines he might write, of pictures he might paint. All the while, reproduced before his mind's eye like a cinematograph, were views of Angela as she had been tonight in his arms, on her knees."[75] The image of Angela on her knees is a reminder of both her physical and emotional vulnerability and the explosive potential of their physical attraction. "No harm had come," he reflects, foreshadowing the impending disaster of their marriage.[76] A little bit later, reading "Darwin, Huxley, Tyndall, Lubbock," he dwells morosely on the temporary nature of any human attraction or relationship:

> To think that his life should endure but for seventy years and then be
> no more was terrible. He and Angela were chance acquaintances—
> chemical affinities—never to meet again in all time. He and Christina, he
> and Ruby—he and anyone—a few bright hours were all they could have
> together, and then would come the great silence, dissolution, and he would
> never be anymore.[77]

Yet that impermanence makes him "all the more eager to live, to be loved while he was here."[78] In this state of mind, he finally persuades Angela to give in to him and then must later come to terms with the fact that in the fulfillment of that desire, something else may have been lost: "This deed shamed him. And he asked himself whether he was wrong to be ashamed or not. Perhaps he was just foolish. Was not life made for living, not worrying? He had not created his passions and desires."[79]

Eugene's inexhaustible attraction to youth and innocence means that he harbors a desire that is forever forced to seek new objects, as the very act of possessing what he wants depletes her value in his eyes, making the women in his life the very sort of limited and disposable commodity he and his art prove to be. The narrator announces this tendency as a weakness, a tragedy waiting to happen:

> The weakness of Eugene was that he was prone in each of these new conquests to see for the time being the sum and substance of bliss, to rise rapidly in the scale of uncontrollable, exaggerated affection, until he felt that here and nowhere else, now and in this particular form was ideal happiness. He had been in love with Stella, with Margaret, with Ruby, with Angela, with Christina, and now with Frieda, quite in this way, and it had taught him nothing as yet concerning love except that it was utterly delightful. He wondered at times how it was that the formation of a particular face could work this spell. There was plain magic in the curl of a lock of hair, the whiteness or roundness of a forehead, the shapeliness of a nose or ear, the arched redness of full-blown petal lips. The cheek, the chin, the eye—in combination with these things—how did they work this witchery? The tragedies to which he laid himself open by yielding to these spells—he never stopped to think of them.[80]

The body, in this configuration of will and desire, is an impenetrable mystery, a force wholly independent of human volition. The isolated components of the female body act almost as their own agents in this passage, just as Eugene's body responds to them before his mind can tease out the implications or contemplate the consequences of acting.

Dreiser dissociates physical attraction from love, an emotion that he locates in some higher function of the mind. Love can be eternal, but attraction is not: "Hypnotic spells of this character like contagion and fever have their period of duration, their beginning, climax and end. It is written that love is deathless, but this was not written of the body nor does it concern the fevers of desire."[81] Dreiser also asks whether human beings have any real agency over these forces:

> It is a question whether the human will, of itself alone, ever has cured or ever can cure any human weakness. Tendencies are subtle things. They are involved in the chemistry of one's being, and those who delve in the mysteries of biology frequently find that curious anomaly, a form of minute animal life born to be the prey of another form of animal life—chemically and physically attracted to its own disaster.[82]

The protagonist's course toward inevitable disaster is resolved only by an adjustment of this chaotic configuration of body and mind, desire and will. The final third of *The "Genius"* proceeds as follows: Eugene recovers from neurasthenia and launches a career as a commercial artist, first in advertising and then in magazine publishing, embracing the world of commodity by becoming one of those creators of desire.[83] He and Angela remain childless, and for a time it seems that the protagonist has found a way of restraining his impulses. When Eugene reaches the pinnacle of his career and he and Angela become the toast of the New York social scene, his eye once again wanders, landing on the young, beautiful, and sophisticated Suzanne Dale. Richard Lingemann characterizes Dreiser's affair with Thelma Cudlipp, whom Suzanne represents, as a sort of midlife crisis, calling the author "acutely, even neurotically conscious of the passage of time."[84] Thelma/Suzanne is a desperate grasp for a taste of youth and beauty, a desire so profound that Theodore/Eugene sacrifices his career and social standing for it. The girl's mother, both in the novel and in real life, alerts Theodore/Eugene's employers to the affair, and Theodore/Eugene is fired. She also convinces the girl to wait a year before seeking some sort of formal arrangement with her paramour, enough time for her desire to cool.[85] In the novel, Eugene's willingness to trim and compromise and his failure to sweep her off her feet, all evidence that he was not "so powerful" as she had imagined, "so much a law unto himself," cause her to reconsider.[86] Meanwhile, "the fullness of what he [Eugene] had been doing began to dawn upon him dimly."[87] Angela succeeds in getting pregnant against Eugene's wishes, and she dies in what was surely one of the most graphic depictions of traumatic childbirth up to that date. It is in the midst of this crisis, a crisis that brings the contingency and consequences of desire into focus that Eugene is introduced to Christian Science.[88]

CHRISTIAN SCIENCE AS SOLUTION TO THE PROBLEM OF DESIRE

Those who were attracted to metaphysical or mental healing found two separate ways to account for the problem of desire. The first, associated with Eddy and her closest followers, was simply to deny its true existence. If matter was not actually real, then desire was only an illusion that could be suppressed by the assertion of the power of Divine Mind. Moreover, "[Eddy] equated the spiritual and the scientific, promoted salvific self-denial rather than aggressive self-assertion, and predicted the final triumph of spiritual 'Woman' over manly desire."[89] The second form, associated with Warren Felt Evans and New Thought, embraced desire as a productive force and gradually evolved into "positive thinking." It is the first form that Eugene Witla encounters in the final chapters of The "Genius."

When Myrtle, Eugene's sister, attempts to use "her knowledge of science to effect a rehabilitation for her brother" at Angela's request, the problem she directly addresses is his wandering eye.[90] While Eugene resists attempts to pathologize his desire, both he and the authorial voice of the novel entertain the possibility that he might find "relief" from it through the study of Mary Baker Eddy's works. At a Christian Science service, he hears the testimony of a man who seems to be very much like himself. Like Eugene, this man threw off the religious principles of his father and led a life of dissipation. He gambled and drank, but "my great weakness was women.... I pursued women as I would any other lure. They were really all that I desired—their bodies. My lust was terrible. It was such a dominant thought with me that I could not look at any good-looking woman except, as the Bible says, to lust after her." The man describes the outcome of his philandering by saying only, "I became diseased." He saw many doctors who were unable to heal him completely and was ultimately "carried into the First Church of Christ Scientist in Chicago," where he became "a well man—not well physically only, but well mentally, and, what is better yet, in so far as I can see the truth, spiritually." Eugene is impressed with this man, not only because of his story but because of his appearance: "He was no beggar or tramp, but a man of some profession—an engineer, very likely." A sense of kinship with this man—"He personally never was diseased, but how often he had looked after a perfectly charming woman to lust after her!"—precipitates his first serious reading of Science and Health. The fact that Eugene seems to pinpoint his promiscuity as the disease to be cured makes it clear that he considers Christian Science a means of "curing" his desire.[91]

Eugene reads Science and Health and considers its claims about the unreality of matter alongside what he takes to be complementary claims by Carlyle, Marcus Aurelius, and Kant as well as the writings of contemporary physicist Edgar Lucien Larkin, who argues that "this micro-universe is rooted and grounded in a mental base."[92] This begins a long philosophical section in which the protagonist finally reaches "a pretty fair confirmation of Mrs. Eddy's contention that all was mind and its infinite variety and that the only difference between her and the British scientific naturalists was that they contended for an ordered hierarchy . . . whereas, she contended for a governing spirit."[93] Ultimately, he comes to see Christian Science as a possible solution to multiple problems pertaining to his marriage, his affair with Suzanne, and his depression. He takes heart in the fact that "Christian Science set aside marriage entirely as a human illusion," alluding to the belief that Mind rendered human reproduction and consequently sex and marriage obsolete.[94]

He visits a practitioner and wonders if her methods would "make him not want Suzanne ever any more? Perhaps that was evil? Yes, no doubt it was. Still. . . . Divinity could aid him if it would. Certainly it could. No doubt of it."[95] After he returns home, his eyes fall upon the following passage from *Science and Health*: "Carnal beliefs defraud us. They make man an involuntary hypocrite—producing evil when he would create good, forming deformity when he would outline grace and beauty, injuring those whom he would bless. He becomes a general mis-creator, who believes he is a semi-God. His touch turns hope to dust, the dust we have all trod."[96] Eugene, applying these allusions to carnality, creation, and the distortion of beauty to his own situation, once again wonders whether Divine Principle might conquer his desire for Suzanne, though he is unsure whether he actually wants this outcome.

After this period of reflection, Angela's moment of crisis arrives. Already weakened by a nervous breakdown brought on by the Suzanne affair, Angela is not expected to survive the delivery of the child she conceived in order to make Eugene stay. The wrenching depiction of surgical delivery that follows serves as another reminder of the physical consequences of sex and of the catastrophic implications of both Eugene's wandering eye and Angela's futile attempts to keep him. Seeing her torment, Eugene is struck by "the subtlety and terror of this great scheme of reproduction, which took all women to the door of the grave, in order that this mortal scheme of things might be continued. He began to think that there might be something in the assertion of the Christian Science leaders that it was a lie and an illusion, a terrible fitful fever outside the rational conscious-ness of God."[97] As Satter reveals, many women embraced the anti-desire aspects of Christian Science as a way of escaping the biological horrors of compulsory heterosexuality: unwanted sexual relations and pregnancy, a condition that was frequently life threatening.[98]

Christian Science does not liberate or cure Angela, though her doctors are also unable to save her. In the end, Dreiser brings his hero to a philo-sophical place that is neither wholly in line with Christian Science nor wholly in line with scientific materialism. The latter, in fact, seems to be as horrifying in its practical implications as Christian Science is improb-able. As Eugene watches the doctors perform a Caesarean section, what most horrifies him is the utter absence of dignity or humanity. Angela, as the patient, becomes a nonperson, the doctors mere mechanics: "They were working like carpenters, cabinet workers, electricians. Angela might have been a clay figure for all they seemed to care." Even the child "might have been a skinned rabbit."[99] Yet this confrontation with mortality as well as the realization that humans are, in a very real way, helpless to overcome its inevitability no matter what theory of mind and body they embrace, brings Eugene to a place of peace. He reconciles with Angela in the mo-ments before her death and embraces sentimental fatherhood, raising his daughter alone. He continues to visit Mrs. Johns, the Christian Science practitioner, even though he can never wholeheartedly believe in what she teaches. In the end, he becomes something of a religious and philosophical eclectic, "an artist who, pagan to the core, enjoyed reading the Bible for its artistry of expression, and Schopenhauer, Nietzsche, Spinoza and James for the mystery of things which they suggested."[100]

This may be very like what Dreiser hoped for himself. As his later novels, particularly *The Bulwark*, demonstrate, the author retained an interest in religion and metaphysics. Christian Science never cured him of his sexual varietism, though it (accompanied by the wisdom of experience) may have helped him make peace with it. As the authorial voice of the novel declares, "the need for religion is impermanent, like all else in life," including desire.[101]

Christian Science, whatever else it might have been, was a strategy for dealing with human frailty and mortality. And for Dreiser, it appears that it never was more than that—"a bandage that man invented to protect a soul made bloody by circumstance" and a bandage that must eventually come off.[102] What we can learn from the Christian Science section of *The "Genius"* is just how deeply he was willing to probe those possibilities and how those preoccupations put him in direct conversation with larger nineteenth- and early twentieth-century concerns about body and mind, desire and rational will, concerns that spanned religious and scientific discourses. This novel unveils the complexities of Dreiser's negotiations with his body, sexuality, and masculinity. Though it is abundantly clear from his biography that Dreiser never fully embraced the model of restraint or passionlessness promoted by some Christian Scientists and social purity advocates, *The "Genius"* suggests that he shared their concerns about desire as both a personal and social problem.

The Dreiser of a certain critical imagination is a Dreiser who flouted convention, who pushed back against Victorian prudery, who championed naturalistic, scientific thinking and shunned moralistic sentimentality. This moment in *The "Genius"* challenges that perception. It presents us with a Dreiser who was profoundly insecure about his philosophical and religious orientation and about his own masculinity, a Dreiser who was attempting to navigate that uncertain territory in print without arriving at any firm conclusions, leaving us instead with a hero who both embraces and restrains his desire, who can mentally accommodate both Eddy and Spencer.

NOTES

This chapter originally appeared in a somewhat different form in L. Ashley Squires, "The Tragedy of Desire: Christian Science in Theodore Dreiser's *The 'Genius,'*" *American Literary Realism* 45, no. 2 (Fall 2013): 328–48.

1. Originally a character in Thomas Morton's *Speed the Plough* (1798), Mrs. Grundy became a common symbol for the forces of moral conservatism, priggishness, and censorship in the nineteenth century.

2. Stephen Alison, "Christian Science versus Organization: An Open Letter to Upton Sinclair," *Christian Scientist* 3, no. 1 (September 1918): 2. Sinclair's response to the Open Letter appears in the October 1918 edition of the *Christian Scientist* and reads as follows: "Dear Comrade—I have read with interest your friendly open letter. I could not say all I had to say about Christian Science in the magazine. You will find more in the book. I have read *Science and Health*. I cannot go with it because I don't believe in any sort of metaphysics. I have given my reasons in the latter part of 'The Profits of Religion.' I went through the whole game when I was in college—the metaphysics game I mean. There is nothing in it for me. Sincerely,

U. Sinclair." Alison prints his own very lengthy response. See "Metaphysics, Socialism, and Religion: A Second Open Letter to Upton Sinclair," *Christian Scientist* 3, no. 2 (October 1918): 1.

3. Richard Lingemann, *Theodore Dreiser: An American Journey* (New York: Wiley, 1993), 264. The other major (recent) biography of Dreiser is Jerome Loving, *The Last Titan: A Life of Theodore Dreiser* (Berkeley: University of California Press, 2005).

4. Jerome Loving, "Theodore Dreiser: The Genius," *American Literary Realism* 43, no. 1 (Fall 2010): 84.

5. Rachel Bowlby, *Just Looking: Consumer Culture in Dreiser, Gissing and Zola* (New York: Routledge, 2009), 72.

6. See Clare Eby, "Historical Commentary," in Theodore Dreiser, *The Genius*, edited by Clare Virginia Eby (Chicago: University of Illinois Press, 2008), 763.

7. See Rahindra Mookerjee's theory of "two Dreisers" in *Theodore Dreiser: His Thought and Social Criticism* (Delhi: National, 1974), and chap. 1 of Walter Benn Michaels, *The Gold Standard and the Logic of Naturalism* (Berkeley: University of California Press, 1987).

8. Theodore Dreiser, *Dreiser's Russian Diary*, edited by Thomas Riggio and James L. West III (Philadelphia: University of Pennsylvania Press, 1996). See also Theodore Dreiser, *Dreiser Looks at Russia* (New York: Liveright, 1928), and Ruth Epperson Kennell, *Theodore Dreiser and the Soviet Union, 1927–1945: A First-Hand Chronicle* (New York: International, 1969).

9. Michael David-Fox, *Showcasing the Great Experiment: Cultural Diplomacy and Western Visitors to the Soviet Union, 1921–1941* (New York: Oxford University Press, 2012), 143.

10. Lingemann, *Theodore Dreiser*, 546.

11. Eby, "Introduction," 763.

12. Theodore Dreiser, *Selected Magazine Articles of Theodore Dreiser: Life and Art in the American 1890's*, edited by Yoshinobu Hakutani (Cranbury, NJ: Associated University Presses, 1985), 275.

13. Theodore Dreiser, *Jennie Gerhardt*, edited by James L. W. West (Philadelphia: University of Pennsylvania Press, 1992), 403.

14. Theodore Dreiser, *A Traveler at Forty*, edited by Renate von Bardeleben (Champaign: University of Illinois Press, 2004), 244–45.

15. Theodore Dreiser, *A Hoosier Holiday* (New York: Lane, 1916), 52.

16. Qtd. in Louis Zanine, *Mechanism and Mysticism: The Influence of Science on the Thought and Work of Theodore Dreiser* (Philadelphia: University of Pennsylvania Press, 1993), 181.

17. Lingemann, *Theodore Dreiser*, 249. This series was not well received. It was considered blasphemous by many religious readers and preposterous by skeptics. He was ultimately forced to withdraw the series.

18. Zanine, *Mechanism and Mysticism*, 141.

19. Theodore Dreiser, *The "Genius"* (New York: Garden City, 1923), 689. Though I have consulted the 1911 holograph edition in the preparation of this manuscript, all quotations— except where indicated—are from the edition originally published in 1915.

20. Ibid., 694.

21. Ibid., 699.

22. Zanine, *Mechanism and Mysticism*, 180.

23. Lingemann, *Theodore Dreiser*, 264.

24. A reference to *Plays of the Natural and Supernatural*, a series of "reading plays" composed while *The "Genius"* was in production.

25. Theodore Dreiser, *Letters of Theodore Dreiser: A Selection, Vol. 1*, edited by Robert H. Elias (Philadelphia: University of Pennsylvania Press, 1959), 335.

26. Ibid., 336.

27. Ibid., 336–37.

28. Satter, *Each Mind a Kingdom*, 26.

29. Herbert Spencer, Social Statics, *together with* The Man versus the State (New York: Appleton, 1899), 137.

30. Satter, *Each Mind a Kingdom*, 27.

31. Gail Bederman, *Manliness and Civilization: A Cultural History of Gender and Race in the United States, 1880–1917* (Chicago: University of Chicago Press, 1995), 7.

32. Satter, *Each Mind a Kingdom*, 27.

33. Ibid., 28.

34. Bederman, *Manliness and Civilization*, 12.

35. George Miller Beard, *American Nervousness: Its Causes and Consequences* (New York: Putnam, 1881).

36. Barbara Ehrenreich and Deirdre English, *Complaints and Disorders: The Sexual Politics of Sickness* (New York: Feminist Press, 1973), 27.

37. Bederman, *Manliness and Civilization*, 12.

38. Ehrenreich and English, *Complaints and Disorders*, 28.

39. Satter, *Each Mind a Kingdom*, 33. According to Bederman, "middle-class manliness had been created in the context of a small-scale, competitive capitalism which had all but disappeared by 1910. Between 1870 and 1910, the proportion of middle class men who were self-employed dropped from 67 percent to 37 percent. At the same time, the rapid expansion of low-level clerical work in stores and offices meant that young men beginning their careers as clerks were unlikely to gain promotion to responsible, well-paid management positions, as their fathers had." Bederman, *Manliness and Civilization*, 12.

40. Satter, *Each Mind a Kingdom*, 35.

41. Bederman, *Manliness and Civilization*, 13.

42. Satter, *Each Mind a Kingdom*, 35.

43. Ibid., 40.

44. Charlotte Perkins Stetson, *Women and Economics* (Boston: Small, Maynard, 1900), 162–63.

45. The argument against forced pregnancy within marriage appropriated evolutionary rhetoric as well: "Men who impregnated their wives against their will or, even worse, who made sexual demands while their wives were pregnant produced offspring who were sickly and doomed to inherit the sensual passions of their fathers, they argued." Satter, *Each Mind a Kingdom*, 41.

46. Ibid., 44.

47. This is Satter's terminology.

48. Ralph Waldo Trine was one prominent contemporary who made the argument for bringing together New Thought and Christian socialism. For more on the socialist dimensions of New Thought, see chap. 7 of Albanese, *Republic of Mind and Spirit*.

49. George B. Day, "Sheep, Shepherd, and Shepherdess," August 1887 (Georgine Milmine Collection, Mary Baker Eddy Library for the Betterment of Humanity, Boston). The location of Day's address is significant. One year later, Mary Baker Eddy would deliver what is widely considered to be one of the most important speeches of her career before Christian Scientists in Chicago. It was so successful, that Eddy considered relocating her entire Boston organization there. But Chicago was also the home of Eddy's former students and rivals, Emma Curtis Hopkins and Ursula Gestefeld, and thus the city would become a particularly fraught space

where her authority would be contested in the ensuing years. Notably, Chicago was also the home of Theodore Dreiser, and the First Church of Christ, Scientist in Chicago is the first Christian Science Church that Eugene Witla attends.

50. They do cover the work of F. L. Rawson, who cooperated extensively with New Thought. The reason for this, however, is emblematic of the difficulty of preserving a too-rigid boundary between the two movements. Rawson was a British engineer who was commissioned by the *Daily Mail* to study Christian Science and write a series of articles about it at the time that it was becoming famous. In the process of studying it, he became a convert, though his writing on Christian Science was rejected by the Mother Church because of an official embargo on any Christian Science writing except Mary Baker Eddy's, a policy that was extremely controversial within the church throughout the twentieth century. Rawson therefore turned to New Thought in order to get his work out. Horatio Dresser himself declared Rawson's thinking to be "almost identical with Christian Science," and one can find corners of the web where Christian Scientists use Rawson as a case example of just how damaging the embargo on outside teaching has been to the modern church. See Horatio Dresser, *A History of the New Thought Movement* (New York: Crowell, 1919), 264, and "Frederick L. Rawson and the Christian Science Movement," Mary Baker Eddy Institute, 12 August 2015, http://mbein stitute.org/Articles/RAWSON.pdf. Rawson's most important work is *Life Understood: From a Scientific and Religious Point of View* (New York: Cosimo Classics, 2007).

51. Stephen Alison, "Christian Socialism," *Christian Scientist* 2, no. 6 (February 1918): 2.

52. "Notes Kept by One of Mrs. Eddy's Students from Her Teaching on the Money Thought," *Christian Scientist* 1, no. 1 (September 1916): 5–6.

53. Alison, "Christian Socialism," 2.

54. "Notes Kept," 6.

55. Satter, *Each Mind a Kingdom*, 152.

56. Ibid.

57. Theodore Dreiser, *Dawn* (New York: Horace Liveright, 1931), 265.

58. Ibid., 268.

59. Lingemann, *Theodore Dreiser*, 31.

60. Dreiser, *The "Genius,"* 246.

61. Beard, *American Nervousness*, vi.

62. Dreiser, *The "Genius,"* 252.

63. Lingemann, *Theodore Dreiser*, 194.

64. Dreiser, *Dawn*, 249.

65. Lingemann, *Theodore Dreiser*, 56.

66. Ibid., 246.

67. Ibid., 59.

68. Dreiser, *The "Genius,"* 122.

69. Ibid., 181.

70. Ibid., 183.

71. Lingemann, *Theodore Dreiser*, 118.

72. Dreiser had himself experienced and witnessed these dramatic cycles, having sunk to the point of starvation and homelessness after the publication of *Sister Carrie*. He also watched his brother Paul, a famous songwriter, lose his fortune and social position, dying without even enough money for the funeral.

73. Ibid., 278.

74. Dreiser, *The "Genius,"* 298.

75. Ibid., 127.

76. Ibid.

77. Ibid., 157.

78. Ibid.

79. Ibid., 181.

80. Ibid., 285.

81. Ibid, 286.

82. Ibid., 285.

83. This episode is based on Dreiser's career at *The Delineator*, which ends following his unconsummated affair with Thelma Cudlipp.

84. Lingemann, *Theodore Dreiser*, 246.

85. Dreiser portrays Suzanne Dale as far more sexually sophisticated and unconventional than Thelma Cudlipp was in real life, possibly a moment of wishful thinking or projection. In actuality, Thelma became horrified by the intensity of Dreiser's need for her, having "blundered into a terrifying grown-ups' world with lurking monsters of convention and sexuality. . . . To make sure that Thelma did not elope with Dreiser on her own, as Thelma recounts in her unpublished memoir, her mother had a friend tell her all about sex and 'man's desire.' It was evidently a graphic lesson, laced with Victorian horrors, for it left Thelma disgusted and angry at Dreiser for wanting to subject her to such a nasty business." Lingemann, *Theodore Dreiser*, 251.

86. Dreiser, *The "Genius,"* 671.

87. Ibid., 669.

88. In the 1911 version of the novel, which never came to print until the publication of Clare Eby's scholarly edition in 2008, Eugene and Suzanne ultimately reunite in a highly sentimental moment. In the official 1915 and 1923 versions, this separation is permanent.

89. Satter, *Each Mind a Kingdom*, 58.

90. Though his problem does later manifest physically as "a new pain in his groin, which had come to him first when her mother first carried Suzanne off to Canada and he was afraid that he should never see her any more. It was a real pain, sharp, physical, like the cut of a knife. He wondered how it was that it could be physical and down there. His eyes hurt him and his finger tips. Wasn't that queer, too?" Dreiser, *The "Genius,"* 687.

91. Ibid., 691–92.

92. Ibid., 697.

93. Ibid., 699.

94. Ibid., 701.

95. Ibid., 708.

96. Ibid., 709.

97. Ibid., 712.

98. For another perspective on the health reform movement and the ideology of female passionlessness as a method of self-defense, see chap. 2 of Regina Morantz-Sanchez, *Sympathy and Science: Women Physicians in American Medicine* (New York: Oxford University Press, 1985).

99. Dreiser, *The "Genius,"* 720.

100. Ibid., 734.

101. Ibid.

102. Ibid., 734.

Conclusion

In 1906, Mark Twain returned to his memoirs after a two-year hiatus and began quoting from and commenting on pieces of a biography his daughter Susy had written about him when she was very young. His autobiographical dictation of Thursday, December 27, 1906, includes the following excerpt (original spelling and punctuation preserved):

> Yes the Mind Cure *does* seem to be working wonderfully, papa who has been using glasses now, for more than a year, has laid them off entirely. And my nearsightedness is realy getting better. It seems marvelous! When Jean has stomack ache Clara and I have tried to divert her, by telling her to lie on her side and try Mind Cure. The novelty of it, has made her willing to try it, and then Clara and I would exclaim about how wonderful it was it was getting better! And she would think it realy was finally, and stop crying, to our delight.

For a few pages, Clemens waxes philosophical on the efficacy of mind cure, which he also calls Christian Science: "It is true that the Mind Cure worked wonders. For a million years the mind has been, in a large degree, master of the body, and has been able to heal many of the body's ailments." He specifically credits the mental method with the alleviation of pain: "To divert the mind from a physical pain, or from a mental one, by the introduction of a new interest, *must* bring relief, because the mind cannot give full and effective attention to two subjects at the same time." Though uncertain that mind cure would be able to heal broken bones, he expresses himself as "quite certain that Christian Science heals many physical and mental ills; but I also feel just as certain that it could call itself by any other name and do the same work without any diminution of its effectiveness."[1]

I have placed Twain at the beginning, middle, and end of this book because he suggests many of its organizing themes. One of these is grief. At the time when Samuel Clemens dictated this entry, Susy had been dead for ten years, having succumbed to meningitis at age twenty-four. And the two-year hiatus that ended in 1906 was occasioned by the death of Olivia Clemens, his wife:

> The dictating of this autobiography, which was begun in Florence in the beginning of 1904, was soon suspended because of the anxieties of the time, and I was never moved to resume the work until January 1906, for I did not see how I was ever going to bring myself to speak in detail of the mournful episodes and experiences of that desolate interval and of the twenty-two months of wearing distress which preceded it.

In fact, those years of distress reached back even further. In the pages immediately subsequent to this explanation, he looks to 1896: "We finally finished our lecture-raid on the 14th of July '96, sailed for England the next day, and landed at Southampton on the 31st. A fortnight later Mrs. Clemens and Clara sailed for home to nurse Susy through a reported illness, and found her in her coffin in her grandmother's house."[2]

These passages on mind cure and Christian Science are haunted. Clemens, as he contemplates the efficacy of Christian Science, is surrounded by ghosts. And throughout this study of what William James called the religion of the "healthy-minded" (contrasted with the religion of the "sick soul"), I find texts that are steeped in grief of the most excruciating kind.[3] The memory of a lost child accompanied Frances Hodgson Burnett throughout the writing of A Little Princess, The Dawn of a To-morrow, and The Secret Garden, texts in which children are the agents and beneficiaries of healing. Burnett sought relief from years of depression and sickness, as did Dreiser, who also looked to Christian Science to overcome the human frailty that threatened to overwhelm his life. Clemens says that he believes Christian Science can alleviate pain, and it is not too much of a reach to extrapolate that to the pain of existence, the anguish of being a conscious thing in a mortal body.

One can argue that the middle of the nineteenth century altered the rational and spiritual orientation of Americans toward death and contingency. This, at least, is what Drew Gilpin Faust suggests in *This Republic of Suffering*: "In the middle of the nineteenth century, the United States embarked on a new relationship with death, entering into a civil war that proved bloodier than any other conflict in American history, a war that would presage the slaughter of World War I's Western Front and the global carnage of the twentieth century."[4] In addition to losses on the battlefield, the Civil War introduced a scale of suffering to the home front that would never be replicated in any subsequent war involving the United States. Mary Baker Eddy was herself touched by it. As Amy Voorhees indicates, "it dominated her life in the 1860s. The war was, in fact, her impetus for contacting Quimby, the new doctor in Portland.... The news of her husband's capture by Confederate forces was the tipping point."[5]

And yet the second theme that Twain suggests is the hope of healing. As I said in chapter 3, scholars often look to the author's biography to explain his attitude toward Christian Science, but this is primarily done in order to explain his rage. When Mary Baker Eddy is the subject of Twain's mockery—and she appears a few times in the autobiography—there is little sense of the personal in any of it. On June 20, 1906, Twain mocks an article defending the doctrine of immaculate conception by Rev. Briggs in *North American Review*: "If the Immaculate Conception could be repeated in New York to-day, there isn't a man, woman, or child, of those four millions, who would believe it—except perhaps some addled Christian Scientist. A person who can believe in Mother Eddy wouldn't strain at an Immaculate Conception, or six of them in a bunch."[6] Clemens believed in the power of the mind, but he remained a believer in the fundamental reality of the material world. And he couldn't go all in for Mary Baker Eddy's apocalyptic vision of her new faith or for the more outlandish, deifying claims of some of her followers. He delighted in poking fun at these more extreme elements of Christian Science.

But when Twain talks about healing in the context of his family and his personal life, he backs down from his comedic register, and instead of mockery and skepticism, we find openness, acceptance, and hope, however attenuated. Mental healing was certainly connected with Susy in her father's mind. Or, at least, it is through his quotation of her that we learn the most about his interest in it. "Papa has been very much interested of late, in the 'Mind Cure' theory. And in fact so have we all," she wrote on March 14, 1886, in an entry that was transcribed by Clemens on December 21, 1906. She continues, "I shouldn't wonder if we finally became firm believers in Mind Cure. The next time papa has a cold, I haven't a doubt, he will send for Miss Holden the young lady who is doctoring in the 'Mind Cure' theory, to cure him of it."[7]

The final theme is contingency. Neither mind cure nor Christian Science saved Susy, but it is not clear that her father ever expected them to or ever blamed them for not doing so. He certainly thought that there was something to it all, but his sense of what such methods could accomplish was limited, and a belief in mind cure did not stop the Clemens family from experimenting with a host of other alternative treatments. Devout Christian Scientists, however, took this reconfigured relationship between the mind and material reality and translated it into a new way of understanding the self and the world, which proved amenable to other ideas about how to move the nation and the human race forward. Christian Scientists wed their theology to journalism, which sought to improve human beings and societies through information. Socialists and feminists used Christian Science (sometimes in unsanctioned forms) and New Thought to critique economic injustice and prevailing attitudes toward gender and even race.[8]

Christian Science, in other words, provided a unified way of understanding complex human experiences. It linked various forms of embodied suffering—the diseases of society as well as the diseases of the body—and provided a direct path to wellness. Its narratives were characterized by their comforting smoothness and satisfying sense of closure: "I once was blind, but now I see." This tendency to produce narratives that reduce all problems to one essential problem and chart the way forward along a single bright path is a feature that Christian Science shares with many of modernity's other master narratives, including the restitution narratives of medicine, with their "single-minded telos of cure."[9] Positioning health as the body's natural state of being, the restitution narrative charts a path from loss to recovery, tracking the interventions of professionals and treatments along the way back to wellness. Journalists provided an analog to this sort of narrative, suggesting that the healing of the nation could be achieved through their profession's diagnoses and suggested remedies. The stories that they told rendered the complexities of social problems legible and remediable by assigning them to discrete pathologies, such as the malignant personality of an oil magnate or a demagogic religious leader.

This is why I find narrative to be such a compelling way of approaching a phenomenon like Christian Science, which made so many of its most compelling appeals through stories and served as an occasion for the production of other stories that linked health and spirituality to the various other ills plaguing the United States in a moment of transition. Narrative provides coherence, suggests connections, rationalizes the irrational, and renders certain kinds of endings almost inevitable—if Colin Craven believes he is well, then he can get well. Looking at Christian Science through the lens of narrative also allows us to mark the places where that coherence starts to fall apart, where the smoothness of narrative becomes too smooth. As I said in chapter 1, the stories of people who died in the care of Christian Scientists are contested, foreclosed, and often ignored, but they speak to the anguish that occurs when the source of all one's hopes proves wholly inadequate to fulfill its promises.

The impossibility of closure becomes most apparent in Twain's writing about Christian Science. His precise feelings about Mary Baker Eddy will probably always remain a bit mysterious. Albert Bigelow Paine, who wrote Twain's authorized biography, once wrote to the author that Christian Science had been a great help to him:

> When I confessed, rather reluctantly, one day, the benefit I had received, he surprised me by answering:
>
>> "Of course you have been benefited. Christian Science is humanity's boon. Mother Eddy deserves a place in the Trinity as much as any member of it. She has organized and made available a healing principle that for two thousand years has never been employed, except as the merest kind of guesswork. She is the benefactor of the age."
>
> It seemed strange, at the time, to hear him speak in this way concerning a practice of which he was generally regarded as the chief public antagonist. It was another angle of his many-sided character.[10]

This seeming change of heart is strange only if one expects a person's sentiments about a thing so complexly woven into one's life to remain stable.

His nonlinear, sometimes meandering, but deeply sincere autobiography demonstrates that Twain's views on many subjects were mutable. A story in which Susy Clemens, Christian Scientist, dies of meningitis and her father makes himself Mary Baker Eddy's number one enemy, committing himself to liberating the world from her tyranny, simply does not emerge from the available evidence. It is no more present than a story in which mental healing fixes Samuel Clemens's eyesight, as his daughter thought it would. That kind of coherence, that promise of closure, is frustratingly elusive.

This is why it is significant that when Twain critiques Christian Science, he folds it into broader critiques of modernity. What is ridiculous about Dr. Briggs's belief in the Immaculate Conception, for Twain, isn't just the belief itself but the fact that Briggs's article is a risible attempt to provide a kind of rationalist, even pseudo-scientific, explanation for it: "If there is anything more amusing than the Immaculate Conception doctrine, it is the quaint reasonings whereby ostensibly intelligent human beings persuade themselves that the impossible fact is proven." In other words, he derides Briggs's argument as faulty reasoning designed to shore up an unprovable belief, something Briggs would never be willing to do if "asked to believe in the Immaculate Conception process as exercised in the cases of Krishna, Osiris, and Buddha."[11]

This tendency to delude ourselves, to rationalize the irrational, is a human attribute that Twain wrestled with throughout his writings. Twain may have acquired this belief empirically, by merely observing his fellow man. But it was a conclusion about human nature that many of his contemporaries (including his friends) were reaching simultaneously. The advancement of science as a set of discrete disciplinary fields of inquiry prompted a great deal of contemplation about the nature of that inquiry itself, about how humans acquire knowledge, about what was provable and what was not. William James blended his laboratory studies with philosophy in order to better understand not only the origin but the function of ideas. According to Louis Menand, he "believed that scientific inquiry, like any other form of inquiry, is an activity inspired and informed by our tastes, values, and hopes. But this does not, in his view, confer any special authority on the conclusions it reaches. On the contrary: it obligates us to regard those conclusions as provisional and partial, since it was for provisional and partial reasons that we undertook to find them."[12]

The invention of statistics sought to quantify the errors produced by human attempts to observe and understand their world. It demanded that measurements be thought of as approximations, capable of being correct not in the absolute but within varying degrees of probability. For a nineteenth-century mathematician like Charles Pierce, what this meant is that better (more probably true) conclusions are arrived at not through individual inquiries but in the aggregate: "Each mind reflects differently— even the same mind reflects differently at different moments—and in any case reality doesn't stand still long enough to be accurately mirrored. Pierce's conclusion was that knowledge must therefore be social."[13] But narrative in the nineteenth century was primarily concerned with the plight of the individual, and perhaps this is why, for Twain, human proneness to error and self-delusion meant that humans were simply doomed to repeat the same mistakes over and over again. *Connecticut Yankee* ends with the horrifying, vaguely prophetic vision of human self-annihilation through modern warfare and of a misguided hero who ultimately doesn't learn anything from participating in it. The dystopia of *Eddypus* remains frozen in Twain's unfinished fragment.

It's a cliché of postmodernism to hold up discontinuity and lack of closure as a superior literary and philosophical virtue, over and against the violence done when a particular narrative is allowed to triumph. That's not really where I wish to leave this. If the closure of the Christian Science narrative and its foreclosure of negative outcomes feels disturbing, the same can be said of Twain's despair. James was always a bit more hopeful. For James, the function of beliefs and philosophies is not to arrive at absolute conformity to some platonic reality. Rather, in the words of Menand, "philosophy is a method of coping" and "what makes beliefs true is not logic but results."[14] James and many others judged mind cure and Christian Science on this basis, and according to this view, its narrative closure has its uses. Twain, despite all his cynicism about human nature, thought Christian Science a useful method for alleviating pain— physical, mental, and spiritual. And in the end, what worried him most about it never came to pass. The ending to the story that Twain never finished and never witnessed is ultimately that Christian Science did not dominate the world. Rather, it became merely one among humanity's many limited attempts to cope with our condition.

NOTES

1. Mark Twain, *Autobiography of Mark Twain, Volume 2: The Complete and Authoritative Edition* (Berkeley: University of California Press, 2010), 516–18.

2. Twain, *Autobiography, Vol. 2*, 133–34.

3. Lawrence Buell has taken James to task for placing Emerson in this group as well: "The thought that Emerson's serenity might have been wrung from melancholy and despair did not occur to William any more than it occurred to his father in 1842 that the ritual presentation of infant William might have felt excruciatingly painful to Emerson, coming little more than a month after the sudden death of his own first-born." But this line of critique could really apply to James's characterization of the entire category. Buell, *Emerson*, Kindle edition, loc. 1586.

4. Faust, *This Republic of Suffering*, xi.

5. Voorhees, "Writing Revelation," 31.

6. Twain, *Autobiography, Vol. 2*, 208.

7. Ibid., 498.

8. What, if anything significant, these movements had to say about race remains woefully underresearched, and admittedly the available primary sources make this a bit of a challenge. Amy Voorhees attempts it in her dissertation, and some of the work on Mina Loy has focused on the resources Christian Science provided her for combating racism and anti-Semitism. See Lara Vetter, "Theories of Spiritual Evolution, Christian Science, and the 'Cosmopolitan Jew': Mina Loy and American Identity," *Journal of Modern Literature* 31, no. 1 (2007): 47–63. The groundwork on the conversion of Jewish Americans to Christian Science and eventually Jewish Science is contained in Ellen Umansky, *From Christian Science to Jewish Science: Spiritual Healing and American Jews* (New York: Oxford University Press, 2005).

9. Frank, *The Wounded Storyteller*, 83.

10. Albert Bigelow Paine, *Mark Twain: A Biography* (New York: Kolthof, 1912).

11. Twain, *Autobiography, Vol. 2*, 207.

12. Louis Menand, *The Metaphysical Club: A Story of Ideas in America* (New York: Farrar, Straus, and Giroux, 2001), 143–44.

13. Ibid., 195.

14. Ibid., 213.

BIBLIOGRAPHY

Abbot, Willis J. "A Force for Clean Journalism." Reprint from *The Quill*, 1933. Clipping, Christian Science Monitor Subject File, Mary Baker Eddy Library for the Betterment of Humanity, Boston.

Ahearn, Amy. "Engaging with the Political: Willa Cather, *McClure's Magazine*, and the Production of National Rhetoric." Dissertation, University of Nebraska, 2008.

Albanese, Catherine. *A Republic of Mind and Spirit: A Cultural History of American Metaphysical Religion*. New Haven, CT: Yale University Press, 2007.

Alison, Stephen. "Christian Science versus Organization: An Open Letter to Upton Sinclair." *Christian Scientist* 3, no. 1 (September 1918): 1–3.

———. "Christian Socialism." *Christian Scientist* 2, no. 6 (February 1918): 1–3.

———. "Metaphysics, Socialism, and Religion: A Second Open Letter to Upton Sinclair." *Christian Scientist* 3, no. 2 (October 1918): 1.

Bauman, Zygmunt. *Mortality, Immortality, and Other Life Strategies*. Stanford, CA: Stanford University Press, 1993.

Beam, Alex. "Appealing to a Higher Authority." *Boston Globe*. 9 June 2005.

Beard, George Miller. *American Nervousness: Its Causes and Consequences*. New York: Putnam, 1881.

Bederman, Gail. *Manliness and Civilization: A Cultural History of Gender and Race in the United States, 1880–1917*. Chicago: University of Chicago Press, 1995.

Bednarowski, Mary Farrell. "Outside the Mainstream: Women's Religion and Women Religious Leaders in Nineteenth-Century America." *Journal of the American Academy of Religion* 48, no. 2 (1980): 207–31.

Bell, Michael Davitt. *The Problem of American Realism: Studies in the Cultural History of a Literary Idea*. Chicago: University of Chicago Press, 1993.

Bennett, Bridget. *The Damnation of Harold Frederic: His Lives and Works*. New York: Syracuse University Press, 1997.

Bercovitch, Sacvan, ed. *The Cambridge History of American Literature, Vol. III: Prose Writing, 1860–1920*. Cambridge: Cambridge University Press, 2005.

Bledstein, Burton. *The Culture of Professionalism: The Middle Class and the Development of Higher Education in America*. New York: Norton, 1976.

Bowlby, Rachel. *Just Looking: Consumer Culture in Dreiser, Gissing and Zola.* New York: Routledge, 2009.

Braden, Charles S. *Christian Science Today: Power, Policy, Practice.* Dallas: Southern Methodist University Press, 1958.

Brooks, Joanna. "From Edwards to Baldwin: Heterodoxy, Discontinuity, and New Narratives of American Religious-Literary History." *American Literary History* 22, no. 2 (2010): 439–53.

Buell, Lawrence. *Emerson.* Boston: Harvard University Press, 2004. Kindle edition.

Burnett, Frances Hodgson. *The Dawn of a To-morrow.* New York: Scribner's, 1906. Project Gutenberg.

———. *A Little Princess.* New York: Penguin, 2014.

———. *The One I Knew the Best of All: A Memory of the Mind of a Child.* New York: Scribner's, 1893. Project Gutenberg.

———. *The Secret Garden.* New York: Norton, 2006.

Cabot, Richard C. "100 Christian Science Cures." *McClure's* 31, no. 3 (1908): 472–76.

Canham, Erwin. *Commitment to Freedom: The Story of the* Christian Science Monitor. Boston: Houghton Mifflin, 1958.

Case, Henry L. Letter to Frederick Peabody. 5 April 1903. Mark Twain Project, University of California at Berkeley.

Cather, Willa. Letter to Edwin Anderson. 24 November 1922. Letter 0649 in *A Calendar of the Letters of Willa Cather: An Expanded, Digital Edition,* edited by Andrew Jewell and Janis P. Stout, 2007–2010. The Willa Cather Archive, http://cather.unl.edu.

Cather, Willa, and Georgine Milmine. *The Life of Mary Baker G. Eddy and the History of Christian Science,* edited by David Stouck. Lincoln: University of Nebraska Press, 1993.

Chernow, Ron. *Titan: The Life of John D. Rockefeller, Sr.* New York: Vintage, 2004. Kindle edition.

"Christian Science and the Law." *Public: A Journal of Democracy* 1, no. 35 (3 December 1898): 7–8. Google Books.

"The Christian Scientist Fraud." *Medical and Surgical "Review of Reviews"* 1, no. 2 (November 1898): 86. Google Books.

Clark, Beverly Lyon. *Kiddie Lit: The Cultural Construction of Children's Literary in America.* Baltimore: Johns Hopkins University Press, 2003.

Clemens, Samuel. Letter to Dr. Hale. 1 November 1899. Mark Twain File, Mary Baker Eddy Library for the Betterment of Humanity, Boston.

———. Letter to Frederick Peabody. 5 December 1902. Mark Twain Project, University of California at Berkeley.

———. Letter to Joe Twichell. 4 April 1903. Mark Twain File, Mary Baker Eddy Library for the Betterment of Humanity, Boston.

Coe, A. S. "Modern Medical Science." *New York Medical Journal* (October 1889): 406–8. Google Books.

Collins, Keith S. *The Christian Science Monitor: Its History, Mission, and People.* Lebanon, NH: Nebbadoon Press, 2012.

Connery, Thomas. *Journalism and Realism: Rendering American Life.* Chicago: Northwestern University Press, 2011.

"Court Transcript: Woodbury v. Eddy." 1899. Typescript, Georgine Milmine Collection, Mary Baker Eddy Library for the Betterment of Humanity, Boston.

Cronkite, Walter. Letter to Erwin Canham. 30 April 1970. Christian Science Monitor Subject File, Mary Baker Eddy Library for the Betterment of Humanity, Boston.

Cushman, Philip. *Constructing the Self, Constructing America: A Cultural History of Psycho-therapy.* Boston: Addison-Wesley, 1995.

Darnton, Robert. *Mesmerism and the End of the Enlightenment in France.* Boston: Harvard University Press, 1986.

David-Fox, Michael. *Showcasing the Great Experiment: Cultural Diplomacy and Western Visitors to the Soviet Union, 1921–1941.* New York: Oxford University Press, 2012. Nook ebook.

Day, George B. "Sheep, Shepherd, and Shepherdess." August 1887. Georgine Milmine Collection, Mary Baker Eddy Library for the Betterment of Humanity, Boston.

"Declares Christian Science All a Fraud." *Sioux City Daily Tribune.* 1899. Newspaper clipping, Alfred Farlow Scrapbooks, Mary Baker Eddy Library for the Betterment of Humanity, Boston.

Deland, Paul. "Helpfulness—Keynote of Christian Science Monitor." Reprint from *The Quill,* 1925. Clipping, CSM Subject File, Mary Baker Eddy Library for the Betterment of Humanity, Boston.

Dicke, William. "Erwin Canham, Longtime Editor of the Christian Science Monitor, Dies." *New York Times,* 4 January 1982.

Dillon, J. "Medical Organization." *Journal of the Kansas Medical Society* 6, no. 8 (August 1906): 311–16.

"The Distress in Italy." *Christian Science Monitor,* 1 January 1909, p. 1.

Dittemore, John V. Letter to Edward Kimball. 31 October 1908. Typescript, Mary Baker Eddy Library for the Betterment of Humanity, Boston.

———. Letter to S. S. McClure. 14 November 1908. Typescript, Mary Baker Eddy Library for the Betterment of Humanity, Boston.

Dittemore, John V., and Ernest Sutherland Bates. *Mary Baker Eddy: The Truth and the Tradition.* New York: Knopf, 1932.

Dixon, Thomas, Geoffrey Cantor, and Stephen Pumfrey, eds. *Science and Religion: New Historical Perspectives.* New York: Cambridge University Press, 2010.

Dresser, Horatio. *A History of the New Thought Movement.* New York: Crowell, 1919.

Dreiser, Theodore. *Dreiser Looks at Russia.* New York: Liveright, 1928.

———. *Dreiser's Russian Diary,* edited by Thomas Riggio and James L. West III. Philadelphia: University of Pennsylvania Press, 1996.

———. *Dawn.* New York: Liveright, 1931.

———. *The Genius,* edited by Clare Virginia Eby. Chicago: University of Illinois Press, 2008.

———. *The Genius.* New York: Garden City, 1923.

———. *A Hoosier Holiday.* New York: Lane, 1916.

———. *Jennie Gerhardt,* edited by James L. W. West. Philadelphia: University of Pennsylvania Press, 1992.

———. *Letters of Theodore Dreiser: A Selection, Vol. 1,* edited by Robert H. Elias. Philadelphia: University of Pennsylvania Press, 1959.

———. *Selected Magazine Articles of Theodore Dreiser: Life and Art in the American 1890's,* edited by Yoshinobu Hakutani. Cranbury, NJ: Associated University Presses, 1985.

———. *A Traveler at Forty,* edited by Renate von Bardeleben. Champaign: University of Illinois Press, 2004.

Eddy, Mary Baker. *Advice to Healers: Selected Letters by Mary Baker Eddy.* Vols. 1–3. Mary Baker Eddy Library for the Betterment of Humanity, Boston.

———. Letter to Archibald McClellan. 22 January 1909. Outgoing Correspondence File, Mary Baker Eddy Library for the Betterment of Humanity, Boston.

————. *Retrospection and Introspection.* Boston: Stewart, 1912.

————. *Science and Health with Key to Scriptures.* Boston: Church of Christ, Scientist, 1910.

"Editorial Announcement." *McClure's* 28, no. 2 (December 1906): 216.

Ehrenreich, Barbara. *Bright-Sided: How Positive Thinking Is Undermining America.* New York: Picador, 2010.

Ehrenreich, Barbara, and Deirdre English. *Complaints and Disorders: The Sexual Politics of Sickness.* New York: Feminist Press, 1973.

————. *For Her Own Good: Two Centuries of the Experts' Advice to Women.* New York: Anchor, 1978.

Emerson, Ralph Waldo. *Nature, Addresses, and Lectures.* Vol. 1 of *The Collected Works of Ralph Waldo Emerson.* Boston: Harvard University Press, 1971.

Ender, Evelyn. *Sexing the Mind: Nineteenth-Century Fictions of Hysteria.* Ithaca, NY: Cornell University Press, 1995.

"Faith Cure Murders." *New York Times,* 11 November 1898. ProQuest Historical Newspapers.

Faust, Drew Gilpin. *This Republic of Suffering: Death and the American Civil War.* New York: Knopf, 2008.

Fessenden, Tracy. *Culture and Redemption.* Princeton, NJ: Princeton University Press, 2007.

Fiedler, Leslie. *Love and Death in the American Novel.* Champaign, IL: Dalkey Archive Press, 1998.

Fluck, Winfried. *Romance with America: Essays on Culture, Literature, and American Studies.* Heidelburg: Winter, 2009.

Foucault, Michel. *The Birth of the Clinic: An Archaeology of Medical Perception.* New York: Vintage, 1994.

Franchot, Jenny. "Religion and American Literary Studies." *American Literature* 67, no. 4 (1995): 833–42.

Frank, Arthur. *The Wounded Storyteller: Body, Illness, and Ethics.* Chicago: University of Chicago Press, 1995.

Fraser, Caroline. *God's Perfect Child: Living and Dying in Christian Science.* New York: Picador, 1999.

"Frederick L. Rawson and the Christian Science Movement." Mary Baker Eddy Institute. 12 August 2015. http://mbeinstitute.org/Articles/RAWSON.pdf.

Gerzina, Gretchen. *Frances Hodgson Burnett: The Unexpected Life of the Author of* The Secret Garden. New Brunswick, NJ: Rutgers University Press, 2004.

Gifford, Sanford. *The Emmanuel Movement: The Origins of Group Treatment and the Assault on Lay Psychotherapy.* Boston: Harvard University Press, 1996.

Gill, Gillian. *Mary Baker Eddy.* Reading, PA: Perseus, 1998.

Good, Howard S. "Epilogue: Muckraking and the Ethic of Caring." In *The Muckrakers: Evangelical Crusaders,* edited by Robert Miraldi. London: Praeger, 2000.

Gottschalk, Stephen. *The Emergence of Christian Science in American Religious Life.* Berkeley: University of California Press, 1978.

————. *Rolling Away the Stone: Mary Baker Eddy's Challenge to Materialism.* Bloomington: Indiana University Press, 2006.

Greenhouse, Lucia. *fathermothergod: My Journey out of Christian Science.* New York: Crown, 2001.

Grier, Peter. "Monitor Correspondent Wins Pulitzer." *Christian Science Monitor,* 10 April 1966.

Haber, Samuel. *The Quest for Authority and Honor in the American Professions: 1750–1900.* Chicago: University of Chicago Press, 1991.

Hansen, Penny. "Women's Hour: The Feminist Implications of Mary Baker Eddy's Christian Science Movement, 1885–1910." Dissertation, University of California Irvine, 1981.

"Harold Frederic and Christian Science." *Buffalo Medical Journal* 38, no. 5 (December 1898): 377–78. Google Books.

"Harold Frederic and the Christian Scientists." *The Outlook* 60, no. 12 (November 1898): 710. Google Books.

"The Harold Frederic Case." *Christian Science Journal* 26, no. 9 (December 1898): 622.

Harrington, Anne. *The Cure Within: A History of Mind-Body Medicine.* New York: Norton, 2008.

Hatch, Nathan O. *The Democratization of American Christianity.* New Haven, CT: Yale University Press, 1989.

H. G. W. "Church Healing." *Long Island Medical Journal* 10, no. 1 (1916): 490–91. Google Books.

Hutchison, William R. *Religious Pluralism in America: The Contentious History of a Founding Ideal.* New Haven, CT: Yale University Press, 2004.

James, William. *The Varieties of Religious Experience.* New York: Penguin, 1982.

Kaplan, Justin. *Lincoln Steffens: Portrait of a Great American Journalist.* New York: Simon and Schuster, 1974. Nook ebook.

Kennell, Ruth Epperson. *Theodore Dreiser and the Soviet Union, 1927–1945: A First-Hand Chronicle.* New York: International, 1969.

Kilmer, Val. *Mark Twain and Mary Baker Eddy.* Accessed June 14, 2015. http://twaineddyfilm .com.

Klassen, Pamela E. *Spirits of Protestantism: Medicine, Healing, and Liberal Christianity.* Berkeley: University of California Press, 2011. Nook ebook.

Klosterman, Chuck. "Crazy Things Seem Normal . . . Normal Things Seem Crazy." *Esquire,* 1 July 2005.

Kolko, Gregory. *The Triumph of Conservatism: A Reinterpretation of American History, 1900–1916.* New York: Free Press, 1963.

Latour, Bruno. *We Have Never Been Modern,* translated by Catherine Porter. Boston: Harvard University Press, 1993.

Levy, Andrew. *Huck Finn's America: Mark Twain and the Era That Shaped His Masterpiece.* New York: Simon and Schuster, 2014. Nook ebook.

"The Life of Mrs. Eddy." *McClure's.* Clipped magazine advertisement, Georgine Milmine Collection, Mary Baker Eddy Library for the Betterment of Humanity, Boston.

Lindley, Susan Hill. "The Ambiguous Feminism of Mary Baker Eddy." *Journal of Religion* 64, no. 3 (1984): 318–31.

Lingemann, Richard. *Theodore Dreiser: An American Journey.* New York: Wiley, 1993.

Lois, Keith. *Take Up Thy Bed and Walk: Disability and Cure in Classic Fiction for Girls.* New York: Routledge, 2001.

Loving, Jerome. *The Last Titan: A Life of Theodore Dreiser.* Berkeley: University of California Press, 2005.

———. "Theodore Dreiser: The Genius." *American Literary Realism* 43, no. 1 (Fall 2010): 84.

Mack, Edwin S. "The Law in Its Relation to Medicine." *Wisconsin Medical Journal* 1 (January 1903): 199. Google Books.

McDonald, Jean A. "Mary Baker Eddy and the Nineteenth-Century 'Public' Woman: A Feminist Reappraisal." *Journal of Feminist Studies in Religion* 2, no. 1 (1986): 89–111.

McGerr, Michael. *A Fierce Discontent: The Rise and Fall of the Progressive Movement in America.* New York: Oxford University Press, 2005. Nook ebook.

Menand, Louis. *The Metaphysical Club: A Story of Ideas in America.* New York: Farrar, Straus, and Giroux, 2001.

"A Message from the Trustees of the Christian Science Publishing Society." 16 March 1936. Memorandum, Christian Science Monitor Subject File, Mary Baker Eddy Library for the Betterment of Humanity, Boston.

Michaels, Walter Benn. *The Gold Standard and the Logic of Naturalism.* Berkeley: University of California Press, 1987.

———. *The Life of Mary Baker G. Eddy.* Long draft. 1905? Typescript, Georgine Milmine Collection, Mary Baker Eddy Library for the Betterment of Humanity, Boston.

———. "Mary Baker Eddy: The Story of Her Life and the History of Christian Science." *McClure's* 28, no. 2 (December 1906): 211–17; 28, no. 3 (January 1907): 227–42; 28, no. 4 (February 1907): 339–54; 28, no. 5 (March 1907): 506–25; 28, no. 5 (April 1907): 608–27; 29, no. 1 (May 1907): 97–116; 29, no. 2 (June 1907): 134; 29, no. 3 (July 1907): 333–48; 29, no. 4 (August 1907): 447–62; 29, no. 5 (September 1907): 567–81; 29, no. 6 (October 1907): 688–700; 30, no. 4 (February 1908): 387–401; 30, no. 5 (March 1908): 577–89; 30, no. 6 (April 1908): 699–712; 31, no. 1 (May 1908): 16–31; 31, no. 2 (June 1908): 179–89.

Mindich, David. *Just the Facts: How "Objectivity" Came to Define American Journalism.* New York: New York University Press, 2000.

Mitchell, S. Weir. *Autobiography of a Quack and Other Stories.* New York: Century, 1905.

"Monitor Judged 'Fairest' Survey Ranks U.S. Publications." *Christian Science Monitor,* 28 August 1970.

Mookherjee, Rahindra. *Theodore Dreiser: His Thought and Social Criticism.* Delhi: National, 1974.

Morantz-Sanchez, Regina. *Sympathy and Science: Women Physicians in American Medicine.* New York: Oxford University Press, 1985.

Morris, Christopher D. "The Deconstruction of the Enlightenment in Mark Twain's *A Connecticut Yankee in King Arthur's Court.*" *JNT: Journal of Narrative Theory* 39, no. 2 (Summer 2009): 159–85.

Morris, James McGrath. *Pulitzer: A Life in Politics, Print, and Power.* New York: HarperCollins, 2010. Nook ebook.

"New Note in Fiction." *Christian Science Monitor,* 7 January 1910.

"New York Letter." *Interstate Medical Journal* 11, no. 10 (October 1899): 534–35. Google Books.

Norris, Frank. "A Plea for Romantic Fiction." In *The Norton Anthology of American Literature,* 8th ed., Vol. C, edited by Nina Baym and Jerome Klinkowitz, 915. New York: Norton, 2007.

Norton, Carol. "Lecture in Concord." *Independent Statesman* (Concord, NH), January 5, 1899. Newspaper clipping, Alfred Farlow Scrapbooks, Mary Baker Eddy Library for the Betterment of Humanity, Boston.

"Notes from the Field." *Christian Science Journal* 9, no. 12 (March 1892): 512.

"Notes from the Field." *Christian Science Journal* 11, no. 5 (August 1893): 229.

"Notes from the Field." *Christian Science Journal* 11, no. 7 (October 1893): 326–27.

"Notes Kept by One of Mrs. Eddy's Students from Her Teaching on the Money Thought." *Christian Scientist* 1, no. 1 (September 1916): 5–6.

Notice from the *Granite State Free Press.* Clipping, Christian Science Monitor Subject File, Mary Baker Eddy Library for the Betterment of Humanity, Boston.

Ober, K. Patrick. *Mark Twain and Medicine: "Any Mummery Will Cure."* St. Louis: University of Missouri Press, 2003.

Ogden, C. K., and I. A. Richards. *The Meaning of Meaning.* New York: Harcourt, 1923.

Paine, Albert Bigelow. *Mark Twain: A Biography.* New York: Kolthof, 1912. Project Gutenberg.

Parker, Gail. "Mary Baker Eddy and Sentimental Womanhood." *New England Quarterly* 43, no. 1 (1970): 3–18.

Peabody, Frederick. *Complete Exposure of Eddyism or Christian Science: The Plain Truth in Plain Terms Regarding Mary Baker Eddy.* Boston: Author, 1904. Google Books.

———. Letter to Samuel Clemens. 2 December 1902. Mark Twain Project, University of California at Berkeley.

Peel, Robert. *Health and Medicine in the Christian Science Tradition.* New York: Crossroad, 1988.

———. *Mary Baker Eddy: Years of Authority.* New York: Holt, Rinehart and Winston, 1977.

Perkins, Eli. "A Word of Appreciation." Undated proof, Christian Science Monitor Subject File, Mary Baker Eddy Library for the Betterment of Humanity, Boston.

———. *On the Divide: The Many Lives of Willa Cather.* Lincoln: University of Nebraska Press, 2008.

———. Letter to Lucia Warren. 13 January 1933. Typescript, Georgine Milmine Collection, Mary Baker Eddy Library for the Betterment of Humanity, Boston.

Rawson, Frederick. *Life Understood: From a Scientific and Religious Point of View.* New York: Cosimo Classics, 2007.

Roggenkamp, Karen. *Narrating the News: New Journalism and Literary Genre in Late Nineteenth-Century American Newspapers and Fiction.* Kent, OH: Kent State University Press, 2005.

Rosenberg, Charles. *The Cholera Years: The United States in 1829, 1842, and 1866.* Chicago: University of Chicago Press, 1987.

Satter, Beryl. *Each Mind a Kingdom: American Women, Sexual Purity, and the New Thought Movement, 1875–1920.* Berkeley: University of California Press, 1999.

Schoepflin, Rennie B. *Christian Science on Trial: Religious Healing in America.* New York: Johns Hopkins University Press, 2003.

Schrager, Cynthia. "Mark Twain and Mary Baker Eddy: Gendering the Transpersonal Subject." *American Literature* 70, no. 1 (March 1998): 29–62.

Schudson, Michael. *Discovering the News: A Social History of American Newspapers.* New York: BasicBooks, 1978. Nook ebook.

Seelye, John. *Jane Eyre's American Daughters: From the Wide, Wide World to Anne of Green Gables.* Newark: University of Delaware Press, 2005.

Shuttleworth, Sally. *The Mind of the Child: Child Development in Literature, Science, and Medicine, 1840–1900.* New York: Oxford University Press, 2010. Kindle edition.

Sinclair, Upton. *The Profits of Religion: An Essay in Economic Interpretation.* Pasadena, CA: Author, 1918.

Skandera-Trombley, Laura E. *Mark Twain in the Company of Women.* Philadelphia: University of Pennsylvania Press, 1994.

"Snap Shots at Current Events." *Gaillard's Medical Journal* 71, no. 5 (November 1899): 725–26. Google Books.

Spencer, Herbert. Social Statics, *together with* The Man versus the State. New York: Appleton, 1899.

Sprague, Frank. Letter to Alfred Farlow. 15 July 1905. Typescript, *McClure's* File, Mary Baker Eddy Library for the Betterment of Humanity, Boston.

Sproul, Robert G. Letter to Wilbur P. Robinson. 31 October 1939. Christian Science Monitor Subject File, Mary Baker Eddy Library for the Betterment of Humanity, Boston.

Squires, Ashley. "The Standard Oil Treatment: Willa Cather, *The Life of Mary Baker G. Eddy*, and Early Twentieth Century Collaborative Authorship." *Studies in the Novel* 45, no. 3 (2013): 1–22.

Starr, Paul. *The Social Transformation of American Medicine.* New York: Basic Books, 1982.

Steffens, Lincoln. *The Autobiography of Lincoln Steffens, Vol. I.* New York: Harcourt, 1931.

Stetson, Charlotte Perkins. *Women and Economics.* Boston: Small, Maynard, 1900.

Stiles, Anne. "Christian Science versus the Rest Cure in Frances Hodgson Burnett's *The Secret Garden.*" *Modern Fiction Studies* 61, no. 2 (Summer 2015): 295–319.

Stokes, Claudia. *The Altar at Home: Sentimental Literature and Nineteenth-Century American Religion.* Philadelphia: University of Pennsylvania Press, 2014.

Tarbell, Ida. *The History of the Standard Oil Company.* New York: McClure, Phillips, 1905. Project Gutenberg.

"Testimonies from the Field." *Christian Science Journal* 24, no. 1 (April 1906): 35.

Tichi, Cecilia. *Exposés and Excess: Muckraking in America 1900–2000.* Philadelphia: University of Pennsylvania Press, 2004.

Twain, Mark. *Autobiography of Mark Twain: The Complete and Authoritative Edition.* Vols. I and II. Berkeley: University of California Press, 2010. Nook ebook.

———. *The Bible according to Mark Twain*, edited by Howard G. Baetzhold and Joseph B. McCullough. New York: Touchstone, 1995.

———. *Christian Science*, edited by Shelley Fisher Fishkin. New York: Oxford University Press, 1997.

———. *A Connecticut Yankee in King Arthur's Court.* New York: Barnes and Noble, 2005.

———. *Mark Twain's Fables of Man*, edited by John S. Tuckey. Berkeley: University of California Press, 1972.

Umansky, Ellen. *From Christian Science to Jewish Science: Spiritual Healing and American Jews.* New York: Oxford University Press, 2005.

Vaughan, Victor C. "An Address before the Alumni Association of the Long Island College Hospital." *Brooklyn Medical Journal* 15, no. 3 (March 1901): 134. Google Books.

Vetter, Lara. "Theories of Spiritual Evolution, Christian Science, and the 'Cosmopolitan Jew': Mina Loy and American Identity." *Journal of Modern Literature* 31, no. 1 (2007): 47–63.

"A Victim of Christian Science." *Medical Herald* 17 (December 1898): 508. Google Books.

Vitello, Paul. "Christian Science Church Seeks Truce with Modern Medicine." *New York Times*, 23 March 2010.

Voorhees, Amy. "Writing Revelation: Mary Baker Eddy and her Early Editions of *Science and Health*, 1875–1891." Dissertation, University of California Santa Barbara, 2013.

Weinburg, Steve. *Taking on the Trust: The Epic Battle of Ida Tarbell and John D. Rockefeller.* New York: Norton, 2008.

Wilson, Harold S. *McClure's Magazine and the Muckrakers.* Princeton, NJ: Princeton University Press, 1970.

Woodbury, Josephine. Letter to Samuel Clemens. 3 February 1902. Mark Twain Project, University of California at Berkeley.

"Woodbury vs. Eddy." *Illinois Medical Journal* 49, no. 5 (November 1899): 223–24.

Wright, John L. Letter to Mary Baker Eddy. 12 March 1908. Incoming Correspondence File, Mary Baker Eddy Library for the Betterment of Humanity, Boston.

Zanine, Louis. *Mechanism and Mysticism: The Influence of Science on the Thought and Work of Theodore Dreiser.* Philadelphia: University of Pennsylvania Press, 1993.

Zimmerman, David. *Panic! Markets, Crises, and Crowds in American Fiction.* Chapel Hill: University of North Carolina Press, 2006. Kindle edition.

INDEX

Note: MBE = Mary Baker Eddy; CS = Christian Science.

L. ASHLEY SQUIRES

was born in Texas and received her PhD from the University of Texas at Austin in 2012. She currently resides in Moscow, Russia, where she teaches American Literature and Culture in a liberal arts program at the New Economic School. She is the author of many articles on American literary and religious history.

CPSIA information can be obtained
at www.ICGtesting.com
Printed in the USA
BVOW03s1830250917
495860BV00001B/24/P